OPERATION PROSPERITY

FIXING AMERICA'S ECONOMY

A Practical And Ecological Guide For Individuals And Governments

by Christopher C. Lai

Published by Candor Press

This book is designed as a prospectus, a guideline to help individuals and governments fix the economy and reduce government debt. It is sold with the understanding that the author is not engaged in providing legal, accounting, or professional services. If legal, accounting, or other expert assistance is required to help fulfill your plans, you should seek a competent professional who can help you execute your goals.

As a prospectus, much information has been purposefully left out to give an overview of how to fix the American economy. For additional information, you can contact sources listed in the Appendix.

This book should be used as a guide since there may be content and typographical mistakes. It is not intended to be the ultimate source of technologies or laws.

This book's purpose is to educate and enlighten the reader about the possibilities that exist within our economy. The author and Candor Press do not endorse any of the products or companies listed within this book. The author offers no warranties on the products or services as well.

PUBLISHED AND DISTRIBUTED BY
Candor Press
Pleasant Hill, CA

Cover and book design and production by Right Angle Productions, Roseville, CA
Cover illustration by Melody Hjerpe, Fair Oaks, CA
Manufactured in the United States of America

Library of Congress Catalog Card Number 96-96522
International Standard Book Number 0-9652728-0-X (hardcover)
International Standard Book Number 0-9652728-1-8 (paperback)

Lai, Christopher C., 1955-
    Operation Prosperity
Fixing America's Economy, A Practical & Ecological Guide for Individuals & Governments

Includes bibliographical references and index

Dedicated To

All Wage Earners

Who Work So Hard

And

Have Very Little To Show

For Their Efforts.

ACKNOWLEDGMENTS

I would like to thank everyone who has contributed to this book. Starting with my mother who gave her time to help run my errands and with research that saved me valuable time. A great thanks goes out to Cathy Nyhan of the San Francisco Library for her excellent work doing research as well. Without Juanita Clifton's attention to detail, this book would not have been done in a timely fashion. Special thanks to my editors who refined my document, they include: Michael O'Laughlin, and Marilyn Pesola. A big thanks to Colleen Nihen of Right Angle Productions for her creative abilities in the cover design and interior layout.

There are literally scores of people who have contributed information or assistance. Unfortunately I do not have their full names or, in some cases, any names of those operators, receptionists, or assistants who have helped immensely by passing me onto the right person or sending me the right information. Without their help, I would not have been able to acquire the information that makes up this book. Those who have contributed and whom I have names for are included here in no particular order. These contributors include: Greg Sanderson, Keith Martin, Dan Tyndall, Holly Gibson, Alia Ghandour, Shane Tyson, David Harrison, Frank Rueckert, David Stephenson, David Swanson, Betty Nelson, Mary Levy, Eric Ridenour, Al Updegrove, Charlie Weinstein, Dick Cooper, Rick Pollack, Gary Van Dorst, David Saltman, Ennio Rea, Ray Enos, Charles

James, Lorena Fee, Jane Turnbull, Dr. Evan Hughes, Randy Turley, Stephen Brand, David Ostlie, Bill Gehoski, Jerry Madeiros, Marianne Costamagna, Steffanie McCorkle, Dr. Charles Dunlap, Ron Breault, Tony Lipka, Mark Carver, Joe Krueger, Margaret Shepard, Peter Riley, Kurt Klunder, Susan Thorneloe, Rose Gray, Bob Marshall, Iris Saunders, Cindy Travers, John Emani, Mr. Kenny, Patricia Pollard, Dori Nielson, Robert Schaefer, Kevin Miller, Richard Shaw, Bob Wichert, Karen Hall, Karen Cohen, Mohammed Farooque, Dr. Pinakin Patel, Patricia Wood, Wendy Black, Marianne Duncanson, Pam Scott, Linda Hennessy, Casey Robb, Bruce Clark, Harvey Brodsky, Steve Gilliand, Kathy Mynarick, Harold Burnham, Pamela Merrit, Carla Stiff, Warren Drayback, Ann Miller, Boyce Thompson, Peter Vanderklaauw, Destiny Hastings, Joe Oldham, Bill Thierrot, Terri Kelly, Kathy Johnston, Byron Lefebvre, Rick Ford, Jeanne Viner Bell, Kathy Ford, Jennifer Fairbanks, Bob Dressler, and David Smith.

TABLE OF CONTENTS

#

T his book is a result and product of one man's frustration. The frustration was born of an economy that is doing poorly and the fact no one currently in power wants to listen to an unknown person. On July 4, 1990, I wrote a letter and sent it to President Bush and every member of his Cabinet on July 5 via certified mail. The letter is printed here in its entirety.

Dear Mr. President:

I am an economist and Republican who voted for you and believes that you can keep your campaign promise of "no new taxes."

Are you interested in eradicating the national debt and salvaging your political future?

Are you open-minded to unique ideas that would require an aggressive position about change? If you feel that a positive change is needed now and you are willing to demonstrate to the Democrats and the rest of the voting public that Republicans have "the right stuff" to run the government, please read on.

In order to achieve the desired results, the economy needs to be stimulated without inflation. The savings rate must increase, interest rates must drop, industries have to grow and compete within global markets, unemployment has to decrease, middle class America has to be happy with your decisions, and special interest groups needs must be met as well.

In order to accomplish an increase in the savings rate, GNP, and tax revenues (with the existing tax rates), a new tax law allowing graduated depreciation and a savings plan on residential housing needs to be implemented.

The other ideas revolve around alternative technologies in the automotive, energy production, and housing industries; re-education of the real estate, banking, and insurance industries; increased stimulation of the farming and recycling industries; and product substitution in the oil and lumber industries.

As a result of implementing these ideas, banks and insurance companies will have less exposure to liability. The banking institutions will have increased revenues and savings. The slumping Midwest economies in farming and oil will also be stimulated. Housing starts will increase and the destruction of our forests will slow down. Acid rain pollution will decrease and smarter uses of all of our resources will be employed.

Anytime new ideas are presented, people and industries will want to resist change because they feel that they have to give up their standard of living and/or profits. To overcome this resistance, my ideas allow the taxpayer to have increased earnings and savings. Industries will benefit by having a larger consumer base to work from, changing technologies will not be difficult since everything we need already exists, and if some of these industries are given some preferential treatment, making product substitutions will be painless, profitable, and good for the environment.

The changes that I am presenting will have the greatest impact, growth, and stimulation on the following industries: housing, real estate, banking, insurance, farming, lumber, oil, energy production, pollution abatement, recycling, and automotive.

By now, you either would be very interested in knowing more about my ideas or you will dismiss this letter and choose to raise taxes and reduce benefits to special interest groups. Would you prefer to implement change that will increase your political popularity or will you take the gamble that increasing taxes and decreasing benefits will not cause a recession and hurt you politically.

If you would like to speak to me in more depth regarding my ideas, I can be contacted by phone or mail to arrange a time to meet with you.

Sincerely,

Christopher Lai

After receiving a form letter for a response, I felt overlooked and unimportant. I knew that the government had its own way of doing business that would eventually bankrupt all of us. Since my message fell on deaf ears, I felt compelled to tell every voting citizen the problems that will eventually bankrupt our country. Without establishing a complete understanding of our problems, we will be doomed to popular and simplified solutions that will end up in disaster. It would be like the three little pigs, two of whom were foolish, arrogant, and pigheaded and believed that their stick and straw homes would survive even the big bad wolf. The third pig built his home of bricks so that it would withstand any disaster. Even though my solutions are integrated with each other and may take some time and effort to understand them, they will be like a house built of bricks. They will be able to withstand the upcoming disaster because they were designed to handle our future problems. Unfortunately, we are a society of instant solutions: fast food, ATM machines, microwaves, etc., which compound our problems. We all want fast and easy solutions that are appealing. In order to make these solutions work, we will have to make some tough choices in the people we elect into office as well as the products we buy. Without making good choices at the polls and in the stores, few of these solutions will be effective.

INTRODUCTION

Forward thinking is the focus of this book. In *Operation Prosperity*, Christopher Lai builds an argument for change. The book elaborates on myths and realities that we all have come to know. The author reveals the myths surrounding topics such as the deficit, taxes, international trade, energy, recycling, unemployment, and natural disasters. By defining them for what they truly are, a strong argument begins to build in favor of change. The argument is only enhanced as Lai enlightens the reader with facts and figures regarding our economy. In an eye-opening presentation, the author exposes the accounting practices of the Federal Government, practices that enable politicians to further their political careers at the expense of taxpayers (allegations supported by a Congressional Research Service report contained in Appendix A). What is frightening about these facts is that they so illuminate the careless piloting of America by politicians toward certain financial crisis by the year 2010. This future awaits us regardless of whether or not the budget is balanced in the promised seven years. Balanced budget or not, current government spending and accounting practices will assure the disaster. America will face runaway inflation. Annual deficits will build at over a trillion dollars a year and grow progressively worse. That is, if nothing is done to begin correcting the problems today. But Christopher Lai is not that figure we have grown so used to seeing, a politician articulating our complaints but with no ideas for solutions. Mr. Lai has a vision for the future. He has a ten step plan with solutions that are easy to understand, but multifaceted. This ten step plan includes:

1. Entitlement Spending Reform
2. Government Fraud Reform
3. Welfare Reform
4. Government Subsidy Reform
5. Tax Reform

He suggests and illustrates in concrete detail real solutions that individuals can employ to help turn aside the tide of disaster. Lai realizes that corporate America must remain strong despite an animosity that may exist between individual taxpayers and corporate America. This book offers an evolutionary and eclectic approach to solving our economic problems with the least amount of disturbance to our economy. It is a master plan which takes into account that the economy cannot be overhauled overnight in the interest of short term solutions to immediate problems. Often solutions create ripple effects that just give rise to new problems. Lai follows these ripples and offers a complex integration of solutions. What he comes up with is an all-encompassing view of a revitalized America.

Lai's solutions are built from creative ideas utilizing specific existing technologies and laws that will enable governments at all levels to minimize expenditures without reducing services. Lai shows how all levels of government can generate revenues by producing real products and services that America needs now. These plans are laid out in an evolutionary path that will allow us to take back control of our government and our economy. *Operation Prosperity* shows how this country's problems can be solved with the least amount of pain and the maximum amount of benefit.

CHEATING AMERICA

merica is getting cheated by deficits and taxes. The reported annual deficit is inaccurate and our tax dollars are being misused by the officials we've put in office. As an honest tax paying citizen, you probably wonder why your taxes are so high, especially in light of the President's claims that the annual deficit is diminishing and the economy is doing well. Like most everyone else, you may very well be more concerned about your standard of living, job security, future Medicare and Social Security benefits than you are with the national debt or the annual deficit. But the hard fact is, issues surrounding the annual deficit directly affect the cost of doing business for industry. Interest payments raise the cost of money higher than it should be. This prohibits your ability to secure a better paying job to earn a decent living and save for the future.

Our future is at stake and what the future holds is controlled by politicians who have little understanding or insight into the problems they have created. To further complicate the situation, politicians often hide the truth about the problems our economy and the Government are having. They sweep the problems under the carpet, so to speak, leaving solutions for another day, probably when they are no longer in office. Since politicians rely on experts for their information, they can claim, from their future cush retirement lifestyles, that their information was either limited, incomplete, or erroneous, thereby absolving themselves of any responsibility for the disaster to our economy. Regardless of whether politicians actually know of, or are ignorant of these impending problems, do we want people running the Federal Government and making important decisions for us who are, at best, unqualified or, at worst, dishonest? At a time when our national debt is heading toward numbers only mathematicians can appreciate, do we want great orators in office, or do we want intelligent, well-educated people who understand the entire picture regarding economics, business, and the welfare of the people?

These are questions that every concerned, well-informed voter should be thinking about. If you are worried about your future, you will need to further investigate the Federal Government, our elected officials, economics, technology, and new possibilities that exist within our economy. This book will introduce you to new ideas that can improve your standard of living as they eradicate inherent problems that exist within the Federal Government and our economy.

America is, indeed, cheating herself in many ways with deficits and taxes. For example, our tax dollars are subsidizing imports. Part of this subsidy manifests itself in the form of favorable tax rates for foreign-owned corporations that do business in America. Another form of tax subsidy results from trade deficit financing. Some of our trade deficits are financed through the sale of Government bonds, which further contributes to the national debt and the annual operating deficit.

Both the annual deficit and the national debt are directly affected when we import oil. We currently import more than 50% of the oil we use and trade deficits are subsidized through normal channels, such as the sale of capital assets. Oil is a special case. The Federal Government spends billions every year for military protection. We have the navy patrolling the oceans and armed forces stationed in and around the oil fields. Since the military provides the protection, oil companies are essentially being subsidized with our tax dollars. Although the actual cost of the subsidy is difficult to assess since military expenditures are part of the unified budget, most of us would agree that the world does not need another Gulf War to remind us how expensive oil can be.

The unified budget is another way America is getting cheated with deficits and taxes. The unified budget includes all the revenues of the Federal Government—from the Social Security trust fund as well as other sources—and Federal expenditures. Ever since the Balanced Budget Act of 1985, the Federal Government has been able to manipulate the books more than they have in the past by excluding Social Security from the unified budget. The Federal Government's accounting method has allowed them to spend our tax dollars as they please, with one caveat: there will be an impending financial disaster that will affect all of us, regardless of our current tax status. This disaster, which will occur around the year

2010, will manifest itself in annual deficits in excess of trillions of dollars per year, even if the budget is balanced in seven years. The deficits will be so high that the Federal Government may be forced to raise taxes that will cripple our economy. If they don't choose to raise taxes or lower benefits, they may print enormous amounts of money that will devalue their debt through inflation.

These future tax increases, or inflation, will result from the demands of Social Security, Medicare, Medicaid, Government pensions, and Welfare. Future tax increases and inflation can be eliminated if steps are taken now to change our view and operation of these programs. By changing the way our economy works, its strength will be increased by building a larger tax base. The Federal Government will be able to carry on its business without raising taxes. If, on the other hand, the Government and our economic system is left as is, America leaves prosperity behind as deficits and taxes pull us deeper into the trap of economic disaster.

Without "Operation Prosperity," our country will face an economic disaster in the near future, even after balancing the budget. "Operation Prosperity" is a blueprint of integrated solutions that will deliver us from the impending financial crisis in the near future. Unfunded entitlement spending will be the major cause of this crisis. Social Security, Medicare, Medicaid, and Government pensions will place heavy demands on the budget that will create annual deficits of over a trillion dollars a year and will get progressively worse.

We need to force our elected officials to tell us the truth about Social Security "stealing." We cannot allow them to juggle the books to further their political careers at our expense. The truth of the matter is, the Social Security and Medicare trust fund programs are already bankrupt. There are no surpluses because these programs do not own any real assets. These trust fund programs only own internal IOUs, which give the illusion of a surplus. Any politician who tells you otherwise, Democrat or Republican, is lying. Government accounting practice regarding trust fund money will assure disaster for our economy (see Appendix A for Congressional Research Report on trust fund accounting).

Essentially, our Government is committing fraud, which will cost us dearly in the near future. Telling Americans that the Social Security and Medicare trust fund programs have a surplus is misleading at best. Since this surplus is simply an accumulation of worthless special issue securities that have to be funded with future tax dollars, their current representation of being solvent is a huge lie. Every politician who perpetuates this lie cannot be trusted. If they claim ignorance to government accounting, then they are incompetent. Regardless of lying or incompetency, we must confront them with the real issue. Once we accomplish that, we must challenge them to create solutions that make sense while acknowledging the problem. Otherwise, our country will be faced with an economic crisis that will bankrupt all of us. This disaster will only be further exacerbated by other demands on the budget that are not cost effective.

One such program is Welfare. Currently, Welfare is neither cost effective nor socially productive. Time limits are being used and the institution discourages hard work by taking away benefits from the recipient who tries to get off the system. Family planning is discouraged by giving financial reward based upon the number of children they have. Since this system is not well thought out, more people will end up back on welfare as the result of poor planning. When this happens, taxes will skyrocket.

Our taxes will get progressively worse unless tax reform is instituted now. We need a system that will encourage investment, savings, and spending that will stimulate the economy if we hope to avert the upcoming financial crisis. We need to develop a fair tax system that will help corporations develop jobs here in America. Our economic base is further eroded when corporations leave America's shores in the name of tax relief. If this happens in large numbers, the Government budget will be greatly affected. This will only accelerate our impending doom.

To help prevent this from happening, our Government will need to institute a plan for revenue reform. Not taxes, but the generation of income by providing real goods and services that our economy needs. When Governments at all levels charge for goods and services our economy needs, a symbiotic relationship develops between private enterprise and Government. For example, a project that has been working for several years exists between Folsom City and the California Prison Industry Authority. The California Prison Industry authority sorts Folsom City's garbage for recyclables. Each partner in this relationship helps each other out, which in turn creates a win-win situation. This is unlike a tax increase, which places a drag on the economy and only benefits the Government. Tax increases are a win-lose proposition that only benefits the Government and does not help stimulate the economy. To prevent this from happening, revenue reform is essential if we wish to move forward into the next century with less debt.

Less Government debt can also be accomplished when appropriation reform is instituted. It is necessary to spend money wisely on technologies that save money in energy and consumables. This will be important if we want to maintain the quantity of Government service without sacrificing the quality. This can be done with existing laws and technologies and can help stimulate private enterprise. As an example, Governments can use alternative fuels that cost less and perform better than gasoline while satisfying the 1992 Energy Policy Act.

Private enterprise will be further stimulated when an aggressive product development program is put into place with the aid of Government. Technologies such as electrical energy, alternative fuels, automobiles, and the like help stimulate the economy and keep it competitive in a global economy. As we change the face of our economy by modifying our perspectives, we will spur the development of new industries, products, and services that our economy needs. We can accomplish this through market-driven incentives that will encourage inventors to develop energy efficient and ecologically sound products and services that will keep America strong in this competitive global economy.

By developing globally competitive technologies and products, America's industries will come alive and further our road to economic stability. Long run economic stability will be important if we are going to stave off this upcoming financial crisis. When our economy suffers from downswings and cycles, the Government has a smaller tax base from which to draw revenue. For this reason, it is imperative to create long-term solutions that will satisfy both the short run and the long haul. Economic stimulation that creates jobs here in America is the focus of this book. Without a strong base of diversified jobs requiring all levels of skill and intelligence, our economy will be stunted, with no hope of getting and keeping welfare recipients out of the system. When welfare recipients become a productive part of our economy, our economic base will grow substantially. Retailers will have a broader base of consumers who will have more purchasing power than they do now. As these people earn more, they will be able to spend more. This will increase our country's GDP as well as the amount of taxes our Government can collect to reduce the deficit. In order to make this happen, we need good paying jobs to be created here in America.

When we create good paying jobs in America, we will be stimulating demand for American-made goods and services. This in part will help us reduce our trade deficits. The other half of the equation will require a combination of ingenuity, laws, and incentives to develop our exports. The more markets we develop overseas, the greater chance we have of reducing our trade deficits while maintaining a balance in free trade. Protectionistic trade policies are a negative way of doing business. These policies hurt everyone who engages in it by building resentment against that country who employs it. This resentment manifests itself in anger and in racism. For example, when Japan keeps its markets closed to Americans, and Americans lose jobs due to our own buying patterns, racism surfaces. Several years ago, some autoworkers were upset over losing their jobs. They blamed their misfortune on the Japanese. An unfortunate Asian was at the wrong place at the wrong time and got the beating of his life. Displaced hatred is wrong and we do not need to perpetuate it with blatant protectionistic trade policies. Rather, we need to use market-driven incentives that will encourage Americans to change their buying patterns. This will result in lowering our trade deficits and stimulating our economy.

TWO

MYTHS & REALITIES

This chapter is intended to give you a better understanding of our economic and political system so you will find it easier to comprehend the logic and options presented throughout this book. It is necessary to first fill the gaps that reporters leave out in the interest of simplicity. As an example, natural disasters directly impact the national debt and our taxes. The general perception is fueled by a lack of information. We are drawn to such shortcuts to simplicity which often fail to reveal the truth.

Due to television and other forms of mass media, many of us have a set of beliefs about our system that may or may not be true. Television, especially, tends to abbreviate the facts to make news stories more appealing. When network news decision makers ask reporters to simplify the news to promote general public comprehension, we often end up with myths about our lives and our socio-economic system. Following are examples of the many myths and the contrasting realities of our situation.

Deficit Myth

The annual deficit figure that politicians talk about is accurate and is the only problem that the politicians need to be concerned about.

Deficit Reality

The annual deficit figure reported by our politicians, especially the President, is false. The figure has been altered to reflect an image of fiscal responsibility. The altered number has been achieved by using money from trust fund programs such as Social Security.

National Debt Myth

The Republicans are most responsible for our national debt.

National Debt Reality

The accumulated national debt is the result of two major factors: Government spending and consumer spending. But these are not the only factors; another major factor is trade deficit financing with Government bonds. As we have incurred huge trade deficits, we have financed some of it with Government bonds, which increases our national debt. Over the years, our Federal Government has spent more money than it has taken in. The accumulation of this national debt has reached the $5 trillion mark. Both Democrats and the Republicans have been responsible for spending money unwisely in Government.

Tax Myth

Tax avoidance by the rich is the reason why middle class America is picking up an unfair share of the tax liability.

Tax Reality

It is true, upper class citizens do not pay their fair share of taxes, but they are not the only reason that middle class Americans are saddled with the lion's share of the tax liability. American and foreign owned corporations are bigger culprits. In the 1950's the corporate share of income taxes was 39%. In the eighties, the corporate share of taxes was only 17%.[1] American owned corporations have many types of tax write offs. Their biggest write-off is Net Operating Loss, otherwise known as interest write-offs. In the eighties, leverage buyouts were the craze. When

---

[1] Figures from: Barlett, Donald L., and Steele, James B. *America: What Went Wrong*, Andrews and McMeel, 1992, p. 47

one company wanted to take another company over, they financed the deal. This financing led to interest expense which could be written off of their taxes. Many companies that were taken over in this fashion became unprofitable and paid no taxes for years, or are still paying no taxes at all. It is estimated that during the 1980's, corporations avoided paying $92.2 billion in income taxes by taking advantage of legal interest deductions.[2]

Corporations that move their operations out of the country into tax havens also avoid taxes. An example of one of the many tax havens is Puerto Rico, where many drug companies, including Johnson and Johnson, have moved their operations in order to avoid paying Federal income taxes. By incorporating in a foreign country, a popular cruise line avoids paying any U.S. taxes but earns billions of dollars in revenue from Americans who continue to book cruises with them.

Foreign-owned corporations are also big offenders. Many of these foreign corporations pay no tax at all, but collect billions of dollars in revenues from American citizens. If these foreign corporations do pay taxes, they pay considerably less than their American counterparts.[3] As these foreign corporations pay less in taxes, they earn more profits from products and services they sell to us.

Another sector of the economy that places an additional burden on tax paying citizens is the underground economy. This is made up of products and services that are purchased in a system popularly known as "under the table." Cash transactions that are not recorded or reported to the Internal Revenue Service is another form of tax avoidance. People who are involved in cash only transactions are just as guilty as corporations who escape their tax liabilities through the use of net operating losses.

The underground community is comprised of not only local thugs, drug dealers, and illegal aliens, but independent contractors as well. Prizate citizens who do not process Internal Revenue Service Form 1099 Miscellaneous to report payments of $600 or more for work performed by independent contractors are part of the problem. Without this form, the Federal Government has no way of knowing how much money an independent contractor actually made during the year. With so many people involved in tax avoidance, it is no wonder why middle class America is being saddled with the lion's share of the tax liability.

---

[2] Figures from: Barlett, Donald L. and Steele, James B. *America: What Went Wrong*, Andrews and McMeel, 1992, p. 40

[3] Barlett, Donald L. and Steele, James B. *America: What Went Wrong*, Andrews and McMeel, 1992, p. 92

International Trade Myth

GATT (General Agreement on Tariffs and Trade) will improve the quality of our lives.

International Trade Reality

GATT was started in 1947 and is an acronym for General Agreement On Tariffs and Trade. The latest version is commonly known as the Uruguay Round and it has twenty-two thousand pages of agreements and related tariff schedules. This latest version was signed in December of 1994. The World Trade Organization (WTO) administers the rules set forth by GATT and can authorize sanctions against violators of GATT. The goal of this document is to cut tariffs and bring trading nations down to a level playing field. The fact that GATT will help improve free trade may at first be viewed as positive, but a side effect of GATT is that dangerous pesticides are entering the country on some fruits and vegetables. Codex Alimentarius Commission (commonly referred to as Codex), which is a unit of the United Nations, has become the governing body that promulgates standards for food safety and how they apply to GATT. Unfortunately, the standards set forth by Codex are less stringent than those of the United States. A study has shown that many pesticides sanctioned by Codex are banned in the U.S., some of which are considered carcinogens by the Environmental Protection Agency.

International Trade Myth

Direct foreign investment in U.S. bonds, companies, and real estate is healthy for our economy.

International Trade Reality

One of the reasons foreigners are able to make investments in the United States is due to the fact that they have a surplus in our balance of trade. This means that these countries have sold more goods and services to America than America has sold to them. When this happens, we must balance our books with the rest of the world. The instruments that enable us to balance the books are capital instruments, such as the selling of stocks, bonds, companies, real estate, and direct investments in new assembly plants. When countries build assembly plants in the United States, we are balancing our books. This situation of selling off America in bits and pieces would probably not have occurred if we didn't have a trade deficit with our foreign trading partners. But our undying thirst for Japanese cars and electronics have provided the Japanese with the capital to come to the United States to buy up our assets. When the Japanese obtain our assets, they also obtain their income streams year after year.

An example of this situation is Japanese-owned Pebble Beach. Americans who golf at Pebble Beach provide profits for the Japanese owners who then have more financial capability to buy up more capital assets of America. Often the Japanese, or some other foreign nation, buys United States Government bonds. The income stream flows to the owner of those bonds for years. This adds to their capital stock and their purchasing power, enabling them to buy more assets from America. Yet another downside of foreign investments is inflation. Sometimes countries with large surpluses spend money foolishly in America for no other reason than that they can afford to, which creates inflation. This happened in Hawaii's real estate market. In total, huge trade deficits and the resulting direct foreign investments can be unhealthy for our economy since there is no way for our economy to respond in equal fashion.

Energy Myth

The price we pay for gasoline at the pump represents the true cost of filling up our tanks.

Energy Reality

The price we pay for gasoline at the pump is only a part of the true cost of gasoline and represents only the wholesale cost of production, profit, and taxes. In addition to the actual hard costs of oil exploration, transportation, and refinement, there are hidden costs that are not readily realized by us when we fill up our tanks. These hidden costs are external non-market costs and subsidies provided by our Government. Examples include military protection of oil sources, depletion allowances for the depreciation of oil wells, and the wide ranging negative effects of pollution from the burning of fossil fuels. If these and other hidden costs were accounted for, the price of oil would be close to $100 per barrel, according to the General Accounting Office.[4]

---

[4] Figures from The Governors' Ethanol Coalition, *Clean Energy & The Environment*, p. 4

Recycling Myth

Due to our recent collective efforts, we are doing a great job recycling.

Recycling Reality

The truth of the matter is that we are doing a very poor job of recycling. It has been estimated by the National Association of Home Builders that 22% of all landfill waste comes from construction and demolition debris.[5] What makes this problem worse is that some states, such as Wyoming, recycle only 5% of their garbage. The District of Columbia incinerates 50% of its garbage. Nationwide, we are recycling only about 23% of the garbage we produce, while 10% of the garbage is incinerated and the remaining 67% is put into landfills!

For your convenience, a table indicating the annual tonnage of garbage produced follows this paragraph, along with the percentage recycled, incinerated, and landfilled. Keep in mind that these numbers are merely estimates and do not take into account products recycled by people who bring recyclables to drop-off facilities.[6]

Waste Generation, Recycling and Disposal Methods (By State)				
State	Solid Waste (tons/yr.)	Recycled[1] (percent)	Incinerated (percent)	Landfilled (percent)
Alabama	5,310,000	15	5	80
Alaska[2]	500,000	6	15	79
Arizona[7]	4,200,000	5 [3]	0	95
Arkansas[2]	2,154,000	25	5	70
California[2]	45,000,000	25	2	73
Colorado[4]	2,800,000	18	1	81
Connecticut	2,905,000	23	63	14
Delaware[2]	1,100,000	27 [5]	13	60
Dist. of Columbia	900,000	25	50	25
Florida	23,561,000	36	23	41
Georgia	8,500,000	12 [6]	3 [6]	85 [6]
Hawaii[2]	2,000,000	17	31	52
Idaho[6]	886,000	10	0	90

[5] Figures from Anderson, Carol. "Green Roofing, Green Siding," *Custom Home*, March/April 1995, p. 71
[6] Figures from Steuteville, Robert. "The State Of Garbage In America," *Biocycle*, April 1995, p. 58

State	Solid Waste (tons/yr.)	Recycled[1] (percent)	Incinerated (percent)	Landfilled (percent)
Illinois[7]	15,000,000	19	2	79
Indiana	5,600,000	19	12	69
Iowa	2,744,000	16 [6]	0 [6]	84 [6]
Kansas	3,500,000	8	0	92
Kentucky[2]	3,750,000	15 [6]	0	85 [6]
Louisiana	3,323,000	8	0	92
Maine	1,293,000	33	39	28
Maryland[7]	5,200,000	26	23	51
Massachusetts	6,750,000	32	48	20
Michigan[8,2]	13,700,000	20	10	70
Minnesota[4]	4,600,000	44	23	33
Mississippi[2]	2,200,000	11	3	86
Missouri	5,600,000	17 [9]	0	83
Montana	790,000 [7]	6 [10]	2	92
Nebraska	1,650,000	19	0	81
Nevada	2,420,000	17	0	83
New Hampshire[2,7]	1,032,000	16	26	58
New Jersey[7]	7,400,000	41 [12]	23	36
New Mexico[7]	1,880,000	9	0	91
New York[2,7]	25,400,000	28	19	53
North Carolina[2]	7,754,000 [3]	8 [3]	1	91
North Dakota	500,000	18	0	82
Ohio[2,7]	22,543,000	32	4	64
Oklahoma	2,500,000	12	10	78
Oregon[7]	3,255,000	30	6	64
Pennsylvania[7]	9,500,000	20	19	61
Rhode Island	1,062,000	24	0	76
South Carolina[2]	5,100,000	9 [3]	5	86
South Dakota	840,000	20	0	80
Tennessee	6,000,000	15	7	78
Texas[2]	25,026,000	14	1	85
Utah	2,000,000	13	7	80
Vermont	700,000 [11]	28	4	68
Virginia[7]	8,000,000	28	18	54
Washington[7]	6,513,000	38	6	56
West Virginia	2,000,000	12 [6]	0 [6]	88 [6]
Wisconsin[7]	5,434,000	28	3	69
Wyoming	504,000	5	0	95
Totals	322,879,000	23%	10%	67%

[1]Includes yard trimmings, composting; [2]Includes some industrial waste; [3]Includes little or no commercial sector recycling; [4]No official estimate - based on actual state recycling tonnage's and national average waste generation; [5]42% including bulky materials; [6]No current estimate; data from previous "State of Garbage in America" surveys; [7]Based on 1993 data; [8]Rough estimates based on limited data; [9]Waste reduction, not recycling; [10]No current data on recycling; based on 1989 estimate; [11]1990 waste generation figure; [12]53% including bulky materials.

Source: BioCycle, JG Press, April 1995 page 58

Recycling Myth

When we recycle paper, that paper is completely eliminated from the landfill.

Recycling Reality

Recycling paper creates unseen landfill waste and only prolongs the inevitable. Paper can only be recycled two or three times before the paper fibers become too short to knit into a sheet of paper. When this happens, this paper fiber ends up as waste sludge. This sludge is sent to the landfill by most, if not all, paper mills that use recycled paper. Even though recycling saves trees, landfill space is still being consumed at a very high rate because progressive technologies are not being employed. This means about one-half of the one hundred million tons of paper we consume each year, ends up in our garbage dumps.[7]

Unemployment Myth

The published unemployment rate is a true representation of the number of people unemployed and how well the country is doing.

Unemployment Reality

This unemployment number only represents the people who file for unemployment. It takes into account no more than the number of known people who have filed for unemployment and who are actively involved with the employment system. This number does not take into account those people who lost their unemployment benefits because they ran out of time in which they were eligible for benefits. Nor does it account for those people who do not wish to be employed or those people such as the homeless, prisoners, and welfare recipients who have slipped through the cracks.

The unemployment figure does not truly represent how well our country is doing. If you research the issue, you will discover that homelessness is on the rise, welfare costs continue to climb, and the President suggests we get tough on welfare recipients. As you dig deeper into newspapers, you will discover stories that indicate how a new WalMart, K-Mart or some fast food outlet has opened their doors to expansion and new jobs. What you won't find in these stories is how many people taking on these jobs

---

[7] Facts from "Paper Pellet Fuels In The Southeast," *Biologue*, 4th Quarter 1994, pp. 18-20

previously had a better paying job that got exported to a less developed nation. In many instances, people who find themselves in the situation of a lost high paying job must now take on several lower paying jobs just to make ends meet. So, when you read or hear about how good a job our President is doing in the area of job creation for the economy, be skeptical and look deeper into your news source to see what other facets and aspects of the news that are not being reported.

Natural Disaster Myth

If you live in the midwest you only have to worry about tornadoes and floods.

Natural Disaster Reality

If you live in the midwest, you will also have to worry about earthquakes if you live anywhere near the New Madrid fault. As earthquakes go, we cannot predict when they will happen or how big they will be. When the next large earthquake results from this fault, it could destroy thousands of square miles of farms and structures and may kill thousands of people.

On December 16, 1811, at about 2:15 P.M., St. Louis and the surrounding country was hit by the most violent earthquake recorded since the discovery of our country. Two more shocks occurred on January 23 and February 7, 1812. Each of the three earthquakes are believed to have been stronger than any earthquakes ever recorded in United States history. These large shocks were felt from the Canadian border to New Orleans and all along the eastern seaboard. Between December 16, 1811 and March 15, 1812, a total of one thousand eight hundred seventy-four shocks were counted. Eight of these were classified as violent, ten were considered severe, thirty-five more were moderate, and the rest were considered insignificant. The initial jolt was so violent that it caused the Mississippi River to flow backwards. Some land was uplifted, other land sank as much as 15 feet. Ponds, swamps, and even lakes were created, including Lake Reelfoot in Tennessee which is 18 miles long.[8]

---

[8] Penick, James Jr. *American Heritage*, Volume XXVII, December 1975, pp. 82-87

THREE

FACTS & TRENDS

This chapter is designed to inform you about the facts that affect our economy as well as set the stage for solutions that are outlined later in the book. When you understand the problems that exist within our economy and how they are interrelated with each other, the solutions become very clear.

Budget Facts

Using 1974 as a starting point, the Federal budget was just over $269 billion. By 1987, the budget reached $1 trillion, and by 1994 the budget is estimated at over $1.4 trillion.

Year	AnnualBudget (In Millions of Dollars)	Annual Percentage Change
1974	269,359	9.6
1975	332,332	23.4
1976	371,792	11.9
1976[1]	95,975	N/A
1977	409,218	10.1
1978	458,746	12.1
1979	503,485	9.8
1980	590,947	17.4
1981	678,249	14.8
1982	745,755	10.0
1983	808,380	8.4
1984	851,846	5.4
1985	946,391	11.1
1986	990,336	4.6
1987	1,003,911	1.4
1988	1,064,140	6.0
1989	1,143,172	7.4
1990	1,252,705	9.6
1991	1,323,793	5.7
1992	1,380,856	4.3
1993	1,408,205	2.0
1994 est.	1,483,829	5.4

[1]Represents transition quarter, July-Sept.

Source: Statistical Abstract of the United States 1994

Budget Trends

As you can tell from the above table, the Federal Budget is growing by leaps and bounds. In just twenty years, the Federal Government's budget has grown five times larger than what it was in 1974. This is a tremendous amount of growth when one considers that inflation over the last few years has been less than 5% per year. If our politicians don't get Government spending under control, our budget will eventually reach $2 trillion a year. This trend can be reversed if positive steps are taken today to downsize the Federal Government, eliminate pork spending, and minimize entitlement spending.

Federal Tax Facts

In Fiscal Year 1994, the Federal Government collected a whopping $1.257 trillion in taxes. This figure includes custom duties, miscellaneous receipts, individual income, corporate, Social Security, excise, estate, and gift taxes. Approximately one-third of that amount ($461.5 billion) is collected from Social Security taxes, while one-fourth of the Federal Government's expenditures is related to Social Security. The cash flow surplus that results from Social Security taxes is being used to finance current consumption in other parts of the Government. The following table is from the Congressional Budget Office and lists the major taxes by categories and years.

	Individual Income Taxes	Corporate Income Taxes	Social Insurance Taxes	Excise Taxes	Estate and Gift Taxes	Custom Duties	Misc. Receipts	Total Revenues
1962	45.6	20.5	17.0	12.5	2.0	1.1	0.8	99.7
1963	47.6	21.6	19.8	13.2	2.2	1.2	1.0	106.6
1964	48.7	23.5	22.0	13.7	2.4	1.3	1.1	112.6
1965	48.8	25.5	22.2	14.6	2.7	1.4	1.6	116.8
1966	55.4	30.1	25.5	13.1	3.1	1.8	1.9	130.8
1967	61.5	34.0	32.6	13.7	3.0	1.9	2.1	148.8
1968	68.7	28.7	33.9	14.1	3.1	2.0	2.5	153.0
1969	87.2	36.7	39.0	15.2	3.5	2.3	2.9	186.9
1970	90.4	32.8	44.4	15.7	3.6	2.4	3.4	192.8
1971	86.2	26.8	47.3	16.6	3.7	2.6	3.9	187.1
1972	94.7	32.2	52.6	15.5	5.4	3.3	3.6	207.3
1973	103.2	36.2	63.1	16.3	4.9	3.2	3.9	230.8
1974	119.0	38.6	75.1	16.8	5.0	3.3	5.4	263.2
1975	122.4	40.6	84.5	16.6	4.6	3.7	6.7	279.1
1976	131.6	41.4	90.8	17.0	5.2	4.1	8.0	298.1
1977	157.6	54.9	106.5	17.5	7.3	5.2	6.5	355.6
1978	181.0	60.0	121.0	18.4	5.3	6.6	7.4	399.6
1979	217.8	65.7	138.9	18.7	5.4	7.4	9.3	463.3
1980	244.1	64.6	157.8	24.3	6.4	7.2	12.7	517.1
1981	285.9	61.1	182.7	40.8	6.8	8.1	13.8	599.3
1982	297.7	49.2	201.5	36.3	8.0	8.9	16.2	617.8
1983	288.9	37.0	209.0	35.3	6.1	8.7	15.6	600.6
1984	298.4	56.9	239.4	37.4	6.0	11.4	17.0	666.5
1985	334.5	61.3	265.2	36.0	6.4	12.1	18.5	734.1
1986	349.0	63.1	283.9	32.9	7.0	13.3	19.9	769.1
1987	392.6	83.9	303.3	32.5	7.5	15.1	19.3	854.1
1988	401.2	94.5	334.3	35.2	7.6	16.2	19.9	909.0
1989	445.7	103.3	359.4	34.4	8.7	16.3	22.8	990.7
1990	466.9	93.5	380.0	35.3	11.5	16.7	27.3	1,031.3
1991	467.8	98.1	396.0	42.4	11.1	15.9	22.8	1,054.3
1992	476.0	100.3	413.7	45.6	11.1	17.4	26.5	1,090.5
1993	509.7	117.5	428.3	48.1	12.6	18.8	18.5	1,153.5
1994	542.7	140.4	461.5	55.2	15.2	20.1	22.1	1,257.2

Revenues By Major Source — Fiscal Years 1962-1994 (In Billions Of Dollars)

Federal Tax Trends

It is obvious that as the years progress, the Government is collecting more money from taxes. This trend will continue until the Government balances the budget and begins to reduce the national debt. Once the budget is balanced, you might experience a slight reprieve from high taxes. However, this reprieve will all but disappear when baby boomers start to retire around the year 2010. When that happens, Medicare and Social Security expenditures will increase dramatically. At that time, all forms of taxes will skyrocket to cover these entitlement programs. This upward trend in taxes can only be averted if progressive plans are enacted today to minimize entitlement spending in the future.

Annual Deficit Facts

Using 1974 as a starting point, the Federal Deficit has grown from $6 billion a year to a high of $290 billion in 1992. The overall growth of the deficit in this twenty-year period is an astounding 3,726.5%.

Year	Annual Deficit (Billions of Dollars)	Annual Percentage Change[2]
1974	6,135	-58.8
1975	53,242	768.0
1976	73,732	38.5
1976[1]	14,744	N/A
1977	53,659	N/A
1978	59,186	10.3
1979	40,183	-32.1
1980	73,835	83.7
1981	78,976	6.9
1982	127,989	62.1
1983	207,818	62.4
1984	185,388	-10.8
1985	212,334	14.5
1986	221,245	4.2
1987	149,769	-32.3
1988	155,187	3.6
1989	152,481	-1.7
1990	221,384	45.2
1991	269,521	21.7
1992	290,403	7.7
1993	254,670	-12.3
1994	234,758	-7.8

[1]Represents transition quarter, July-Sept.
[2]These figures were calculated by the author
Source: Statistical Abstract of the United States 1994

Annual Deficit Trends

It is obvious that the deficit has been growing steadily for some years. The President and Congress have promised us that these deficits will continue for at least another seven years. This promise is based on a prediction of what the economy will do in that period of time, but if their predictions are too optimistic and wind up being wrong, the deficits will go on longer. Several factors that will determine the future deficits will include who becomes President in the next election and what type of corporate and personal income tax system is adopted during the next several years. The performance of the economy during that time and how much capital is imported through the sale of Government bonds to foreigners will depend on the price of money. The size of the deficit will be directly affected by how much trust fund money the Government uses. Regardless of what happens in the next several years, the annual deficits will be outrageous within the first decade of the next century. Starting around the year 2010, annual deficits will exceed a trillion dollars every year and will continue to expand unless progressive plans are enacted today to minimize entitlement spending in the future.

National Debt Facts

The national debt is an accumulation of the recurring annual deficit. Back in 1955 the total debt was only $274 billion. By 1974, almost twenty years later, the national debt grew to only $483 billion, less than twice the amount it was in 1955. In the ensuing twenty years to 1994, the national debt has grown to the shocking figure of nearly $5 trillion. This national debt consists of two parts. One part is publicly owned debt and the other part is Government owned debt. Publicly owned debt occurs when the Federal Government sells bonds to the public to finance the deficit. Government owned debt occurs when the Treasury uses money generated from trust fund accounts for general spending. When the Government uses trust fund money for general spending, the Treasury replaces the money with non-negotiable bonds which are essentially internal IOUs. These bonds have maturity dates and bear interest. Even though these bonds bear interest, they are not paid with cash, but rather "paid" with another worthless IOU.

Year	Gov. Debt (Millions of Dollars)	Public Debt (Millions of Dollars)	National Debt (Millions of Dollars)	Debt as Percentage of Gross Domestic Product
1974	140,194	343,699	483,893	34.5
1975	147,225	394,700	541,925	35.9
1976	151,566	477,404	628,970	37.3
1976[1]	148,052	495,509	643,561	36.2
1977	157,295	549,103	706,398	36.8
1978	169,477	607,125	776,602	36.0
1979	189,162	639,761	828,923	34.1
1980	199,212	709,291	908,503	34.4
1981	209,507	784,791	994,298	33.5
1982	217,560	919,238	1,136,798	36.4
1983	240,114	1,131,049	1,371,164	41.3
1984	264,159	1,299,951	1,564,110	42.3
1985	317,612	1,499,362	1,816,974	45.8
1986	383,919	1,736,163	2,120,082	50.3
1987	457,444	1,888,134	2,345,578	52.7
1988	550,507	2,050,252	2,600,760	54.1
1989	678,157	2,189,336	2,867,538	55.4
1990	795,841	2,410,366	3,206,207	58.5
1991	910,362	2,687,942	3,598,303	63.4
1992	1,003,302	2,998,639	4,001,941	67.4
1993	1,104,045	3,247,178	4,351,223	69.1
1994[2]	1,203,617	3,472,412	4,676,029	70.4

[1]Represents transition quarter, July-Sept.
[2]These numbers are estimates

Source: Statistical Abstract of the United States 1994

National Debt Trends

As you can clearly see from the chart, the national debt began to skyrocket once it exceeded a trillion dollars in 1982. In just twelve years, that trillion dollar debt has grown almost five times as big. This growth is in great part due to compound interest. Consider the national debt as if it were a credit card with an unlimited balance and the country never made any payments on the principal balance. Since no payments are made on the principal debt, the interest calculated each payment period becomes part of the principal debt. Since our Government is unable to balance its budget and it never reduces the national debt, more interest is being compounded each year until the budget is balanced.

Another statistic to help you see how far out of hand this problem has gotten is to look at a percentage figure. As a percentage of the Gross Domestic Product, our national debt was only 34.5% in 1974. By 1994, it had grown to 70.4%. At this pace, it won't take long for the national debt to equal our entire country's Gross Domestic Product! It would be like owing more on a credit card than the amount you make in an entire year. This trend will not go away until our Government balances the budget and future entitlement spending is brought under control. This can happen if we sell less Government bonds to pay for our trade deficits. We can start now by changing our consumer buying habits that directly affect our trade deficits. Even though this may take some time, it will produce long run solutions that will benefit our pocketbooks.

Interest On National Debt Facts

In 1974, the Federal Government made interest payments of $28.1 billion. By 1994, that interest expense had grown to a whopping $203 billion. These interest payments reflect only public debt. To clarify, this interest expense represents only the interest that has been paid on Government bonds sold to the public, not on internal debt.

Year	National Debt (Billions of Dollars)	Interest (Billions of Dollars)
1974	483.9	28.1
1975	541.9	31.0
1976	643.6	26.7
1977	706.4	29.9
1978	776.6	35.5
1979	828.9	42.6
1980	908.5	52.5
1981	994.3	68.8
1982	1,136.8	85.5
1983	1,371.2	89.8
1984	1,564.1	111.1
1985	1,817.0	129.5
1986	2,120.1	136.0
1987	2,345.6	138.7
1988	2,600.8	151.8
1989	2,867.5	169.3
1990	3,206.2	184.2
1991	3,598.3	194.5
1992	4,001.9	199.4
1993	4,351.2	198.8
1994	4,676.0	203.0

Source: Statistical Abstract of the United States 1994
Source: Economic Indicators, January 1976 & October 1995

Interest On National Debt Trends

Since the Federal Government is unable to balance the budget, the national debt continues to climb. Since none of the actual debt is ever reduced, the interest that is calculated and owed each and every year becomes part of the new principal balance. This trend will continue until the Government balances the budget and begins retiring the national debt. The first step our Government must take is to implement new progressive plans that will reduce entitlement spending and help build a strong economy. In order to reduce entitlement spending, we can decrease Social Security spending by raising the retirement age ten years over a twenty year period. If this is done in conjunction with expanding our manufacturing sector, more people will be able to acquire better paying jobs that will yield more tax revenues for the government. In this way, the Government will be able to obtain more tax revenues at a faster pace. If such steps are not taken, the national debt will continue to grow and the amount of interest paid out every year will skyrocket.

World Trade Fact

The Pacific Rim nations now account for 19% of global trade.

World Trade Trend

The Pacific Rim nations will become stronger trading partners with the rest of the world, and it is anticipated that their share of world trade will grow to account for at least one-third of the world trade by the year 2000.[9] This trend will continue unless changes in our tax laws and in GATT are implemented to encourage more fair and free trade. Without either, America will become a second rate economic power in the global marketplace.

Trade Deficit Facts: Japan

Back in 1980, the United States began to incur sizable trade deficits with Japan. In that year, the trade deficit was just over $12 billion. From that year forward, the annual trade deficit grew. In the years between 1980 and 1985, the trade deficit grew to nearly $50 billion. In 1990, the trade deficit actually shrank down to $41 billion, but a look at the following chart will show you the result of years of trade deficits with Japan. The

---

[9] Stein, Tom. "Emerging Markets In Asia," *Success*, June 1995, p. 10

total has now grown to nearly $600 billion, this explosion in just fourteen years! Most of that is attributed to production of automobiles.

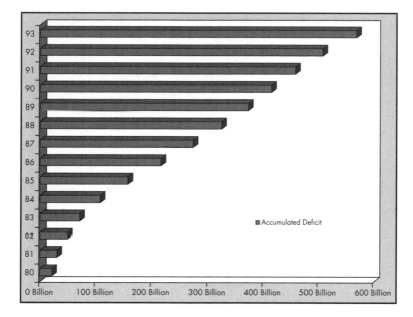

Source: Commerce Dept.

Trade Deficit Trends: Japan

As the above chart indicates, each year the United States has incurred a trade deficit with Japan. This trend will continue as long as we maintain our insatiable demand for Japanese goods. However, this trend could be reversed if Japan were to open its markets to American products and American automobile companies were to change their products to accommodate the Japanese market. Such a reversal will require smart marketing on the part of American companies in conjunction with an open market in Japan. Another way to reverse this upward trend is to manufacture more Japanese products here in America using American-made components. Changes in GATT and in our own tax system can help make this happen. One such change is to make automobiles depreciable under the new tax system. This system would allow for a greater tax write off for an automobile with a higher percentage of American-made content. If we can get these changes implemented, it will be an important step in improving the outlook of our trade deficits.

Trade Deficit Facts: OPEC

Using 1980 as a starting date, the United States has been incurring large trade deficits with the OPEC nations. In 1980, the trade deficit was just over $37 billion. In five years, the annual trade deficit actually shrank down to $11 billion. However, by 1990, the trade deficit grew back up to $29 billion, and by the end of 1993, the trade deficit shrank back down to just over $17 billion. In this short fourteen-year period, the United States incurred a total of nearly $250 billion in trade deficits with the OPEC nations.

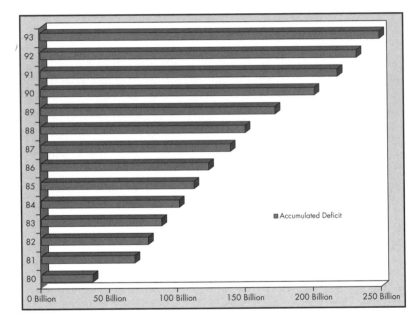

Source: Commerce Dept.

Trade Deficit Trends: OPEC

Each year, the United States has incurred trade deficits with the OPEC nations. Some years have seen smaller figures than others, but our trend of incurring trade deficits will continue as our population grows and the demand for gasoline increases. This trend can be reversed if there is a higher domestic production of crude oil or our vehicles become extremely energy efficient overnight. Alternative fuels, electric and hybrid vehicles will have an impact upon the demand for imported oil. We will have to invest more money into research and development for these changes to occur. Also, each one of us will need to contact the automobile manufacturers demanding them to manufactue automobiles that can handle alternative fuels and accelerate the progress toward the commercialization of a hybrid vehicle. Changes in GATT and in our own tax codes can have a positive effect on reducing our trade deficits with the OPEC nations.

Trade Deficit Facts: Germany

In 1980, our trade deficit with Germany was minimal, but by 1985, the trade deficit grew to over $12 billion. The annual trade deficit peaked in 1986 at almost $16 billion. The greatest portion of this trade deficit was attributed to German automobiles. During this fourteen-year span, we incurred nearly $120 billion in trade deficits with Germany.

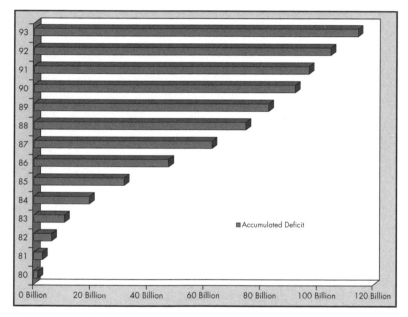

Source: Commerce Dept.

Trade Deficit Trends: Germany

This upward trend in trade deficits will continue until Americans decide to buy fewer German automobiles. This trend could be reversed if German automobiles utilized a higher percentage of American-made parts. Again, obtaining help through GATT and our own tax laws can accomplish goals that will reverse this trend.

Trade Deficit Facts: China

The United States did not incur a trade deficit with China until 1983. From 1980 to 1982, we had a trade surplus with China totaling over $4.5 billion. During the three years from 1983 to 1985, inclusive, the United States incurred less than a billion dollars in trade deficits. Then, in the eleven years that followed, the United States managed to accumulate nearly $80 billion in trade deficits with China.

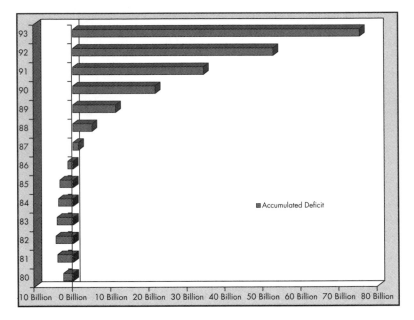

Source: Commerce Dept.

Trade Deficit Trends: China

Our trade deficits with China will continue so long as China maintains its most favored nation's status. As more American companies have their products manufactured in China, we will continue to import more products of all types that are made there. However, if we export more food, automobiles, and infrastructural improvements to China, this trend can be reversed. Technologies such as waste gasification, sewage treatment, and power plants are key. Helping China develop into an industrialized society will create their need for more of the things America can provide. This new demand will eventually bring our trade deficits into balance.

World Trade Deficit Facts

From 1980 to 1993, the United States incurred nearly $1.2 trillion in trade deficits with the rest of the *entire* world. Nearly 80%, or nearly $1 trillion, of that total came from Japan, the OPEC nations, Germany, and China. The biggest offender was Japan at nearly $600 billion, followed by the OPEC nations at $250 billion. In third place was Germany at nearly $120 billion, followed by China at $80 billion.

World Trade Deficit Trends

Our trade deficits with the rest of the world will continue to get worse every year because our country believes in free trade. This open door policy allows countries (that have closed markets with the United States) to enter our country and dump their cheap goods into our markets. These goods eventually drive out American competition. This trend will continue until the United States Government takes a more aggressive stance in helping American entrepreneurs penetrate foreign markets. This can be accomplished by requesting our Congressmen/Congresswomen to implement U.S. Government Online, an online service that will help entrepreneurs penetrate world markets.

Automobile Industry Facts

As of 1994, imported automobiles had a whopping 35.4% of the market share here in America. Chrysler only had 9%, while Ford had 21.6%, and General Motors 34%. Even though General Motors was the leader in market share, their share was less than all of the imported cars sold during that year. By comparison, all imports in 1985 accounted for only 27% of the market share, while Chrysler had 11.3%, Ford had 18.9%, and General Motors had 42.7%.[10]

---

[10] Ward's Automotive Yearbook, 1995, p. 196

Year	Chrysler	Ford	GM	Honda	Nissan	Toyota	Mazda	Mitsubishi	VW	Others
1985	11.3	18.9	42.7	5.0	5.2	5.3	1.9	0.5	2.5	6.6
1986	11.5	18.2	41.2	6.1	4.8	5.3	2.0	0.4	2.3	8.2
1987	10.8	20.2	36.6	7.2	5.2	6.0	2.0	0.6	2.2	9.2
1988	11.3	21.7	36.3	7.3	4.5	6.2	2.4	0.6	1.8	8.0
1989	10.4	22.3	35.2	8.0	5.2	6.9	2.3	1.1	1.5	7.0
1990	9.3	20.8	35.6	9.2	4.9	8.4	2.4	1.6	1.6	6.3
1991	8.6	20.0	35.6	9.8	5.1	9.1	2.7	2.0	1.3	5.9
1992	8.3	21.6	34.6	9.4	5.1	9.3	3.0	1.9	1.1	5.8
1993	9.8	22.0	34.1	8.4	5.7	8.7	3.1	2.0	0.7	5.5
1994	9.0	21.6	34.0	8.5	6.0	8.5	3.1	2.2	1.2	5.9

U.S. Market Share, 1985 - 1994

Source: Ward's Automotive 1995

Automobile Industry Trends

As you can tell from the previous table, the Japanese are increasing their market share while American car companies are losing theirs. This trend can be reversed if new tax laws and provisions in GATT are implemented. In the future, American car companies may start to lose more market share to the Japanese as alternative-fueled vehicles gain momentum in our markets. The loss in market share will result from competing technologies trying to establish themselves as industry standards. This fracturing of the market will result from not having a master plan allowing automobile and oil companies to make a smooth transition that will keep our economy strong. We must communicate to the oil and automobile companies a need for alternative fueled and hybrid vehicles. At the same time we need to show these industries a way to develop other markets for their products.

Lumber Industry Facts

It is estimated that 47% of the softwood timber inventory (pine, spruce, and fir) is located in the publicly-owned national forests in the Pacific Northwest. This softwood inventory has only grown by 4% between 1952 and 1992. In 1991, the softwood inventory growth exceeded the removal rate by only 9%, and about two-thirds of all the wood harvested in the United States is softwood which is used primarily for construction and paper pulp.[11]

Lumber Industry Trends

Lumber availability and prices will remain uncertain as environmental concerns for the spotted owl (that resides in the northwest forests) increase. As more forest lands become unavailable to loggers, the supply of lumber will continue to decrease despite increases in new plantings. Even though there are more trees today than there were in the early 1900s, many of them are not yet ready to be harvested, which can affect prices and availability. As prices become more unstable in the future, wood will be substituted with other building materials such as plastics and steel. As this product substitution occurs, more people will lose their jobs in the lumber industry. In fact, due to the spotted owl crisis, more than thirty thousand lumber jobs were lost and lumber prices went up by 50%.[12] This job loss trend will continue as long as we reduce the amount of forests that can be harvested for *traditional* lumber use. This trend can be reversed if more trees are harvested for *engineered wood products* that can be sold here in the United States and abroad. By engineered wood products, I mean things like laminated beams, engineered floor joists, and Parallam® beams, which may be harvested from orchards of young trees, thereby saving old growth forests.

Steel Industry Facts

Skyscrapers, bridges, and automobiles are just a few examples of items that are made of steel. Unfortunately, many steel products that we consume here in America are not made from recycled or virgin steel made in the United States. A great percentage of the steel used for our products comes from Japan. We sell our scrap steel to the Japanese and in turn they transform it into finished products that we end up buying back to use for pipelines, bridges, automobiles, and other consumer products. In fact, our biggest export to Japan is scrap steel.

The Japanese have dominated the steel industry for some years now. They were able to accomplish this task after we gave them the necessary money and technology when we rebuilt their economy after WW II. Since then, they have reinvested their profits into their steel industry to make it the most modern in the world. As a result of this advantage, they have dominated the steel market even here in America.

---

[11] Facts from "Evergreen, The Truth About America's Forest," *Builder*, August 1995, p. S-66
[12] Facts from "White House Urged To Ax Timber Plan," *Builder*, February 1994, p. 29

Steel Industry Trends

The dominance in the steel market will remain with the Japanese for some years to come unless the price of electricity drops substantially. When electrical prices are very cheap, smelting steel in electric arc furnaces becomes very cost competitive with the Japanese. When the Government eliminates the deficit and the national debt, the money supply will be larger and borrowing will be cheaper. This will enable existing steel companies to rebuild their industry with the latest and most energy efficient technologies.

Electrical Energy Facts

There are approximately four thousand three hundred sixty electrical power plants in America. Of these, one hundred seventy-seven burn coal exclusively.[13] Of these one hundred seventy-seven coal-fired power plants, one hundred ten are hazardous to us and therefore subject to Phase I of the acid rain reduction plan of the 1990 Clean Air Act.[14] These coal-fired power plants are also hazardous in another way that is not highly publicized. Research has shown that a large coal-fired power plant releases large amounts of uranium and thorium. Tons of this radioactive material are released through smokestacks or disposed of in dumps or ash ponds. Considering that a nuclear power plant of approximately the same size releases hundreds of times less radioactivity than a coal-fired power plant, is all the more reason to find safe, cost-effective alternative energy sources.[15]

Electrical Energy Trends

As a result of the 1990 Clean Air Act, coal-fired power plants have begun to use low sulfur coal. This has resulted in lower prices for emission allowance credits which has kept solar, biomass, and renewable energy technologies out of the market. Not only is the alternative energy market being thwarted in this way, but it is also thwarted by the results of the 1992 Energy Policy Act. This act was supposed to create competition and help develop the alternative energy technologies, but its effect has been just the opposite. Due to deregulation of the industry, many power companies are merging to keep their costs low. As they drive down their costs, competition from the alternative energy industry is driven out. Even

---

[13] *The U.S. Cogeneration and Independent power Plant Directory,* 1994 Edition
[14] EPA, *The Plain English Guide To The Clean Air Act,* 1993, p. 15
[15] Nadis, Steve. "Radioactive Coal," *Popular Science,* April 1995, p. 35

though the power companies are making progress in reducing their pollution, all of it will not be eliminated unless a new, clean coal technology is developed, or unless we help subsidize the alternative electrical energy market so that it can begin replacing outdated coal-fired power plants. For example, Sierra Pacific Power company has one generator producing electricity using an alternative fuel developed from water and naphtha, called A-21.

Energy Conservation Facts

Twenty years ago, homes did not function as efficiently as they do today. Homes built in that period had inferior insulation, less efficient appliances, and single pane windows. Today's homes are designed for energy efficiency with improvements in all areas of construction. The biggest gains in energy efficiency came from heating and cooling. In twenty years, energy consumption was reduced by 55%. In this same period of time, lighting and cooking reduced their energy consumption by 20%. Water heating had the third largest gain by saving 15%, while refrigerators and freezers cut their consumption of energy down by 10%. As we spend money in research and development, we will continue to make strides toward improved energy efficiency. This will ultimately save all of us money that we can use in other areas of our lives.

Energy Conservation Trends

Future homes will be more energy efficient than the homes we build today. These gains in energy efficiency will result from better energy management as more homes become automated. Automatic washing of clothing and dishes will be done during off-peak periods when electricity is cheaper. The waste heat can be captured and utilized for space and/or water heating. This will reduce space heating costs during cooler months and/or water heating costs year round. During the summer months, air conditioning usage will be minimized. Lighting will also be automated to help reduce electrical needs while insuring security for the homeowner who is away. When a better building envelope is developed to minimize heat transfer, additional gains in energy efficiency will occur. Other improvements in wall, window, and door construction will also help accomplish this goal, and the widespread use of plastics in building construction will help reduce our energy consumption. As consumers, we have to question the builders and developers regarding the materials they use in the construction of our homes. We should refuse to buy homes that do not use advanced energy efficient technologies.

Energy Conservation Fact

During the 1970's, a high efficiency electronic ballast in fluorescent lights was developed as a result of the Department of Energy's efficiency program. These ballasts have already saved United States businesses $850 million in energy costs. A study performed by the Department of Energy indicates that if businesses could eliminate 10% to 20% of waste in all areas, this would give businesses additional capital to create two million new jobs.[16]

Energy Conservation Trend

Every business will look for energy saving technologies that will save them money in the long run, especially since businesses are downsizing to keep their costs low. This will be especially true for businesses that depend on energy for their processes of production. If, for example, steel mills can reduce their usage of electricity in electric arc furnaces, their charges for steel will be cheaper than their competitors, thus giving them market advantage and greater market share and profitability. Even though new energy production technologies will not sprout up over night, large electrical power users will be able to keep their electrical costs low due to the deregulation of the electric power industry which allows large electrical users to shop for power across state lines where electrical rates may be cheaper. As these companies find cheaper power, they will be able to hire some of the people who were laid off due to the deregulation and downsizing of the power industry. As more companies seek energy efficient technologies, more capital will be available for other needs that will help keep a company in business and our economy strong. Unless new energy efficient and cheaper energy production technologies are developed quickly in the next few years, we could possibly see more manufacturing jobs exported out of the country. We can help prevent this from happening by buying smarter. This would include purchasing more energy efficient products made in America. As an example, the purchase of compact flourescents over incandescent bulbs will save you money in the long run and help create jobs here in America.

Biomass Energy Facts

Biomass for energy production can come from many different sources. It can be commercially harvested from a stand of trees or it can come from yard clippings, construction debris, or waste from a sawmill. So long

---

[16] Figures from Romm, Joseph J. "The Benefits of Lean and Clean," *Technology Review*, February/March 1995, p. 71

as the material is woody in nature and reasonably dry, it can be used as fuel in an electrical power plant.

California has more than fifty-five biomass-powered electrical generation facilities that produce nearly 950 megawatts of electricity. This amount roughly equals 2% to 3% of the total electrical generating capacity of the state.[17] It is estimated that 2.5 trillion tons of cellulosic biomass are produced annually throughout the United States. This could be converted into 300 billion gallons of ethanol.[18]

The California Biomass industry represents over $2 billion worth of fuel collection, processing, transportation, and energy conversion equipment that produces over $110 million in state and local taxes. This industry has contributed over thirty thousand skilled jobs and has eliminated nearly 70,000 tons of air pollution while saving landfill capacity of approximately 320 million cubic feet which is approximately 4 million tons per year.[19]

In 1992, thirteen states including Arizona, California, Colorado, Kansas, Nebraska, Nevada, New Mexico, North Dakota, Oklahoma, South Dakota, Texas, Utah, and Wyoming spent approximately $1.4 billion in wood consuming equipment that employed sixty thousand workers. As a result of that expenditure, nearly $2.5 billion of income was generated that resulted in $621 million in taxes.[20]

The same thirteen states produce about 3.3 billion pounds of beef tallow annually. If converted to biodiesel, the tallow would replace 416 million gallons of diesel fuel.[21]

In 1992, in the Northeast, due to the expansion of the wood energy industry, there was a net gain of thirty-four thousand jobs and $1.8 billion of income. This expansion also saved approximately 1 billion gallons of oil that year.[22]

Biomass energy only represents approximately 3.4% of the country's total energy consumption. Only 2% is used for transportation fuels while the other 1.4% is used for electrical generation.[23]

[17] Morris, Gregory. "The Current State of the California Biomass Energy Industry," *Biologue* 4th Qtr 1994, pp. 4 & 8

[18] Morrer, Richard. "Biofuels System Research," *Department of Energy Biofuels Program*, p. 6

[19] Figures from Simons, George; Johannis, Mary; Miller, William; Swanson, Dave; and Wiltsee, George. "Institutional Issues Facing California's Biomass Energy Industry and the Role of a Collaborative," *BioEnergy '94, Technical Papers, Volume 2*, p. 547

[20] Figures from Quinn, Michael W.; Whittier, Jack; Hasse, Scott; High, Colin; Swanson, Dave; and Wood, Ed. "Economic Impact Of Industrial Wood Energy Use In Thirteen Western States," *BioEnergy '94, Technical Papers, Volume 2*, p. 398

[21] Figures from Hanns, Milford and Nelson, Richard. "Biodiesel Fuels Could Reduce Dependence On Foreign Oil," *Biologue* 4th Qtr 94, p. 25

[22] Figures from "Economic Impacts of Biomass Energy Development," *Biologue* 1st Qtr 95, p. 15

[23] "Pacific Northwest Power Planning Council Receives Biomass Resource Briefing," *Biologue* 1st Qtr 95, p. 18

Biomass Energy Trends

Biomass fuels will find it hard to compete with fossil fuels. Due to the 1992 Energy Policy Act, the electrical power industry is being deregulated. This situation is causing many utility companies to merge in order to save costs. As these power companies grow in size, they squeeze out less competitive companies and technologies. Since biomass energy has less energy on a pound for pound basis, it will not be able to compete with coal-powered electrical generation plants. As a result, these less efficient biomass operations will be forced to close down, resulting in lost jobs.

The net gains in employment may not look good for the biomass liquid fuels industry. Biodiesel and ethanol costs more to manufacture than gasoline or diesel. Without tax credits and incentives, the biofuel industry does not have a chance of surviving the oil companies competition. Compounding the problem, the oil industry has no interest in promoting these fuels because it would create additional competition in their markets. If the 1988 Alternative Motor Fuel Act is ever funded by Congress and conscientious citizens voice their concerns for a cleaner environment, the result might be local demand for biodiesel. This negative trend towards the elimination of biofuels can be reversed if all of us voice our concerns and opinions to Congress and to the automobile and oil companies. Reaching Congress can be done by buying one of the products listed at the end of Chapter 10. Automobile companies can be reached by writing or calling their alternative fuels division listed in Chapter 9.

Garbage Facts

The United States is the biggest producer of garbage in the world. With a population of two hundred fifty million, we throw away nearly 200 million tons of municipal solid waste every year, which is approximately 3-1/2 pounds per person per day. It is estimated that 30% of all garbage is made up of packaging and 45 billion pounds of plastic are hauled to the garbage dumps every year.[24] It has been estimated that we throw away enough office and writing paper to build a wall from Los Angeles to New York that would stand twelve feet high. On a daily basis, we buy sixty-two million newspapers and throw out about forty-four million of them. This much paper is the equivalent of twenty-six million trees a year! If we recycled just half of the magazines that are printed every year, we would save over twelve million cubic yards of landfill space.[25] From each ton of

[24] Figures from Motavalli, Jim. "The Real Conservatives," E Magazine, August 1995, p. 28
[25] Alameda County Recycling Guide, 1995, Inside Cover

garbage that is processed in recycling plants, it is estimated that 180 pounds of glass, 160 pounds of metals, 60 pounds of nonrecyclable material, and about 1,500 pounds of cellulosic material can be obtained.[26] In addition to municipal solid waste, we generate approximately two hundred fifty million scrap tires every year and we have approximately three to five billion tires stockpiled throughout the United States.[27]

Garbage Trends

Every year, more of our garbage is recycled, composted, or turned into energy. This trend will accelerate as landfill space disappears and tipping fees become exorbitant. New gasification and liquefaction technologies now entering the marketplace will help reduce the amount of garbage being landfilled by producing feedstocks for either energy or plastics production. We can help accelerate this process by voting people in to all levels of Government who are environmentally concerned. Or our Government can develop joint ventures such as the one between Folsom City and the California Prison Industry Authority which sorts the garbage for recyclables and composting.

Pollution Facts

The 1990 Clean Air Act is mandating tougher automobile smog checks in eighty-three urban areas where they don't meet Federal air quality standards. The new tests are called I/M 240, which stands for inspection and maintenance for 240 seconds. The cars are to be tested on a dynamometer while the vehicle "drives" at 55 mph for four minutes.

Pollution Trends

Due to the greater pressures of the 1990 Clean Air Act, clean fuel technologies are becoming more important. As a result of these pressures, reformulated gasolines, ethanol, and other alternative fuels are beginning to enter the marketplace. We can help this process along by buying alternative-fueled vehicles and by writing to the automobile and oil companies and strongly suggesting that they supply more alternative-fueled vehicles and fuels.

---

[26] National Fertilizer & Environmental Research Center Resource Group, Tennessee Valley Authority, "Fuels & Chemicals from Municipal Solid Waste"

[27] Metz, Robert. "N.M. Firm Is Ready To Roll Into The Tire Recycling Industry," *The Boston Globe*, Dec. 28, 1993, p. 34

Employment Facts

One of the largest employers in America is Manpower Inc.—a temporary employment agency with five hundred sixty thousand workers.[28] This is a frightening thought. At the present time there is no job security in the United States. This is a result of American companies moving their operations overseas. Since 1980, two and one-half million manufacturing jobs have left North America and moved to Asia, the Middle East, and the Caribbean.[29]

Employment Trends

As our economy evolves, corporations will continue to downsize, merge, and consolidate. Many of them will lay off their staff and hire temporaries and independent contractors to keep their costs low. This practice will erode the confidence each of us has in our economy. With less confidence, the economy will remain flat, despite improving productivity. When people are afraid of losing their jobs, few of them will encumber themselves with car and home loans, and these spending practices keep our economy strong. This trend will continue until our Government can balance the budget and begin to eliminate the national debt. Without low borrowing costs, corporations will do whatever is necessary to keep their bottom line in the black. Until a new prosperity in our country is achieved, the employment market will remain volatile. The United States will no longer be an economic power house unless we achieve economic prosperity.

Since the United States is the most economically powerful nation in the world, practically every other nation will pay its workers less than we do here. One of the major factors in the ability of these nations to keep their wages lower than those in America is they usually have lower and fewer infrastructural costs. They are not burdened with OSHA, workers compensation, insurance, employee taxes, and other benefits. As these countries become more industrialized, advanced, and in debt, they too will adopt some of these costs that will eventually drive up their price of labor. As this happens, a balance will eventually occur. This will not happen overnight since most less developed nations have few natural resources other than cheap labor. Until the day when all countries become equally industrialized and a world currency is established, our manufacturing jobs will continue to leave the country, and we will always feel the urge to promote protectionistic trade policies in an attempt to protect

---

[28] Castro, Janice. "Disposable Workers," *Time*, March 29, 1993, p. 43
[29] Figures from Wasny, Garrett. "Mission Possible," *World Trade*, November 1994, p. 38

our jobs here in America. A way to avoid this trend of job exportation is to implement creative tax laws that reward products that are made in America or products that have a higher percentage of American-made parts.

Crime Facts

By the end of fiscal year 1993, the Federal Government spent a total of **$1.26 trillion** on prison systems within the United States and its territories! In 1992, the state prison systems incarcerated 883,593 people.[30]

Crime Trends

Tougher legislation like California's "Three strikes and you're out" law will become the norm throughout our nation. As a result of this tougher legislation, there will be more prisoners and a greater demand for prisons. Costs of incarceration will escalate. Cities, counties, and states will need to create ways to help reduce this burden. They might use private companies to guard the prisoners. They might create joint ventures such as the one at Folsom Prison in California to help reduce their costs of incarceration. Some prisoners are reducing their prison stays and their cost of incarceration by sorting through garbage for recyclables. The revenues generated go directly to the City of Folsom, while the California Prison Industry Authority earns a processing fee. As the prison population increases throughout our nation, creative joint ventures that generate revenues for the prison system will be the wave of the future. This will not only help defray costs but protect the small communities from footing the bill. This will result in the development of new industries and the employment of more people.

Housing Facts

According to the Joint Center for Housing Studies at Harvard University, a family's home makes up 60% of that family's net worth. Of people surveyed, 60% would prefer buying a new home compared to only 17% of them who wanted a previously owned home. About two-thirds of them felt it was very important to have the interest deduction on their income taxes.[31]

In 1991, middle income taxpayers claimed almost two-thirds of the $45 billion in mortgage interest deductions.

---

[30] *The Book of the States* Volume 30, 1994-95 Edition, pp. 392 & 530
[31] Thompson, Thomas. "Housing Sentiments," *Builder*, February 1994, p. 46

Mortgage Interest Deduction: Who Benefits	
Household Income	**Percent of Benefit**
Less than $10,000	1.3%
$10,000 - $19,000	4.1%
$20,000 - $29,999	8.0%
$30,000 - $49,999	23.1%
$50,000 - $74,999	27.4%
$75,000 - $99,999	12.8%
$100,000 - $199,000	13.7%
$200,000 - $499,999	5.7%
$500,000 and up	3.0%
Source: Builder Magazine, December 1993, p. 19	

Housing Trends

Despite low inflation rates over the past few years, new and used home prices will continue to rise every year except for a few anomalies in the real estate market. The increase in prices is partly the result of a growing population with a pent up demand for homes near employment centers. Marketing costs associated with reselling a home also keep home prices high. This problem is further exacerbated by the current real estate appraisal and loan system that makes little or no distinction between new and old homes within the same neighborhood. As land becomes more scarce and prime locations disappear, existing home prices will continue to get higher even though they are second rate compared to new home construction. Older homes are usually less energy efficient, are not engineered for natural disasters, and develop structural problems over time resulting from dry rot, termite infestation, and settling. Clogged plumbing, faded paint, and a leaky roof are other types of problems that one inherits with an older home. Yet for some reason, appraisers will give a close or equal value to a home that is thirty years old compared to a new home of the same square footage. Their reasoning defies logic, but at the same time they reinforce the three most important aspects of real estate: location, location, and location. It is the location of the home that is valuable and not the home itself. There are of course exceptions to this point. Historical structures will need to be treated differently than homes stamped out of a cookie cutter. Until the real estate system makes this distinction, real estate prices will continue to go through the roof, making it more difficult for first-time and low-income buyers to acquire a home.

FOUR

FEDERAL TRUST FUND DECEPTION

As you may have heard by now, many of us will not see the benefits of our Social Security taxes by the time we retire. Social Security and other trust fund programs are financially insolvent due to Federal Government accounting practices and irresponsible spending behavior on the part of our legislators.

Government Accounting

You and I have to comply with general accounting practices that do not apply to the Federal Government. To most of us, trust funds are considered protected financial entities with specific purposes and rules. To the Government, trust funds are merely considered accounting devices that have no special meaning. When the Federal Government collects revenues from trust fund activities such as Social Security, the money goes directly into the general fund where it is spent for *current* Social Security benefits and other *nonrelated* Social Security expenditures.

Every dollar collected and deposited into the general fund on behalf of Social Security and any other trust fund programs increases the national debt. For example, $50 million of Social Security taxes are deposited into the Treasury, the Treasury delivers $50 million of special issue securities to the Social Security trust fund and makes two corresponding ledger marks. The national debt is increased by $50 million, and the Social Security trust fund ledger card is increased by $50 million as well. By the same token, when the Government spends $100 million for the Social Security trust fund, it retires $100 million worth of special issue securities from the Social Security trust fund and makes two corresponding ledger marks. The first ledger mark reduces the national debt by $100 million. The corresponding mark reduces the amount of surplus in the Social Security trust fund account. The remaining sum of special issue securities in a trust fund account represents a "surplus." From a glance, one would reason that the Social Security trust fund is solvent since it has these special issue securities. This is far from the truth. These special issue securities have no market value. They cannot be sold on the open market and they do not generate real interest. The interest that is paid on these special issue securities is done with more special issue securities. Essentially, the Government issues worthless IOUs to itself and it pays itself interest with more worthless IOUs.

When the Government reports to us that the Social Security trust fund has a surplus, they are referring to two different things. First, a cash flow surplus. This cash flow surplus exists when our current Social Security tax dollars are being used to finance current Social Security demands. After all payments are made on current Social Security recipients demands, a cash flow surplus exists. This surplus is illusory since the cash flow surplus is immediately spent on other Government expenditures such as salaries, bombs, and perks. In reality, this surplus does not really exist since it is not being used to purchase marketable securities on behalf of the Social Security trust fund program. This would be like having a Christmas savings account where you were able to put away $10 a week for a year and accumulated over $500. If you drew names for gifts for six people and you were not allowed to spend more than $50 per gift, your expected expenditure would be $300 for Christmas gifts. That would leave you $200. Since you are always running short of money, you decide to take the remaining $200 and make your car payment with it. Later, you call your banker and ask him/her if he/she would pay you interest on an IOU that you would replace for the money that was taken out for the car payment. Your banker laughs at you first, but agrees to pay you interest not with money, but with more worthless IOUs. Elated, you decide to call your family and tell them your great news: you balanced your budget and you still have money for next year's Christmas presents. At first you had a surplus in your Christmas savings account, but it disappeared as soon as you took the money for your car payment. You could claim that you had a surplus after making the car payment, but it is totally illusory and only would exist if the money was left in the savings account. Since the money was misappropriated for a car payment, no surplus exists at all.

Another surplus that doesn't exist is the one that politicians refer to when they speak of the Social Security or Medicare trust fund programs. Politicians speak of surpluses as if these trust fund accounts had real assets or money within them. This is far from the truth. In actuality, the trust fund accounts only own special issue securities that have no value. These surpluses represent a total of the annual cash flow surplus plus interest and they do not represent what we have paid into Social Security taxes or Medicare premiums. They only represent what is left over after the Government has spent our taxes on current Social Security or Medicare demands. At the end of 1994, the Government collected $461 billion in Social Security taxes, and only ended up with at $57 billion surplus.[32] This means that approximately 88¢ of every dollar we pay in goes towards current Social Security demands. The remaining 12¢ is used for other Government expenses, which means there is no surplus. Yet the Government wants us to believe there is a surplus. Can you imagine depositing your savings into a bank where the bank automatically takes 88¢ of every dollar as bank charges and uses it to pay off other depositors "withdrawals?" The remaining 12¢ is also spent, but the bank gives you a worthless IOU for it. The bank tells you that they will allow you to withdraw the money (12¢ for every dollar deposited), but they won't guarantee how much of the remaining money (12¢ per dollar) you will be able to withdraw when you retire (assuming they have new depositors to collect bank charges from at that time). This is essentially what the Government is doing with our Social Security trust fund program. To reiterate, the surplus is only a small fraction of what was originally deposited and there is no guarantee that it will be there for us when we retire.

If the Government were truly fair in regards to our trust fund money, it would have real assets contained within the trust fund accounts that represent our total deposits into the system. They would also only use these assets for their intended purposes and rightful beneficiaries. Since the Government only creates special issue securities for the cash flow surpluses, they are cheating us out of a tremendous amount of money. The problem becomes worse when it comes time to fund them. Because the securities don't have any value, the cash will have to come from the sale of real Government bonds, income taxes, trust fund revenues, printing of money, and cash flow surpluses from other trust fund accounts. If this scenario is allowed to play out, it will have many negative ramifications. Regardless of how the money is obtained to finance these trust fund programs, all of us will have to pay for it one way or another, even if

---

[32] Congressional Budget Office, *The Economic & Budget Outlook: Fiscal Years, 1996-2000,* 1995, pp. 92 & 94

we are retired. It will affect the elderly the most, since they won't have the same earning capacity as they did before retirement. The elderly will either see reduced benefits or higher income taxes or both. This dilemma is a result of government accounting practices that drive its spending patterns. It's like the tail wagging the dog.

Almost twenty-five years ago, the budget deficit was very small and could have easily been balanced if our legislators had been more responsible and eliminated wasteful spending. Since they could use trust fund money to help balance the budget, they felt they could continue their irresponsible deficit spending. This sentiment was reflected by traditional economists of that time. I remember one of my economics professors. The statement he made was approximately, if not exactly, the following: "It's okay for the Federal Government to engage in deficit spending so long as there is excess demand in the private sector." At that time, I felt this professor was nuts, but we now have the results of that global belief: an annual deficit that has grown over the years and a national debt that is out of hand.

Every year, the national debt grows larger and a greater portion of the annual budget is used to service the national debt. At the time of this writing, interest expense on the national debt was over $200 billion a year. The amount of interest will continue to grow every year until the budget is balanced. What is amazing about the interest expense and the deficit is that our legislators have taken twenty years to realize that this issue was important enough to make it part of their political campaigns. What was even more amazing about the Presidential candidates of 1996 is that some of them have claimed to be visionaries who had fresh ideas that can deliver our country into the 21st century without debt.

Visionaries tend to be nonconformists who are progressive thinkers who resist traditional thinking. Career politicians have to be very traditional in their thinking in order to survive the political process. After years of thinking in a certain manner, people develop a mindset that determines their behavior. Humans are creatures of habit. This includes their spending behaviors. Fiscal responsibility is learned behavior and most of us have had to learn how to balance our own budgets or else suffer the consequences. If a person is not challenged on a daily basis to make ends meet or is not punished for their irresponsible spending habits, a person can turn out to be financially reckless. Over years of learned recklessness, a person's mindset starts to condone irresponsible behavior and eventually the person loses perspective of what is right or wrong and continues to act in the irresponsible manner they have grown comfortable with.

Career politicians who have learned to become fiscally irresponsible are unlikely to change their mindsets overnight. Political promises, driven by the emotional enthusiasm of eloquent speeches, are nothing more than fancy rhetoric with no substance. At a time when Government spending has gotten out of hand, traditional thinking will not solve the problem. It will require an honest assessment of the problem. This includes realizing the truth about trust funds and the deficit. If this is not done and our legislators continue to lie to us about the real problem, politicians will further their political careers at the expense of the deficit, interest rates, taxes, and the demise of trust fund programs.

Political Games

Our elected officials are furthering their political careers by using the trust fund programs to their advantage. The accounting of trust funds are confusing and for your convenience, a Congressional report titled *Trust Funds and The Federal Deficit*, dated February 26, 1990, is printed in its entirety in Appendix A. It was authored by David Koitz, Gene Falk, and Philip Winters, and explains how the Treasury collects, spends, and creates debt for our trust funds.

The report tries to make light of the impending financial disaster of trust funds by using the analogy of an extended family. In this analogy, each family member contributes to the general fund and receives IOUs for their contributions. Their collected contributions are then used to pay for all of the basic necessities of living within that family such as food, rent, and utilities. This analogy neglects the individual needs and desires of each family member. Even though the basic needs of the family are being met, it does not account for the day when one of the family members wishes to use his or her IOUs to purchase a car and go to college. These IOUs are worthless to the car dealer and to the college. If one family member wishes to acquire a car and go to college, the rest of the family will have to reduce its expenditures, steal from its food budget, not pay rent, and/or borrow money. This analogy tries to justify that it is okay for the Government to use trust fund money for current consumption, regardless of the long term consequences. This attitude toward trust fund programs prevails throughout the legislative and executive branches of our Government. Our legislators and the President feel it is okay to take money from trust funds and use it to finance current consumption while creating an impending financial disaster.

This insidious attitude transcends good judgment and honesty and places every member of Congress and the President (who use the trust fund money to their advantage) in contempt with the American public. Their condescending action is not only irresponsible, but insulting as well.

Since none of our elected officials has had the courage to tell us about this mismanagement of our trust funds and the impending financial crisis, one has to wonder about their integrity and their agendas. Will our elected officials do what is right for the country or will they hide the truth from us to further their political careers? If one looks at legislation enacted in 1985 (the Gramm-Rudmann-Hollings Balanced Budget Act) to remove Social Security from the unified budget, it would seem to be latter. In doing so, the cash flow surplus became "found money" that could be applied to the budget deficit and announced to the media as superior fiscal policy by the current administration that resulted in lowering the deficit. This deception has its definitions embedded in the 1974 Budget Act under Section 401(c)(2), which defines offsetting receipts, contract authority, borrowing authority, entitlement and residual authority.

For years, both the Republicans and Democrats have been using trust fund money to make their deficit numbers appear better than they really are. The only recent difference has been the accounting of Social Security trust fund money in the unified budget. Prior to the Balanced Budget Act of 1985, all income and expenses of trust fund programs were reported on the unified budget. The only difference between pre- and post-Balanced Budget Act of 1985 is how the administration claims the cash flow surplus from the Social Security trust fund as "found money." Regardless of how cash flow surpluses are reported to the media, all the trust fund programs (especially Social Security and Medicare) are in deep trouble and will experience a financial crisis in about the tenth year of the next century. When that happens, cash flow surpluses from other trust funds may be used or benefits will be reduced. Social Security and/or income taxes may be raised, funds may be borrowed, money may be printed, or a combination of these solutions may be used to pay for Social Security and Medicare expenditures. This constant robbing of Peter to pay Paul will continue until the voting public demands an honest accounting from our elected officials. Until then, cash flow surpluses will be used by elected officials to hide the true plight of the deficit.

When you examine claims made by elected officials on how they would not balance the budget on the backs of the sick and the elderly, you find more hypocrisy. The mere fact that trust funds are not being treated in a fiduciary manner and that revenues are being used to finance other Government activities means our elected officials *are* trying to balance the budget on the backs of the sick and the elderly. If legislators weren't trying to balance the budget this way, the Social Security and Medicare trust fund programs would be fiduciary instruments. To fulfill the modern needs of a downsizing Government, visionary plans need to be put into place that will satisfy both current and future needs while limiting Government expenses. Trust funds managed in a non-fiduciary manner prove that elected officials are using rhetoric to twist the numbers in the interest of furthering their political careers.

This ladder climbing was demonstrated by both Republicans and the Democrats in 1995 and 1996. Our country was held hostage when the President and Congress could not agree on how they would balance the budget in seven years. They closed the Government down and both parties blamed each other for the closure and the country lost productivity and money. President Clinton did not want to compromise his standing in regard to education, the environment, and the elderly, while the Republicans were interested in giving tax cuts and downsizing Government expenditures. This difference in agendas created a stalemate. At the beginning of their stalemate, the Government was shut down and workers were sent home. Eventually, a debt extension was given and laid off workers were paid for their time not at work. This did not accomplish anything except to waste money and anger the voting public. During that period of time when there were no debt extensions, the Government ran its operations by using trust fund revenues. It was reported to the media as a last resort measure, but in reality, the use of trust fund revenues for daily operations has been going on for years. The Government did not want to let this fact out since it would have pointed a finger at them for their dishonest, incompetent, and irresponsible behavior. In fact, allegations were flying around on how certain politicians wanted to impeach other politicians and Government officials for doing their jobs, even though their behavior was governed by prescribed accounting procedures and laws. One such instance involved a member of Congress wanting to impeach Treasury Secretary Rubin for circumventing Congress's constitutional authority of raising the debt limit. Another instance revolved around wanting to impeach President Clinton for juggling the books.

Since both parties have been guilty of using trust fund cash flow surpluses and revenues to finance current consumption and advance their political careers, they probably decided to keep trust fund accounting a secret. In doing so, they averted the negative opinion polls that would result from the public's knowledge of their actions. Since none of our elected officials have had either the intelligence or the ability to figure out a better way of handling the trust fund programs and the deficit, they have opted for choices that become well publicized and popular with the voting public. These choices may indeed be popular, but not necessarily good or intelligent ones that will benefit all of us in the long run. Our elected officials are great spokesmen, adept at handling delicate situations diplomatically. Because their speeches have been effective on the level of high-sounding rhetoric, the majority of people have trusted that they are qualified and educated enough to make good decisions for us. But now we are in a pickle, along with the politicians. Making good long-term decisions requires time, research, intelligence, and foresight, and it appears that many of our elected officials are lacking in several of the requirements needed to find good solutions.

A politician's logic is not hard to see. Making good decisions for the country sometimes can be devastating to a politician's career. One example a politician may be faced with is pork spending that has gone on for years and has been financed with our trust fund money. If politicians had eliminated their pork spending during their term in office, they probably wouldn't have gotten re-elected and would have lost their jobs and the perks that go with it.

Since our elected officials find themselves with this dilemma regarding trust fund programs, they probably feel the best thing they can do is to treat us like mushrooms: "keep us in the dark and feed us shit." They reason that what the public doesn't know can't hurt them. Besides, by the time the trust fund programs are in deep financial crisis, many of the current Congressmen/Congresswomen will have outlived their popularity and will no longer be in office; they will be retired, collecting their Government pensions. If some of them are still in office by the time the crisis hits, they will tell us that the Congressional Research Service did not apprise them of any long-term negative ramifications as they are written in the report reprinted in this book.

As an example of this misguided information, the report states:

> But even when a trust fund program actually does run a cash surplus, as in the case with Social Security today, to conclude that these funds provide the Government with a substitute form of borrowing is speculative. There is no way of knowing whether over time a surplus leads to a reduction in Government borrowing from the public or whether it permits the Government to spend more or tax less.

These statements are very ambiguous, confusing, and inconclusive. Congressmen/Congresswomen who have read this report and do not question or challenge the information and conclusions will undoubtedly absolve themselves of any future crisis by claiming ignorance. Anyone with any amount of intelligence should be able to read this report and see it is sugar coated. If our elected officials had spent any time reading this report, they would have come up with the same conclusions I have: the trust fund programs are in deep trouble and will put our Government further into debt.

What I propose is this: If our elected officials want to bury their heads in the sand like ostriches, then we should clean out Congress and eliminate everyone who is not willing to look at the problem for what it is and deal with it on a serious problem-solving level. If we present Congress with real solutions that will work and encourage them to support these policies, everyone will win. The country wins, and the politicians win by being part of the solution. They will be the heroes who saved our country. If they fail to respond to our needs, we should boot them out of office for continuing this masquerade regarding trust funds and the deficit.

Deficit Masking

For years, trust fund revenues have always been included in the unified budget and are used to finance current consumption. The unified budget included all the revenues of the Federal Government—from the Social Security trust fund as well as other sources—and Federal expenditures. The unified budget deficit is the difference between total revenues and total expenditures.[33] In 1983, legislation was enacted to remove the Social Security trust fund from the unified budget, effective in fiscal year 1993. Later, in 1985, The Gramm-Rudman-Hollings Balanced Budget Act made the removal effective immediately.[34]

Since the Balanced Budget Act, Social Security revenues, expenses, and cash flow surpluses have been removed from the unified budget. This gives the President extra political leverage to use to his advantage. After the projected unified budget deficit was announced, the President chose a time that was politically advantageous to hold a press conference and announce the unified budget deficit had just been lowered by billions of dollars due to his superior fiscal policies. In actuality, the President simply applied the cash flow surplus from the Social Security program to the unified budget deficit and announced a new, lower figure. At the end of Fiscal Year 1993, our Government had used over $366 billion worth of Social Security trust fund surpluses to mask the size of the annual deficits.[35]

The picture gets worse when you include the Medicare trust fund cash flow surpluses (includes the Hospital Insurance trust fund and the Supplementary Medical trust fund) in the amount of $149 billion.[36] The Unemployment trust fund has contributed over $47 billion,[37] while the Highway trust fund contributed over $22 billion over the years.[38] So by the end of Fiscal Year 1993, Social Security, Medicare, Unemployment, and Highway trust fund programs have contributed over $584 billion worth of cash flow surpluses to mask the size of our annual deficits. Even though the Medicare, Unemployment and Highway trust fund programs are included in the unified budget, their cash flow surpluses are used to mask the true size of the deficit. This masking is not readily evident when you consider that most of the trust fund programs do not have sufficient revenues to cover their expenses. Trust fund programs that have cash flow surpluses are basically subsidizing other trust fund programs that receive little or no income from their benefactors. This includes the Civil Service and Military Retirement trust fund programs.

---

[33] General Accounting Office, "Social Security Trust Fund Reserves" 1989, p. 36
[34] General Accounting Office, "Social Security Trust Fund Reserves" 1989, pp. 2-3
[35] Historical Tables, Budget of the United States Government, Fiscal Year 1996, p. 226
[36] Historical Tables, Budget of the United States Government, Fiscal Year 1996, p. 227
[37] Treasury Bulletin, December 1994, p. 134
[38] Treasury Bulletin, March 1994, p. 139

This deficit masking in the short run saves the Government from borrowing money from the public. The downside of using trust fund money in this manner is that future deficits will become outrageous as cash flow surpluses evaporate and turn into deficits. This will be especially true for Social Security and Medicare. These two entitlement programs will become more expensive every year as our population grows older and life expectancy is increased. A huge financial crisis will occur when the baby boomers begin to retire in the year 2010.

At that point, the cost of living will be substantially higher than it is today. The problem gets compounded because the trust fund programs have no real assets that can appreciate or generate revenues. Funding these entitlement programs will place a tremendous strain on the Federal budget. The Government may raise taxes, borrow funds, print money, or default on government programs or debt. As our Government borrows more money, a greater percentage of the budget will be used to service the national debt and we will no longer have cash flow surpluses from either Social Security or Medicare trust fund programs to help offset the size of the deficit.

Interest Rates

As the national debt gets bigger, the Government will use a greater percentage of its budget to pay interest on the debt. At this time, the national debt is $5 trillion and more than $200 billion of the annual budget is being used to pay interest on the debt. By the time the Government balances the budget, the national debt will be close to $7 trillion and the amount of interest paid out on an annual basis will be astronomical. The problem will get worse when baby boomers start to retire since there are no cash reserves to finance their retirement. The financing will have to result from the sale of Government bonds, increased taxes, or the printing of money. If the choice is to sell bonds, the government will have to offer high yields in order to compete with other financial instruments. When bond yields are attractive, foreign capital will flow to our country. When this happens, it will help perpetuate the myth that in order to keep inflation low, we must keep interest rates high. This is especially true when the dollar is strong and we have favorable exchange rates. With a strong dollar, imports are cheap and our inflation is kept low due to the fact we are importing low-cost goods. Also, when interest rates are high, the attraction of foreign capital will accomplish two things simultaneously: it will settle the balance of payment issue and it will help finance the annual deficit through the sale of Government bonds.

Higher Taxes

As more Government bonds are sold and interest rates rise, the Government will need more revenues to cover its interest expense on the national debt. With fewer cash flow surpluses to steal from, the Government will be forced to raise revenues through the tax system. This will include increased income, Social Security, and Medicare taxes. The tax burden will become overwhelming as the national debt grows.

Because Social Security taxes are being used for current consumption for the Social Security trust fund program and other Government expenditures, Social Security taxes can be considered as another form of income tax. This disguise is more apparent when you consider the Earned Income Tax Credit that was put into place in 1975. The tax credit was designed to counteract the antiwork incentives of Social Security taxes. Our legislators knew they were using Social Security taxes as income taxes, but they didn't tell us that. To give the working poor a break on their taxes, our legislators decided to give them the Earned Income Tax Credit. Between income taxes and "Social Security taxes," all of us are paying a much higher amount of income taxes than most of us realize. As Social Security taxes rose, so did the Earned Income Tax Credit. The creation of the Earned Income Tax Credit almost coincides with the Social Security Act Amendments of 1977 and 1983 which moved the Old-Age, Survivors' and Disability Insurance (OASDI) trust funds away from their traditional pay-as-you-go financing basis toward the accumulation of a substantial, though temporary, reserve.[39] Again, this reserve only represents future spending authorities because special issue securities have no real value.

Trust Fund Solvency

Since trust funds only own special issue securities and our Government does not comply with general accounting practices, our trust fund programs are insolvent. The Social Security trust fund is insolvent despite the fact that the trust fund generates a cash flow surplus. This cash flow surplus is illusory because current Social Security taxes are being used to finance current Social Security recipient benefits. Our taxes are not being used to buy real interest-bearing instruments to build a nest egg for us in the future; they are being used to finance current consumption. If all of our Social Security taxes from 1962 to 1994 had been used to purchase interest-bearing financial instruments, the Government could have funded our retirement with over $6.1573 trillion worth of revenues.[40]

---

[39] General Accounting Office, "Social Security Trust Fund Reserves," 1989, p. 1
[40] Congressional Budget Office, "The Economic & Budget Outlook: Fiscal Years, 1996-2000," p. 94

Since only cash flow surpluses are being accumulated in our trust fund programs, the Government only owns $1.2 trillion worth of these "worthless" internal IOUs in *all* trust fund programs as of 1994.[41] As you can clearly determine, our Government has been spending our trust fund money recklessly, causing them to become insolvent. In the next few years, without any changes to the system, our Government will be in a financial crisis that will make the $5 trillion national debt seem like peanuts. To prevent this from happening, and to avoid this crisis, your enlightenment on this subject is imperative. For this reason the report titled "Trust Fund Programs and The Federal Deficit" is printed in Appendix A in its entirety.

---

[41] Statistical Abstract of the United States, 1994, p. 330

FUNDAMENTALS & PERSPECTIVES

Government's Function

When you are up to your ass in alligators, you forget that your main objective is to drain the swamp. This is the dilemma that our Government is faced with. We have a staggering national debt and an unbalanced budget with an anemic economy. This deficit and the national debt is keeping our legislators from seeing what their main objective is, which is to maintain competition, correct market failures due to externalities, provide economic stability, and achieve economic equity.

Maintain Competition

One of the most important economic functions of Government is to maintain competition. In order to achieve this goal, incentives, not impediments, are needed to stimulate ingenuity that will result in new technologies and efficiencies, new products, lower prices, and a growing economy. Sometimes subsidies, Government sponsored research, tax credits, and cash payments are needed to stimulate competition. In any case, without establishing healthy competition in all sectors of our economy, monopolies and oligopolies creep in. When this happens, they drive out competition and push prices up. Eventually, this action will stunt the growth of our economy.

Correct Market Failures Due To Externalities

An externality occurs when a person's or a group's activities affects other peoples' well being and there is no payment or compensation to the affected party. It is the Government's function to make sure that the damaging party makes some form of restitution, if not to the individuals, then to the system, whereby the money can be used to help develop solutions to mitigate the externality.

Without Government acting as policeman for the environment, big business would eventually destroy the environment as they are doing in less developed nations. If pollution goes unchecked, it will cost ten to one hundred times more to clean up the problems in the future than it costs now. To keep future costs under control, it is imperative that our Government keep a strong arm in the policing of the environment, otherwise our world will be unfit to live in.

Provide Economic Stability

Recession, high unemployment, high interest rates, economic stagflation (stagnation with inflation), and inflation are the enemies of a healthy economy. It is the Government's function to insure that none of this happens. The Government can accomplish economic stability through monetary, spending or tax policies.

Achieve Economic Equity

One of Government's main functions is to achieve greater economic equity; a fair distribution of personal income and resources. In part, this can be accomplished through the tax system, but achieving equity is very subjective. All classes of people will agree on one thing: they need more money. However, none of them are willing to give up their share to make the system more equitable.

Economics

If you put one hundred economists in a room, you will get one hundred different predictions about what will happen in the future regarding our economy. Economics is a soft science. On a scale of one to ten, where ten is exact, mathematics would hold this spot. Meteorology is much less accurate and would score about a five. Economics would score around three. Economists look to different indicators in our economy to help them determine what will happen, but very few economists are proven correct on a constant, regular basis. This is one of the reasons why it is so difficult for the Government to keep its promises regarding economic growth and the elimination of the deficit.

The world is large and diverse, with people following many different agendas, priorities, and perspectives. At any moment, any group could decide that their values are more important than anyone else's and go on strike, engage in terrorist activities, or even start a war. With such extremes of possibilities, economic prediction is not the goal of this chapter. Neither is teaching you everything there is to know about economics. Rather, the goal is to establish a foundation of knowledge that will help you to understand the solutions and conclusions that I am proposing.

Constraints On The Economy

There are three constraints of basic economic theory that govern the potential growth of our economy. They include: Technology, Resources, and a blend of Social Customs and Written Laws governing the use of our resources.

The first constraint is Technology. Our economic growth is in part constrained by how much technological know-how we can apply to production. The more technological advances we achieve, the more possibilities for potential growth can occur. Take for example the use of the personal computer in manufacturing. Personal computers are great machines for remembering redundant operations and sequences. A set of instructions can be programmed into the computer to perform precise, repetitive machine operations. Previous to the advent of computers, a machinist had to manually machine parts and check their work for tolerances as they went along. Due to the implementation of the computer, productivity in machining has been greatly enhanced.[42] As productivity increases, production prices tend to drop and demand for that product usually increases. This in turn results in the growth of our economy.

The second constraint of economic growth is Resources. Resources consist of three main categories: Land, Labor, and Capital. Land includes items such as mineral deposits, water resources, and fertile soil, as well as the climatic conditions of the land in question. Labor includes everyone

---

[42] The negative effects of computerization in the workforce are not accounted for in the productivity picture. This includes the disruption of people's lives, especially when technology puts people out of work and they don't have the required skills to be reabsorbed into the marketplace. Even though you sometimes increase productivity through computerization, you can create waste by creating unemployment.

in our work force, whether it be a fry cook at Burger King or a rocket scientist at NASA. Capital includes items such as money, durable machinery, buildings, roads, and other forms of construction.

The third constraint of economic growth is Social Customs and Written Laws. Building codes are one example of this constraint. The building code specifically enforces standards of safety, sanitation, and the use of materials. Unfortunately, some building codes are outdated and prevent the use of certain specific building materials that would increase productivity. When this happens, productivity is held down, prices are kept up and growth is stunted.

Economic Efficiency

Economic Efficiency is an elusive term that is very hard to measure, but the constraint of our economy is dependent on how much waste occurs within it. The concept of efficiency to most people means the avoidance of waste. Waste can be something as simple as a forest fire where precious trees and wildlife are lost. Another form of waste is discrimination. If talented people with training and education are not allowed to fill a job because of sex, race, or sexual preference, waste and productivity losses occur. Another example of waste occurs when monopolies exist. Our Government can be viewed as a monopoly. Since it would be impractical and chaotic for more than one form of Government in our country, the monopoly must exist. Because it does, waste occurs, placing a constraint on the economy's potential for growth. Our economy would grow more than it does now if Government was more efficient and less wasteful.

Opportunity Costs

When a resource is used for one activity over another, the lost value of the forgone activity is called the opportunity cost. For example, you have $10 to either buy lunch or go to the movies. You choose to go to the movies so your opportunity cost is the lost value of not having lunch. This definition works under the assumption that everything in life is finite, and that there are no free lunches. Everything has a cost.

Law Of Increasing Opportunity Costs

Understanding the Law of Increasing Opportunity Costs demands that you understand that life is finite and there are no free lunches. Money, energy, and all resources have their limits, and no matter what goods or services are produced, the goods or services require a given amount of resources in order to be produced.

When our economy decides to reduce production of one product in favor of increased production of another product, the product being reduced suffers increased opportunity costs because of decreased efficiency, lost revenues, and lower profitability. The increase in production of the second product requires that resources of the first product are given up.

If for example, gasoline production is reduced while ethanol production is increased, the oil companies will suffer from increasing opportunity costs since fewer resources are being employed to produce gasoline. Oil companies lose their efficiencies through smaller economies of scales, which in turn results in lower revenues and profits. As they lose more profits and revenues their opportunity costs increase.

Elastic Demand Curve

Having an elastic demand for a product/service means that when the price of that product/service goes up, we decide that our demand for that product/service is less important than the price increase. As a result, we decide not to make that purchase. As an example, many consumers have an elastic demand for fresh fruits and vegetables. When fresh fruits and vegetables show a substantial price increase, most consumers choose not to buy fresh fruits and vegetables.

Inelastic Demand Curve

Having an inelastic demand for a product/service means that if the price goes up, we are inflexible or inelastic about our demand for that product/service. When consumers have an inelastic demand for a product/service, a price increase will mean that they will pay the higher price.

An example of an inelastic demand for a product is gasoline or diesel fuel. Since all of our vehicles need gasoline or diesel to power them, and most of us need our vehicles to help us get to work, a price increase at the gas pumps means that most of us will pay the higher price. A lot of us will grumble and complain about the price, but we will still consume the same amount. Some people will shop around for a lower price, but their opportunity cost for doing so is wasted time, gasoline, and increased frustration.

Economic Multiplier

The economic multiplier is also known as the multiplier effect. This term represents the measurement of how much economic growth can be accomplished through combinations of spending, tax cuts, and/or investments. For the sake of explanation and ease of understanding, we will arbitrarily assume that the multiplier effect within our generic economy is a factor of two. This means that for every $1 injected into the economy from an outside source, a total of $2 will be generated. For example, say you have just moved to the United States from a foreign country and brought $10,000 with you. Applying the multiplier effect of the factor of two with this sum of money, the economy will grow by an additional $20,000. This growth is accomplished when the dollars are re-spent throughout the economy.

Externalities

An externality occurs when a person's or a group's activities affects other peoples' well being (good or bad), and there is no payment or compensation to the affected party. For example, sulfur dioxide emissions from coal-fired power plants affects everything in the world. People with respiratory problems are afflicted, historical buildings and statues are eroded by acid rain, watersheds are polluted with sulfuric acid, plants and trees are damaged by acid rain, and the paint on our automobiles is slowly destroyed by the acid rain. No one is being compensated for these damages.

Trade Deficits

When we buy imported oil, cars, or electronics, as well as any other imported goods, and we fail to sell an equal value of U.S. made goods to the rest of the world, we incur a negative Current Account Balance. This is commonly called a trade deficit.

The United States employs different financial instruments through-out the year to settle up our trade deficits with the rest of the world. These instruments include Government bonds, stocks, currency, bank loans, real estate, and companies. Instead of buying American goods and services to balance the trade deficits, the rest of the world is buying up America one piece at a time and gaining more control of our economic base. To help you understand how trade deficits and balance of payments works, a simple analogy will be used.

Pretend that you live and work in a very special town. This is the only town on the planet and the company that you work for owns everything in the town. Everyone who lives in this town works for the company and everyone has a debit card that can be used anywhere in town. You can use this debit card as much as you like, but at the end of your pay period (every three months), you must settle up with the company.

At the end of the pay period, you have spent more than you have earned. This is something you have done for the last fifteen years so your spending habits won't change. The company doesn't worry, since you cannot leave the town or work anywhere else. Besides, the company is very flexible regarding your debt. They will allow you to sell back personal property that you have acquired over the years, or they will take a promissory note. Toasters, televisions sets, your car, and even the clothes on your back are acceptable forms of payment for the company. If they take a promissory note, they expect interest payments and a balloon payment for the principal amount to be paid back by a negotiated date. Unfortunately, you have been spending more than you have been making for fifteen years and you had to sell off practically everything you own except your home. This company is very liberal about payments and has devised another way for you to make ends meet. They create a revolving promissory note system. It is much like having unlimited credit limit on an American Express credit card with extended payoff dates. You also may have as many of these cards as you wish. Whatever you owe at the end of your pay period is placed on this account. The company expects you to pay interest every month and the principal balance in a predetermined amount of time. If you cannot make an interest payment or the principal balance, the company will allow you to close that account and open up a new account with different terms. The terms could be better or they could be worse. Most likely they will be worse, since you will be paying interest on top of interest. The unpaid interest now becomes part of the principal balance that you owe and you must pay interest on the entire sum. Unfortunately, you are terrible about your spending habits and you cannot make the minimum interest payment and you have to renegotiate a new account. In this last account you negotiated twenty four monthly interest payments of $20 a month with a balloon payment of $500 at the end of the twenty-fourth month. You only made two interest payments and defaulted, which means you still owe twenty two interest payments plus the principal amount. The interest is $440 (22 X $20) and the principal amount is $500 which makes your new account balance $940.

This debt problem continues pay period after pay period. Eventually, you are so far in debt that you decide to have children and promise the company that your children will pay off your debt. The company agrees and allows you to continue spending since you are now buying things for your child and the company's future debt servicer.

In this analogy, earnings represent our exports and purchases represent imports. For the last fifteen years, the worker has been buying more than he has been earning, just like the United States has been buying more than it has been selling abroad. The company represents the rest of the world, and settling the account is the same with them. Our country sells off assets to balance the trade deficits just as the worker did to settle up his account. The United States sells real estate, companies, stocks, and bonds. Government bonds would represent the revolving promissory notes in the example. The rest of the world trusts that the United States will pay its debt in the future since the world believes the future generations of the United States will continue to make America strong and pay its debt. The difference lies in the settlement period. In the example, the settlement period is three months. In real life, this settlement process is year round and it does not just happen on the last day of every quarter. We have official reports for every quarter of the year that represents what happened during those three months of the quarter.

There are many drawbacks in the way we settle our chronic trade deficit problems:

1. **Recurring Interest Payments:** When we sell Government bonds instead of goods and services, we must continue to pay interest year after year until that bond matures. When it does, we must pay the principal as well.

2. **Trade Deficit Financing Becomes Part of the Annual Deficit:** Even though cash is being exchanged for a bond which helps finance our fiscal deficit in the short run, the annual interest payments on those bonds become part of our annual deficit. Eventually, those bonds will mature and payment on the principal balance will become due. That payment will have to come out of the Government's pocket.

3. **Subsidizes Imports:** Even though the initial cost of buying imports is lower than buying domestic made products, trade deficit financing are hidden costs that we do not realize when we purchase imports. Those hidden costs come in the form of interest payments on bonds, profits and dividends that leave the country, and lost tax revenue on assets sold to individuals and countries that have favorable tax status in the United States.

4. **Shrinking Tax Base:** When taxpaying American-owned assets are sold to foreigners who have preferential tax treatment, America loses tax dollars. Some foreigners pay very little or no income taxes at all to America. If these individuals or companies gobble up high tax paying industries, our Government's tax receipts suffer and the liability is then transferred to the American public.

5. **Less Money for Expansion:** Since we have a chronic debt problem and part of our trade deficit financing is in the form of Government bond sales, our Government must continue to borrow greater sums of money every year in order to meet those obligations. When more money is drained from the system to finance Government debt, there is less money for the private sector. The money that is available is more expensive than it would be if the Government wasn't borrowing as much as it is. Higher costs of borrowing translates into slower or marginal growth. If the economy stalls or recedes, then there will be fewer jobs, fewer taxpayers, more extended unemployment insurance, higher Government deficits, and less money available for expansion.

6. **Capital Outflows To Foreigners:** When we sell capital assets to foreigners in order to finance our trade deficits, we are selling that income stream as well. Whether it be stocks, companies, or real estate, these assets generate dividends and profits that go to the holder of that asset. Those dividends and profits leave the country and gives the holder of those profits additional means to purchase more of America.

7. **Losing Control Of America:** When we sell assets to foreigners, we are selling off America one piece at a time. Pebble Beach, Rockefeller Center, and the Empire State Building (one half foreign ownership) are some examples of foreign ownership of American assets. As we sell off more of our assets, foreigners will be able to dictate policy to those who interact with those companies. They can set prices or determine how business will be conducted here in the United States.

8. **Create Inflation:** Foreigners who accumulate cash reserves from income streams on American assets or excess profits from foreign trade have been known to create inflation here in America. These foreigners with too much cash and too little American business savvy end up paying too much for assets. This drives up the values of similar assets. The Japanese have done this in the real estate market which has made it more difficult for average people to own their own home. Their reckless buying behavior can be partially blamed on anyone who buys foreign goods. Without our trade deficits, foreigners would not have excess cash to spend foolishly here in America.

9. **Foreign Profit Subsidies:** Our excess foreign spending leads to foreign profit subsidies through our tax system. Take for example the BMW assembly plant in South Carolina. When BMW first announced its plans to locate a billion dollar assembly plant in that state, other states such as Nebraska, Massachusetts, and Arizona wanted BMW to locate that assembly plant in their state. To induce BMW to do so, each of these states offered incentives to BMW. As a result, the bidding war got out of hand, and South Carolina had the best package to offer BMW. Their package resulted in tax breaks and incentives totaling about $150 million. Included in this $150 million was free land that cost the state $25 million, not to mention the interest costs on the bonds that were sold to buy the land. To make matters worse, the Germans did not build a billion dollar plant. They only spent about $300 million, then decided to pay the assembly line workers substandard wages. Not a bad deal for BMW, considering they would have made money anyway by moving their plant to America regardless of the incentives.[43]

---

[43] Figures from Barlett, Donald L. and Steele, James B. *America: Who Really Pays The Taxes*, Touchstone, 1994, pp. 301-306

Simply put, cheap imports have many hidden costs that are not reflected in the price we pay at the register. These hidden costs affect inflation, our tax system, Government debt, and our ability as an economy to grow and prosper. By settling our trade deficits through our Capital Accounts, profits get exported out of the country, we lose tax revenues, we become indebted to foreigners for years, the national debt gets bigger, the cost of money becomes more expensive, and our foreign exchange rate becomes unfavorable.

Many traditional economists may argue that there should be no concern for huge trade deficits since the accounts must always balance. Their reasoning stems from the equation:

Current Account = Capital Accounts + Statistical Discrepancy
+ Official Reserve Transactions

Remember, Current Account is simply the trade deficit. Capital Accounts represent the capital assets sold to pay for the trade deficit. The statistical discrepancy is a number the Government uses to balance the books—their fudge factor. Since data comes from different sources, it is impossible to make all of it balance and they must resort to using a number called statistical discrepancy. Official Reserve Transactions involve purchase or sale of official reserve assets by central banks. In the case of America, the central bank is the Federal Reserve System and the most common asset used by the Federal Reserve is the Treasury Bill. Other assets include gold, foreign exchange reserves, credits issued by the International Monetary Fund, and Special Drawing Rights.

With this equation and a given set of variables, several conclusions are drawn. The most popular conclusion stated today is that interest rates must remain high in order to keep inflation low. Keeping inflation low is an ancillary benefit of high interest rates. The real reason for high interest rates is the need to finance trade deficits and fiscal deficits. The three arguments below are not always true because predicting foreign exchange rates is empirical and a rise in interest rates does not always mean a strong foreign exchange rate. This was true in 1995 when interest rates were high, but the U.S. dollar was weak against foreign currencies. The strength of the U.S. dollar is in great part a reflection of the Current Account Balance. Since the United States had been running huge trade deficits, the currency market responded accordingly and the U.S. dollar was weak against foreign currencies. This eventually changed when The Swiss National Bank, The German Central Bank, the Bank of Japan, and the Federal Reserve intervened to prop up the value of the dollar against the Yen in mid August of 1995. After these banks bought dollars, the U.S. dollar's value improved greatly against the Yen.

ARGUMENT 1

High domestic interest rates in the U.S.	Equals	An attractive investment to foreigners
An attractive investment to foreigners	Equals	A large inflow of foreign capital
A large inflow of foreign capital	Equals	An overvalued dollar in foreign markets
An overvalued dollar in foreign markets	Equals	Strong U.S. exchange rates
Strong U.S. exchange rates	Equals	Cheaper imports
Cheaper imports	Equals	Increased consumption of cheap imports
Increased consumption of cheap imports	Equals	Low inflation

ARGUMENT 2

High domestic interest rates in the U.S.	Equals	An attractive investment to foreigners
An attractive investment to foreigners	Equals	A large inflow of foreign capital
A large inflow of foreign capital	Equals	An overvalued dollar in foreign markets
An overvalued dollar in foreign markets	Equals	Strong U.S. exchange rates
Strong U.S. exchange rates	Equals	Cheap imports
Cheap imports	Equals	Increased consumption of cheap imports
Increased consumption of cheap imports	Equals	Growing trade deficit
Growing trade deficit	Equals	Growing capital account surplus
Growing capital account surplus	Equals	Trade deficit financing

ARGUMENT 3

High domestic interest rates in the U.S.	Equals	An attractive investment to foreigners
An attractive investment to foreigners	Equals	A large flow of foreign capital
A large flow of foreign capital	Equals	Government bond sales
Government bond sales	Equals	Fiscal financing

In each argument, we start with high domestic interest rates. This leads to three distinct conclusions: We have low inflation, we finance the trade deficits and our annual fiscal deficit. So when you hear politicians alleging the reason why interest rates must remain high is to keep inflation low, this is only partially correct. The real reason is to finance trade and fiscal deficits.

SIX

INCOME CONSERVATION

This chapter deals with income conservation. Income conservation, unlike budget cuts, helps retain essential Government services while reducing Government expenditures. Today, governmental solutions to deficits usually include massive budget cuts that result in employee layoffs and/or reduction of services. When layoffs in Government jobs occur, it usually has a shrinking effect upon the rest of the economy. The exception to this would be a scenario involving other positive factors that would cause the economy to grow whereby new or existing industries would absorb laid-off Government workers.

Your input to your elected officials can prevent massive layoffs and cuts in services. You need to advocate specific plans to reduce Government expenditures while stimulating the private sector. This goal can be accomplished by reducing expenditures for consumables, energy, subsidies, and negative productivity. The broad areas that will be affected by these plans include automotive expenses, energy expenses, farm subsidies, FEMA, and Welfare.

Automotive

Local, state, and Federal Government deficits can be reduced by implementing long term solutions that will save money. There are three very simple things that all Government agencies can do to save money in the long run: use the TF Purifiner™ On-board Oil Purification System, retreaded tires, and install a base of alternative fuel vehicles. Since every Government agency owns vehicles that consume motor oil, tires, and fuel, reducing the consumption of these items will save money.

TF Purifiner™ On-board Oil Purification System

The TF Purifiner™ On-board Oil Purification System, which can be attached to most major equipment that uses oil, offers many benefits to operators of large transportation vehicles, manufacturing machinery, heavy off-road equipment, boats, locomotives, automobiles, and other applications that use up to 50 weight lubricating oils. This easy-to-install device keeps oil continually clean and would enable Government agencies to realize substantial savings on operating expenses, maintenance costs, capital outlay, and the costs and problems associated with the disposal of waste oil.

Since used oil is defined as a hazardous substance in the Hazardous and Solid Waste Amendments of 1984, it is very important to limit Governments' liability regarding clean up and mitigation costs due to mishandling of this hazardous substance. By installing the TF Purifiner™ On-board Oil Purification System, Government agencies will be able to limit their liability exposure. See Appendix C for a more detailed list of benefits and how this product works.

Retreaded Tires

Government agencies can save money by using retreaded tires. Under Section 506 of Executive order 12873 titled **Federal Acquisition, Recycling, and Waste Prevention,** this order mandates the use of retreaded tires on all Government vehicles. The guidelines for acquiring these tires are defined in Section 6002 of the Resource Conservation and Recovery Act. Even though this executive order mandates the use of retreaded tires, it does not specify how many tires or how often they must be used. Their usage is dependent upon the fleet managers' perception of retreaded tires. This is unfortunate since many people believe that the tire casings they see strewn on the highway are the result of retreaded tires. The reality is, if you were to look more closely at those casings, you would see that most of them have steel strands protruding from them. This indicates that the tire casing failed. The failure was not a result of retreading. Tire failure of any tire, whether it be new or a retread, will come about from driver error. Causes include:

➤ Inadequate attention to air pressure and maintenance.

➤ Overloading beyond a tire's rated capacity.

➤ Using tires which are unsuited for particular applications.

➤ Lack of vehicle maintenance, especially wheel alignment and front tire balancing.

➤ Cracking caused by weather and age.

As observational experience may have shown you, these situations happen easily and occur quite often. Unfortunately, tire failure from such driver abuse and error is what gives retreaded tires a bad image. If driver error can be minimized or eliminated, the perception of retreaded tires will be improved greatly, and fleet managers or individuals would probably use retreaded tires more extensively. As more retreaded tires are employed, more money will be saved by Government agencies. Taking into consideration the fact that a retreaded tire can cost 30% to 50% less than a new tire, savings would be substantial. This savings is attributable to the fact that retreaded tires consist of up to 85% recycled materials (the worn casing itself). The secondary savings occurs when oil consumption is lessened and the costs of trade deficit financing is thereby reduced. Oil savings can be considerable since retreading can save 15 gallons of oil for a retreaded truck tire and 4-1/2 gallons per passenger car tire. With the potential for millions of tires being retreaded by Government agencies, billions of foreign exchange dollars would be saved. This simple solution would also eliminate Government's related financing costs.

Alternative Fuel Vehicle

Installing a large base of cost saving alternative-fueled vehicles will require some time and energy. Fortunately, there are three supporting pieces of legislation to help push this goal along: the 1988 Alternative Motor Fuel Act, the 1990 Clean Air Act, and the 1992 Energy Policy Act.

The 1988 Alternative Motor Fuel Act provides a budgetary avenue of promoting alternative-fueled vehicles. Both the 1990 Clean Air Act and the 1992 Energy Policy Act defines what alternative fuels are and sets a buying schedule for alternative-fueled vehicles. These vehicles would clean up the air and reduce our dependency on imported oil, but savings to the budget are questionable. The most common alternative-fueled vehicles used today are compressed natural gas and natural gas vehicles. These vehicles require conversions that cost over a $1,000 per vehicle, plus a special fuel handling system that costs a substantial amount of money.

A better solution to these natural gas vehicles is to convert vehicles to accommodate A-21 fuel. At the time of this writing, A-21 is not designated as an alternative fuel but hopefully that will change soon. The cost of conversion per vehicle will be substantially less and there is no special fuel handling infrastructure needed. Considering the fact that wholesale cost of production could be less than 40¢ per gallon, retail cost to Government shouldn't be that much. If Government can reduce their fuel costs by 25% to 50%, deficits would be substantially impacted. Even though each vehicle would need to be converted, the pay back period would be very short, considering the possible savings per gallon.

There are also ancillary benefits in the use of naphtha as the feedstock for this fuel. Naphtha costs less to produce and we would only need half as much crude oil as we do today. Considering the fact that we are importing 50% of the crude oil we now use, A-21 fuel would have a substantial impact on the trade deficit picture. If every vehicle was converted to run on this fuel, the trade deficit and its associated financing costs would disappear, saving the Government billions of dollars.

Building Energy Conservation

Solar lighting is an important topic to discuss since buildings account for about 40% of the Government's total energy consumption. Of that 40% consumed, approximately 35% of it is used for lighting.[44] There are two important pieces of legislation that affect this subject. The first is Executive order 12759 and the other is the 1992 Energy Policy Act. Executive order 12759 was signed on April 17, 1991, by President George Bush, and titled Federal Energy Management. Under Section 3 of this order, it mandates that buildings use alternative energy sources other than petroleum products. Under Title I of The 1992 Energy Policy Act, the Federal Government is mandated to spearhead energy efficiency in the buildings they own or lease.[45] Between these two acts, they define what needs to be done and set minimum energy efficiencies. The 1992 Energy Policy Act establishes deadlines for energy efficiency conversion. Provisions are included to promote the use of solar energy.

Solar lighting can satisfy both pieces of legislation while reducing the expenditures that the Government makes for electrical energy. Solar lighting replaces electrical lamps with sunshine. During the evenings and dark days, energy efficient lamps can be turned on when needed. Otherwise,

---

[44] Williams, Dan R. and Good, Larry. *Guide To The Energy Policy Act Of 1992*, Fairmont Press, 1994, pp. 78 &163
[45] Williams, Dan R. and Good, Larry. *Guide To The Energy Policy Act Of 1992*, Fairmont Press, 1994, p. 348

free sunshine will lower Governments' utility bills while improving environmental quality. Products such as the Sunpipe, Sun Tunnel, Sola Tube, or So-Luminaire are good examples of how direct sunlight can reduce expenses for electrical lighting and improve air quality with a one-time capital improvement expense.

Federal Pension

As you discovered in Chapter 4, the Civil Service and Military Retirement pension plans are not cost effective. The Civil Service Retirement plan only receives a small portion of income from its benefactors while the Military Retirement plan receives no income at all. These two retirement programs represent a huge amount of money funded by our tax dollars. Our taxes could be smaller and the deficit reduced more rapidly if these pension programs are brought under control.

In 1984, our Government started the Federal Employee Retirement System which is designed for civil service employees. The program is outrageous and sucks up tax dollars in three ways:
1. **EMPLOYEE CONTRIBUTION**: Civil service employees contribute **only 1%** of their salary to their pension program.
2. **SOCIAL SECURITY**: Civil service employees contribute their share of Social Security taxes and the Government matches it dollar for dollar.
3. **INVESTMENT PLAN**: The employee has an investment plan where he/she can contribute up to 5% of their salary and the Government matches it dollar for dollar.

These three plans (Civil Service Retirement plan, Social Security, and Civil Service Investment plan) are the major reasons why the Social Security and Civil Service Retirement trust fund programs have created so much debt. The national debt grows bigger each year as money is spent to finance these retirement programs. When a Federal employee retires from his or her branch of Government, their pension can be as high as 70% of the highest annual salary received during their last three years at work. Included in their pensions is an automatic cost of living adjustment which further increases the annual deficit and the national debt.

By the time a Government employee retires, it is possible for this person to receive income from three Government sources: from Social Security as well as two Federally-funded retirement programs. Except for small contributions made to Social Security and the Civil Service Retirement program, the rest of the money used to finance their retirement comes from our tax dollars.

The Military Retirement program is another offender when it comes to increasing the deficit and the national debt. Military personnel are not required to contribute anything to their pension programs. If a person joins the military at age eighteen and retires after twenty years of service, that person retires at thirty-eight with a pension. At that age, they are still young enough to start new careers in either the private sector or in another branch of Government. If this person decides to enter another branch of Government, they will be eligible for another pension program (double dipping) that is funded by our tax dollars.

Both the national debt and the annual deficit will be lowered if the Government implemented several policies:

1. Insist that all military personnel contribute 10% of their gross wages to their pension program.
2. If any military personnel retires before serving twenty or thirty years and moves to another branch of Government, their contributions will be taken from the Military Retirement fund and placed into the respective pension plan (no double dipping).
3. If any military person or civil service employee leaves the military and the Government entirely before retirement, all of their paid contributions plus interest should be placed into a Government approved mutual fund.
4. Eliminate the pension program for civil service employees who have less than ten years serving the Government and have it replaced with the new Personal Security tax system explained in this book.
5. Civil service employees who have more than ten years of service must contribute 10% of their gross wages to their pension program.
6. If civil service employees have more than ten years of service and leave the Government entirely before retirement, all of their paid in contributions plus interest should be placed into a Government approved mutual fund.
7. Have a 30% ceiling limit on a thirty-year service for civil service employees. This percentage reflects how much their pension will be based upon their salary at retirement.
8. Make the Federal Government one employer. This will make it impossible for an employee who has served in more than one branch of the Government to collect more than one pension. If a person moves from one branch to another, their pension contributions follow them into the next branch.
9. Eliminate Social Security taxes entirely for all Federal employees who are thirty years old and younger. Reimburse paid in contributions plus interest. These funds will be deposited into a Government approved mutual fund.

10. Federal employees who are thirty years or older and who wish to be reimbursed for their contributions and interest from the Social Security trust fund have the option of doing so. The funds should be deposited into a Government approved mutual fund.
11. Federal employees who are thirty years and older who choose not to be reimbursed for their contribution may remain on the Social Security program, but employees must pay their Social Security taxes as they do today.
12. Raise the retirement age one year for every two years that passes until the retirement age of seventy-five is reached.
13. Funds can only be withdrawn from Government pension plans at official retirement age.

These cuts might seem painful for those involved, but it is almost like gangrene in one toe of your foot. If it goes unchecked too long, we may have to cut off your leg. It is better to lose a toe than a whole leg. This will happen as we get closer to the year 2010 when baby boomers start to retire. Their demands on the Social Security trust fund program will be enormous. The budget deficit will exceed $1 trillion in the first year and could cause the economic collapse of our system if we try to fund these entitlement programs.

To recap what was discussed in Chapter 4, trust fund programs do not have any real assets and only own special issue securities. These securities are non-marketable securities which are essentially internal IOUs and part of the national debt. These securities simply give trust fund programs the ability to spend in the future. When money is needed to pay for trust fund programs, the money is either taken out of tax receipts, or the Government sells bonds to the public to finance its operations. As more future spending authorities are issued and money is borrowed to finance current consumption, the national debt rises in both the Government and publicly owned debt.

Because the Civil Service and Military Retirement trust fund programs are currently underfunded by their benefactors, a good portion of the deficit is attributed to these trust fund program expenditures. If the cash flow deficits of these trust fund programs were eliminated from the budget, the deficit would be much closer to being balanced than it is today. In order to reduce the cash flow deficits from these trust fund programs, military personnel and civil service employees should be required to contribute 10% of their gross wages to their pension plans. If this is done, billions of dollars in revenues will be generated from Federal employees. This will ease the deficit problem.

The deficit can be further reduced if pensions are limited to a more reasonable level. Receiving 30% of their last year's salary, plus cost of living adjustments, is very generous for a pension. Knocking it down from 70% to 30% for civil service employees will save several billions of dollars a year. Additional savings will also result when double dipping is no longer allowed. It is ridiculous to allow Federal employees multiple pensions when they retire from one branch and move to another part of the Government. The Government is a single entity. It is one employer and the pension programs should reflect this. By making all of these changes, the Government will save billions of dollars a year.

Some might want to see pension programs eliminated completely and have them replaced by the new Personal Security tax system described within this book. Some might even suggest having Congress and the President give up their pensions as well, but Congress would never vote for it, just as they did not vote to pass term limits in their "Contract With America." Eliminating pensions might sound very attractive to us as voters, but it would be extremely unsettling to those affected by such a drastic change. If the change is too drastic, our National Security might be at stake. Disgruntled servicemen, civil service employees, and Congressmen/Congresswomen may try to prevent a major change from happening by shutting the Government down. We have already experienced Government shut down. It didn't solve anything, and it wasted millions of dollars. In the budget crisis of 1995 and 1996, Federal employees were sent home not knowing if they were going to be paid for their time away from work. When they eventually went back to work, they were paid for the days they did not come in. Trying to take away pension programs from our Congressmen/Congresswomen may be brought up in Congress, but it will suffer the same fate term limits did: was voted on and defeated. Eliminating all pensions may look good on paper, but it can cause the Government more problems than it would solve. A better way to save money without causing too many problems is to reduce benefits for civil service employees and change Social Security for all Federal employees.

Big savings in future deficits will result if we can eliminate Social Security for Federal employees. Since the Government is using our Social Security receipts to pay for everything from Social Security expenditures to Government salaries, the Social Security trust fund program is insolvent. The trust fund program owns special-issue securities which gives the trust fund program the right to spend in the future—does not give the trust fund program any real money. In the future, when Social Security needs more money than it receives, Government will have to borrow huge sums of money just to make minimal payments to its beneficiaries. This process of robbing Peter to pay Paul will cause our future deficits to become even more outrageous than they are today since it will require trillions of dollars to finance the Social Security trust fund program.

Social Security

Future deficits will be reduced substantially if Social Security becomes privatized and the proposed income tax system (explained in Chapter 8) is enacted. Within the new tax system, all savings and investments plus other deductions would be subtracted from one's earnings to determine the person's taxable wages (this amount is subject to one's marital status). If the remaining number is below the "tax free" amount, then no income tax is due. If the income is above the "tax free" amount, the person must pay a flat rate on that amount. This tax system encourages saving and investing for the individual by avoiding double taxation on savings. If people are prudent with their savings and investments, they will have a sizable nest-egg at the time of retirement. Consequently, their lives will be much more comfortable than they would have been had they depended only upon Social Security.

By eliminating Social Security taxes and replacing them with Personal Security taxes, our Government will not have to spend trillions of dollars in the first part of the next century financing Social Security expenditures. If Social Security remains unchanged, our Government will have to begin spending huge sums of money by the year 2010. In that year, large numbers of baby boomers will begin to retire and their demands on the Social Security trust fund program will be enormous.

Despite the reported Social Security trust fund "surpluses" (see Chapter 4), the Social Security trust fund program is already bankrupt from constant robbing of Peter to pay Paul by our elected officials. Using Social Security taxes to pay for non-Social Security spending is irresponsible and dishonest, especially when our politicians report that the Social Security trust fund program has "surpluses" and the deficit was reduced due to superior fiscal policies. These surpluses are simply future spending authorities and using cash flow surpluses from trust funds only masks the true size of the deficit. This practice is only creating a future financial disaster. When it comes time to fund these spending authorities, the Government will have to either borrow huge sums of money or charge higher Social Security or income taxes, reduce the benefits in either the Social Security or other trust fund programs, and/or print huge sums of money to pay for these entitlement spendings.

To prevent this scenario from happening, we can choose to bite the bullet now by reimbursing all the contributions paid into the system plus interest to those who are interested in taking responsibility for their own retirement, or else ignore the problem until its too late. By taking action, we will save trillions of dollars in future taxes and save the Government trillions of dollars in debt and interest expenditures. With the national debt over $5 trillion, it now costs over $200 billion a year in interest to service this debt. As the national debt gets larger, a greater percentage of the Government budget will be used to finance the debt. Since the budget is still out of balance and will be for some time, future Social Security benefits may be reduced substantially or almost eliminated when demands from its recipients overwhelm the "surpluses" in the Social Security trust fund program. Since these surpluses are only spending authorities, all cash outlays will have to come from the general fund, which will place heavy demands on the budget. Assuming that the numbers and projections provided by the Congressional Budget Office were accurate in predicting the future economy, the budget will be balanced in seven years. If the numbers and projections are wrong, our Government may not be able to balance the budget in seven years. If the budget is still unbalanced by the time baby boomers start to retire, Social Security recipients will probably get the short end of the stick.

If you are concerned about your future and your retirement, you need to ask yourself this question: Who do you think is best qualified to look out for your future interests and retirement? Is it the Federal Government or is it yourself? The obvious answer to these questions is ourselves. Most of us believe that we have more good sense in managing money than the Federal Government does. Since most of us feel that way, we should replace Social Security taxes with Personal Security taxes.

Personal Security taxes would be deducted from everyone's earnings. It would be mandatory and the employer would have to contribute an equal share just like the case with Social Security taxes. The rate can be the same as current Social Security taxes, or it can be raised to 10%. Regardless of the rate chosen, the employer will contribute an equal amount into your personal retirement plan. The money can be used to buy whatever Government approved mutual fund each person feels comfortable with. The withdrawl rate would be determined by the fund balance and actuarial tables. These Personal Security taxes will be separate from any other money that a person is able to save during the year, assuming the new tax system suggested within this book is enacted.

To facilitate the Personal Security Tax system, the Government must make Social Security optional to everyone above the age of thirty. Everyone who is below the age of thirty or who participates in the Personal Security tax system will be required to start their own Personal Security accounts. Those who wish to stay on the Social Security system and are above the age of thirty will continue to pay Social Security taxes and have their employers contribute their share as they do today. There will be one caveat to the system: raise the retirement age one year every two years until the official retirement age is seventy-five. The Social Security trust fund program needs to become a fiduciary entity whereby the Government will not be able to use Social Security trust fund money. For people who do not wish to participate in the Social Security system, they will have their Social Security taxes reimbursed, plus interest.

To prevent a run on the Government, reimbursements should be done over several years. In the first year, people between the ages of fifty and sixty-four should be reimbursed. Most, if not all, of these taxpayers may elect to stay on the Social Security system since they have very few years left to build a retirement fund. In the next reimbursement period, people age forty to forty-nine should be reimbursed. In this group there might be a greater number of individuals than in the first group who would partake in their own retirement program because many of these individuals have by this age already achieved financial success. They might want to capitalize on their "found money" by reinvesting their reimbursements into their own retirement programs. In the next reimbursement period, people who are between thirty-five and thirty-nine should be reimbursed, followed by the thirty-two to thirty-four year olds, and then by thirty to thirty-one year olds. Everyone who is below thirty years of age will be taken one year at a time until the entire population is reimbursed. People who decide late to get reimbursed can do so at a later date with no penalty. Since they are older than the reimbursing age group, their reimbursement will be given priority over their younger counterparts. To apply for a reimbursement, each person will fill out a form one month in advance of his/her birthday. This will give the Government time to process the paperwork and the employer time to respond as well. By reimbursing people on a monthly basis, the system should not get bogged down with paperwork.

By taking several years to reimburse everyone who partakes in this plan, the cash flow requirements will not experience peaks or valleys. By estimating how many people will take a reimbursement and setting a reasonable budget for it, the cash flow peaks and valleys should not exist. To insure this does not happen, a survey should be taken one year prior to the planned reimbursement period and every year thereafter until every age group is reimbursed. This survey will establish an approximate number of eligible recipients and the cash needs for the subsequent year. Once this is established, a reasonable budget and time frame can be set. If there is an overwhelming amount of people who want to partake in this plan, the reimbursement period will have to be adjusted to insure the Government has sufficient funds for everyone. If all the solutions outlined in this book are in place, the Government should not have any trouble reimbursing people who want to take charge of their own retirements. This reimbursement period may take some time, but it can be done at an up front cost that will save the Government trillions of dollars of interest expense, not to mention the trillions of dollars in income and Social Security taxes that we would have to pay.

Currently, our Government is using our Social Security taxes as if they were income taxes. Instead of being used to build up our retirement fund, they are being used to pay for current Social Security demands and to finance current consumption in non-Social Security expenditures. Since this is happening, we might as well use Social Security and income taxes to build a mutual fund nestegg and to pay for all Social Security demands. If we do this now, we will be reducing the national debt and the annual deficits of the future.

One major caveat to privatizing Social Security are low income people. Low income people will not be able to earn enough wages in their life-times to make their retirement funds large enough to live on. These people will need to have their incomes supplemented by the Government so they can make ends meet. Under the tax system proposed in this book, their retirement income, plus wages, plus Government assistance, can add up to $22,500 (arbitrary) for a single person, tax free, and even more for married couples. Those retired people who cannot survive on their own Personal Security plan may have to take assistance from the Government. If they do take "Social Security" it should be done so without strings attached. By the time a person reaches retirement age, they might be in poor health and generally worn out, especially if they have low incomes. Low income people usually do not have the luxury of living well and taking care of themselves. Regardless of who ends up on Social Security, or why they are there, our income taxes should fund their "retirements" (i.e., if you call receiving a sum of $500 to $600 a month a retirement). The amount of money they are eligible to receive from the Government would be based on the balances of their individual retirement fund, actu-arial tables, and a predetermined amount of money which is considered to be a reasonable amount set by the Government.

Each year, the withdrawl rate and the basic living costs will be re-evaluated and redefined so that people will get a fair amount of assis-tance. People who make more than $50,000 (arbitrary) a year without their Social Security benefits will have their paid in contributions (plus interest) reimbursed. By privatizing the Social Security system and mak-ing people take more responsibility for their own futures, the new stream-lined Social Security system will not experience a financial crisis as will happen in the early part of the next century if the system remains un-changed.

Medicare & Medicaid

Future deficits will be reduced if the hemorrhaging of the Medicare and Medicaid programs are eliminated by "privatizing" them. This can be done through the issuance of insurance premium vouchers to those who are currently receiving Medicaid and Medicare benefits. These vouchers would be counted as income to the individual receiving them (under the proposed tax system in this book), but the insurance premiums would be considered as a deduction from their gross income, which essentially would create a wash. Individuals under this plan would have to take responsibility for their own health care by shopping for health insurance suitable for their needs, just like the rest of us. By eliminating the fee-for-service program that currently exists with Medicare and Medicaid, fraud would be greatly reduced or practically eliminated since private insurance companies and health carriers are interested in their bottom lines and will not stand for fraud and abuse.

In order for this plan to work, our legislators will have to make sure that all insurance carriers eliminate any pre-existing conditions that may exclude these people from getting decent health coverage. As these people get absorbed by private insurance programs, their additional expense of coverage will be shared by everyone who is insured.

Premiums may go up slightly for everyone who is insured, but the additional premium expense will be substantially less than what the present Government program costs us in fraud, deficits, and future taxes by financing these entitlement expenditures.

Farm Subsidies

Farm subsidies can be eliminated by using two avenues that will not affect the farmers' ability to survive in this highly volatile and competitive economy. This would entail developing business relationships with the oil and the electrical power companies. The common denominator between oil companies and electrical companies is the ability of the farm to produce ethanol. Dilute and fuel grade ethanol can be the basis whereby the farmer can generate additional income while eliminating the farm subsidy payment. When farm subsidy payments are eliminated, the Federal Government will no longer be saddled with an expense that places a strain on the Federal annual operating budget. The annual operating budget will also improve when the economy begins to grow as the result of farmers making direct investments in equipment and technology made here in America. As this happens, more people will be employed and there will be a larger tax base from which to collect taxes. Besides increased tax revenues, the costs associated with trade deficits will be avoided, saving the Federal Government money. In addition to reducing trade deficits and their costs, we will have lower prices for fuel, home heating oil, and electricity.

These lower costs will result from the farms' ability to produce biomass that is usable for ethanol production. Conventional and non-conventional feedstocks can be used in the production of fuel grade ethanol.

Today, at least 95% or more of the ethanol produced is made from corn. By using corn as the feedstock, byproducts add value to the ethanol production. One byproduct is corn oil that can be used to make margarine or biodiesel. The second byproduct is the concentrated protein meal that can be used to feed animals on farms. The third byproduct is carbon dioxide that can be captured and sold to bottlers. The fourth byproduct is heat, and this can be used in the fermentation and drying processes associated with ethanol production.

Ethanol production from nonconventional feedstocks would include the use of the corn cobs or any crop residues that are considered waste. These feedstocks can be made into ethanol from commercial processes that are now entering the market. When these residues are made into ethanol, the overall cost of ethanol drops, making it more attractive as a fuel additive and/or substitute. As the cost of production drops, the need for imported oil will decrease, which in turn will help our trade deficit and the environment. Environment and air quality are enhanced when biomass is used for fuels because no additional carbon dioxide is emitted into the atmosphere. This occurs when the amount of biomass consumed for energy is equal to the same amount of new biomass produced through new plantings and/or new growth of existing biomass.

The atmosphere is further enhanced when energy farms are created. Energy farms are farms specifically designed to create electrical energy using dilute ethanol as a fuel. This dilute ethanol can be created from conventional and nonconventional feedstocks. Depending on the need for fuel grade ethanol, some or all of the dilute ethanol can be diverted to electrical production with the use of the Direct Fuel Cell. By providing electricity through biomass production, these energy farms will have certain incentives to make their production cost even more attractive. The first is Internal Revenue Code §40 that resulted from the 1992 Energy Policy Act. This gives the producer of electricity from "closed loop biomass" systems a tax credit of 1.5¢ per kilowatt hour. Additional incentives are given to the producer who makes ethanol for fuel purposes. These provisions are covered under Internal Revenue Codes §4041, §4081, and §4091, giving the farmer additional benefits.

Additional benefits can be acquired by the farmers through provisions of the 1990 Clean Air Act. If a utility company buys electricity from the farmer and is willing to pay the farmer the avoided costs of acquiring sulfur dioxide emission credits, the farmer would increase his revenue base while lessening the dependency upon the Federal Government for farm subsidies.

FEMA

The Federal Emergency Management Agency (FEMA) was established in June, 1979, by President Jimmy Carter to improve the responsiveness of the Federal Government to catastrophes in the United States. The Federal Emergency Management Agency gets hammered every time there is a substantial disaster. From 1989 to 1993, the President issued one hundred eighty-five major declarations under the Stafford Authority Act. Nine major disasters alone account for more than $10 billion. Listed below are those disasters and how much is expected to be spent by conclusion.

Comparative Costs of Major Disasters FEMA Stafford Act Costs Only (Dollars in Millions; Data as of February 4, 1994)			
FEMA Disaster #	Disaster Name	Current Project FEMA Costs	Obligated to-date
841-844	Hurricane Hugo	$1,513	$1,487
845	Loma Prieta	636	578
942	LA Civil Unrest	171	162
955,956	Hurricane Andrew	1,875	1,717
957	Hurricane Omar	80	75
991	Hurricane Iniki	304	269
993-1001	Midwest Floods	1,087	740
1005	California Fires	98	51
1008	Northridge	4,885	538
Source: FEMA, Office of Congressional Affairs.			

As you can tell from this table, earthquakes, hurricanes, and flooding represent the biggest and most costly disasters. The Northridge earthquake was the most expensive, over $4.8 billion, followed by Hurricane Andrew at $1.8 billion. The Midwest floods came in fourth at just over $1 billion. In order to protect FEMA from these costly disasters, progressive building codes, advanced construction technologies, and common sense will have to be implemented. In addition, builders will have to be willing to use progressive technologies that will save money for themselves and for FEMA. Regardless of the natural disaster, an equitable insurance program that spreads the financial burden across all insured policy holders will lessen the financial impact that FEMA must endure.

Constructing buildings that can survive in earthquake country requires the use of common sense, progressive building codes, and advanced construction technologies. Common sense tells us not to put heavy roofing materials on homes that are built in earthquake country. Even though homes are designed to withstand earthquakes and the loads that are placed upon their roofs, many of these engineered homes fell apart during the Northridge earthquake of January 17, 1994. Putting heavy loads on the roof, just puts additional strain on the structure when an earthquake hits. Lighter substitutes exist to replace heavy cement or clay tiles. Steel or aluminum roofing panels are now made to look like Spanish tiles or slate. Many of these roofing products come with a fifty-year warranty and weigh one-tenth as much as a concrete tile. These products perform better in an earthquake and are accepted by all building codes.

Progressive building codes will be necessary to insure common sense and advanced construction technologies are used in potentially hazardous areas. Even though California is known for its earthquakes, people overlook the New Madrid fault zone because it is in the midwest, an area most of us do not associate with earthquakes. But on December 16, 1811, about 2:15 P.M., St. Louis and the surrounding country was visited by the most violent earthquake recorded in the history of our country. The initial jolt was so violent that it caused the Mississippi River to flow backwards. The entire eastern half of the United States is susceptible to another earthquake of comparable magnitude. FEMA's financial exposure will be limited only if we implement long range plans and use progressive building codes to insure that advanced construction technologies are used throughout the United States.

These new building codes should specify the use of base isolators on buildings that are between two and fourteen stories high. One such building that lies in the New Madrid fault zone is the Auto Zone Headquarters in Memphis, Tennessee. This building is eight stories, with 250,000 square feet of space, and cost $27 million to build. Since this building used forty-three base isolators, it did not require additional materials to strengthen the building and added costs were minor.

Building costs are not the only factors to be considered when approaching the problems associated with earthquake damage. Once an earthquake hits and buildings are damaged, there are disruption costs that are associated with the damages. People are thrown out of their homes and businesses. There is lost rent, revenue, and productivity. A look at two examples will illustrate the point. During the 1994 Northridge earthquake, the USC University Hospital, a building protected with base isolators, sustained no damage. However, Los Angeles County General Hospital, which was less than a mile away from the USC University Hospital, suffered $389 million in damage with two wings of the hospital permanently closed. This is proof of the capacity of an existing building technology to save money.

Other building technologies capable of saving FEMA money while strengthening the buildings without additional costs, would include the use of framing systems such as Wallframe™ building systems. Since this product is made from steel and expanded polystyrene foam, it has a high shear strength and will bend and give before it will break. If new building codes would mandate the use of this type of product, there would be less damage in the event of an earthquake. Today's building codes require conventional construction to have high shear strengths. This requirement is usually accomplished with plywood. Unfortunately, plywood adds rigidity to the structure and in the event of an earthquake, the energy is not dissipated but is absorbed by the building. If the energy released by the earthquake is greater than the building can absorb, the building will break apart, causing damage and huge expenses.

When buildings fail in hurricanes, huge expenses mount up. Many of these failures can be avoided if common sense and superior building codes and materials are used in the construction of those buildings. After Hurricane Andrew, Dade County come up with Protocol PA 202-94 which covers procedures for conducting a uniform static air pressure test for materials and products such as wall cladding, glass block, exterior doors, garage doors, skylights, exterior windows, storm shutters, and any other external building component that helps maintain the integrity of the building envelope. They also devised Protocol PA 201-94 which covers procedures for conducting impact tests on materials required by section 2315 of the South Florida Building Code. Products are tested to determine if they can survive the forces of a hurricane. This is done by shooting a 9-pound 2x4 at the test subject at 34 mph. Many products fail this test, but concrete walls can pass them easily. Unfortunately, concrete does not lend itself to easy modification in the field or to recycling after the structure has outlived its useful life. For the time being, there are windows, doors, and shutters that perform to the new standards. By protecting the most vulnerable parts of the building with these products, the potential of having the roof blown off the building when doors and windows fail due to increased air pressure inside the house will be minimized. Until a time when the "perfect" building envelope is invented and we can replace our entire housing stock with this new structure, common sense will be needed to protect existing structures.

Building in a flood plain also requires common sense and progressive building technologies. Common sense should tell you to build on higher ground or at least elevate your structure so when it does flood, your home is not destroyed. Native islanders in the Pacific have done this for years, but for some reason our homes and cities along the Mississippi River are built at ground level. Every time the river threatens to overflow its banks, people scramble to sandbag the banks of the river and/or their homes and businesses. Homes that exist in a flood plain can be retrofitted by lifting the structure high enough to build a lower story that can be used for parking or storage. LiftPlate International has a patented process suited for this purpose.

The great flood of 1993 covered some fourteen million acres in seven states and caused $2 billion in damage to some fifty thousand homes, virtually all of them older homes. Credit this to the National Flood Insurance Program (NFIP) rules discouraging new construction in the one hundred year floodplain.

The National Flood Insurance Program was created in 1968 and currently insures $239 billion worth of property in eighteen thousand communities that comply with Federal Emergency Management Agency (FEMA) flood control rules. Within the last two years NFIP's $400 million fund was wiped out by hurricane and blizzard damage. This problem is further exacerbated by the fact that some lenders in the thirty year season coast erosion zone (areas FEMA deems vulnerable to high erosion) continue to finance uninsured properties which puts additional strains upon NFIP.[46]

The problem with NFIP is that the Government is subsidizing stupidity. Homes are built behind levies below the water level of the Mississippi River while NFIP insures these homes from floods. It makes more sense to elevate these homes above the water level of the Mississippi River by either berms or stilts. If the Mississippi River overflows its banks, the damage will hopefully be minimal and FEMA's financial exposure limited. FEMA is also further protected due to a new rule enacted by NFIP. Their 50% rule requires the homeowner to elevate their structure if the cost of repairs to the home equals or exceeds 50% of the "fair market value" or "replacement cost." If a home meets this 50% rule, it must be elevated. If the home does not meet this rule, then the homeowner can choose to repair the structure and face another flood in the future, costing the Government and the homeowner more money later. Since this rule is hard to enforce because people are ignorant of it, homeowners and the Government will face another financial crisis when more floods destroy their homes. It only makes sense to employ common sense technologies that will save homeowners and FEMA money in the future.

FEMA can also be protected if a national insurance program is devised to cover everyone in the United States. Funding for this insurance program can be a surcharge on everyone's policy. A few additional dollars from each and everyone of us will not place a financial burden on any of us and would build a substantial nest egg for FEMA in the event of a natural disaster. This fund can be managed for profit and growth, just like any other insurance company. This would give the commercial carriers relief from the expense of natural disasters such as the Northridge earthquake, an earthquake so devastating to the insurance market that all but three insurance companies have left California's market.

---

[46] German, Brad. "Flood Spares Builder," *Builder*, October 1993, p. 52

At this writing, California requires all insurance companies to offer earthquake insurance to anyone who buys a homeowner's policy. If another financially disastrous earthquake hits California, it will cause the remaining insurance companies to leave the state. If this happens, California homeowners will be left out in the cold without any form of insurance. By providing a national insurance program to cover natural disasters such as earthquakes, hurricanes, tornadoes and flooding, the liability will be shared by every policy-holder in the United States. Since the fund would be managed for profit and growth, it would be kept out of the hands of Congress. Keeping the funds and its administration away from Government will be a big step toward insuring its profitability and its ability to help out in times of crisis.

Welfare System AFDC

Even though President Clinton has boasted about how he has reduced Welfare, he does not mention why he expanded the Earned Income Tax Credit in 1993 and how much this expansion increased the deficit. One of the big obstacles in getting people off Welfare is the disincentive created by the Earned Income Tax Credit (EITC). The EITC was established in 1975 and was originally designed to create work incentives by providing people with tax credits. The current tax credit for a qualifying child is $2,094.00, and if there is more than one qualifying child, the tax credit can be as much as $3,110.00. The credit does not affect eligibility or benefit levels for families already receiving food stamps, housing subsidies or AFDC (Aid to Families with Dependent Children). If a person doesn't owe any tax and uses the tax credit, this person can get a tax refund from the Government. It has been estimated that the cost of these tax credits exceed the cost of Aid to Families with Dependent Children, which is running approximately $15 to $20 billion a year.

Further compounding the problem is the added cost of training programs that are not viable in the current job market. Training welfare recipients for jobs that don't exist is a waste of money, time, and resources. Welfare recipients may have better skills, but their efforts and skills are wasted if the economy cannot absorb them. This is one of the reasons why our elected officials have never really put much stock into training welfare recipients. They realize training is very expensive and there is no guarantee that the training will result in removing people from Welfare. If a welfare recipient learns to become a truck driver, fork lift driver, or keyboard operator, and the economy is not expanding sufficiently to absorb these people, their presence in the job market will keep other people on unemployment. If other people are kept on unemployment due to an expanding workforce made up of welfare recipients, the net result is higher costs due to training and daycare expenses. For this reason, it is cheaper to keep welfare recipients on Welfare than it is to train them and displace other workers into unemployment. This is extremely true when companies are downsizing and merging to improve their profitability, since their actions usually result in job losses.

If we want to put all welfare recipients and those who are unemployed back to work, our economy has to expand and grow much more than it has today. Since the economy has only had moderate growth, the prospect of taking people off Welfare through job training is dismal. Given the state of the economy, working society does not have the capacity to absorb these people. It is naive for anyone to believe that simple training will magically reduce the amount of people on Welfare. In order to achieve the goal of removing people from Welfare, more lower skilled and manufacturing jobs will have to be created.

In addition, we will need to eliminate the disincentives of the Earned Income Tax Credit. These tax credits were supposed to counteract the anti-work incentives of Social Security taxes. If anything, these tax credits, combined with the current income and Social Security tax system, have discouraged people from working harder. First, the more one works, the more Social Security taxes are taken out of one's paycheck, and as you learned in Chapter 4, what we call Social Security taxes is just another term for income taxes. Since the revenue collected from Social Security taxes is used for everything but building a retirement fund, it can be considered another form of income tax. Second, people can automatically increase their income just by qualifying for the credit with one caveat: the more one makes, the less credit they will receive. The system was designed to reward those for working harder, but it achieves just the opposite. In fact, the General Accounting Office published a report in 1993 which stated: "Before qualifying for the credit, a worker may view taking a second job as worth the sacrifice of forgoing leisure time. But after qualifying for the credit, the extra income the credit offers partly replaces the income the worker would lose if he or she were to quit the second job. Also, full time workers may shift to part-time jobs to get the leisure time they now prefer." To further back up their claims, the General Accounting Office found that those receiving the Earned Income Tax Credit worked 700 hours less than the average person.[47] In order to get people off Welfare and interested in working more, they must be able to keep more of what they earn.

To accomplish this goal, Social Security needs to be privatized so that the Government won't use our Social Security taxes as if they were income taxes. Next, the income tax system needs to be revised as suggested

---

[47] Howard, James. "Clinton's Biggest Welfare Fraud," *Wall Street Journal*, May 10, 1994

in Chapter 8. Finally, Welfare needs to be reformed to eliminate the free-loaders.

Welfare has too many freeloaders on the payroll. As the system stands, we pay welfare recipients to get pregnant, have more children, and to waste their time being unproductive citizens who do not contribute to the growth and betterment of our society. Welfare encourages laziness, learned helplessness, and promiscuity amongst its recipients. The system has been the same for years, and for now it is the most economical way of dealing with the problem. As of 1994, the Federal Government spends about $14 billion a year on Welfare which is about 1% of the Federal budget. This amount is down from 1970, when Welfare accounted for approximately 1.4% of the budget. This is largely due to the fact that Welfare hasn't been adjusted for inflation.[48]

Congress felt it was much cheaper to send these people a welfare check than it is to spend money for daycare, education, and job training. This conclusion does make sense considering the state of our economic base. Manufacturing jobs are being exported to less developed countries where labor is cheaper. More and more fast food restaurants and retailing operations are opening and absorbing people who were previously employed in factories. We have only ourselves to blame for this problem. Due to our shortsightedness as consumers, many of us have bought, and continue to buy, imported goods. This continual buying pattern has accelerated the exportation of jobs to less developed nations that can assemble products more cheaply than American workers can. This process continues daily and our economic base continues to erode.

Without a strong economic base to absorb additional workers, it is much cheaper for the Government to send welfare checks to recipients rather than train them for jobs that do not exist. This fact seems to elude some politicians. By ignoring the fact that many overqualified people are taking minimum wage or very low paying jobs, their solution of putting time limits on welfare recipients that require them to enter the job force will only place additional pressures on the job market. With an over abundance of cheap labor, wages will be pushed down, putting additional hardships on those people who are barely making ends meet. Until our buying patterns change and more jobs are created here in the United States, the next best way to deal with the welfare recipient is to send them a check.

Of course, sending these people checks does nothing for their self-worth or their desire to get off Welfare. The only thing it seems to accomplish is more Government debt. With each passing day, it seems more

---

[48] Figures from Bernstein, Aaron. "Why Clinton's Workfare Won't Work," *Business Week*, March 7, 1994, p. 92

and more welfare recipients commit fraud by collecting more than one welfare check. This is accomplished very easily by the recipient who maintains more than one address. Once this has been established, the recipient can then receive multiple checks and defraud the system. An example of this was found in New Jersey and Manhattan in 1994. Since 1991, four hundred twenty-five New Jersey residents came to defraud New York City of over $1 million. These were people who were stupid enough to use the same name in both places. But this does not account for the people who were smart enough to use different names in each city.[49]

To prevent fraud within the system, a national ID card for welfare recipients needs to be put into place. The card can be used as an identification card as well as a debit card. As an identification card, it would contain the recipient's picture, date of birth, Social Security number, driver's license number, fingerprint information, and address. With this type of information encoded on the card, it would be impossible for a welfare recipient to try to defraud the system by collecting benefits from more than one address or name, especially since fingerprints are unique.

The debit card should be used for all of the welfare recipients benefits. Each recipient should be given a monthly credit limit (each case will be different, depending upon the number of children and other circumstances) to be used for their housing, food, AFDC payments, Social Security, and medical benefits. If they exceed their limit before the end of the month, they are cut off from further benefits until they can make arrangements for more credit, assuming they can justify the need. Otherwise, they will need to learn how to budget their credits. Placing welfare recipients on a budget will make their lives more realistic and hopefully they will learn how to make more responsible decisions. A statement will be sent to them each month indicating their usage of the system. If the recipients are frugal with their credits, they can bank them until they need them.

Fraud would be eliminated and money saved if the existing phone networks, ATMs, and store debit systems are modified to accommodate this new debit card that allows for fingerprint verification. The interface screen of the ATM could have a new option that would include "Welfare Payment Options." Once this option is selected, an electronic transfer of funds could occur for rent, phone, utilities, and health insurance payments. The software should be designed to place reasonable limits on how much each person can spend on phone and utilities. Without these limits, recipients will spend all of their credits on the wrong items. If they run up their phone or utility bills beyond their credit limit, they will have to deal with the respective companies themselves. If, on the other hand, they are frugal, they should be able to use their unspent phone or utility

---

[49] Faison, Seth. "Welfare Rolls In Manhattan Lists Jerseyans," *New York Times*, March 3, 1994

credits for food. At the grocery stores, the credit card/debit machines should have fingerprint verification systems installed as well.[50]

As each transaction is made for food and miscellaneous cash transactions, the amount is deducted from their credit and a receipt would be printed reflecting their balance. If no card readers are available for certain transactions such as housing, the landlord can verify the transaction over the phone and produce a handwritten transaction record. By establishing this system, welfare recipients will be unable to defraud the system and will be forced to be more responsible for their lives by making better decisions.

Food stamp fraud occurs when recipients sell their food stamps for cash and possibly use the money for some illicit habit or behavior. This process involves one or several steps, depending on how many middlemen are involved. These middlemen take a profit along the way until they sell the food stamps to a merchant for about 50¢ on the dollar. Once the merchant receives the food stamps at this price, he deposits them into the bank as if he had sold groceries to receive them. When this type of fraud exists, the children lose out, the system is defrauded, and the cheaters are not held accountable. By eliminating printed paper food stamps, at least $1 billion of the $30 billion food stamp program can be eliminated.[51] Some of these problems could have been avoided if a sophisticated debit card system were installed as promised in the 1990 Farm Bill Provision. In that bill, the Federal Government promised to install at least 15% of the grocery stores with special devices, at the Agriculture Department's expense.[52]

As proof of how sophisticated systems can save money for the Government, we have an example in the Los Angeles area. A fingerprint system to catch cheaters was installed in 1991. After one year, the county reported saving $5.4 million, which represented more than half its welfare costs. Over two hundred people were denied assistance because they refused to be fingerprinted: over three thousand people were suspected of fraud and lost their assistance. Obviously, this system works and Los Angeles County is now the first place in the nation to require welfare applicants to submit to fingerprint checks.[53]

The Federal Government can save money by off-loading the cost of Welfare through block grants to states. These block grants need to be

---

[50] Credit card fraud would be reduced substantially if all merchants and banks upgraded their card systems to include fingerprint verification. With fingerprint verification, PIN numbers wouldn't be necessary, furthering system security.

[51] Figures from Holstrom, David. "Food Stamp Use—and Abuse—Reaches All-Time High in US," *Christian Science Monitor*, March 15, 1994, p. 1

[52] *Congressional Quarterly Almanac*, 101st Congress, 2nd Session, Volume XLVI 1990, p. 346

[53] Figures from Associated Press. "A Welfare Fingerprint Program," *New York Times*, March 31, 1994

adjusted for area differences. States such as California and New York have higher living costs than states such as Mississippi or Arkansas. States should keep the level of welfare payments the same throughout the state and encourage welfare recipients to move away from more densely populated and crime-ridden areas to less populated areas where living costs and crime rates are lower. Funds for moving assistance can come from the system since the proposed program will be generating real products and income. If welfare recipients move to areas of lower cost, their benefits will stretch farther and their standard of living will improve without increasing the need for larger benefits and Government debt.

Government debt will not go away until our economic system can absorb these people into the workforce, but until that time happens, we can minimize expenses of Welfare through Government-run energy farms.

In order to make these energy farms work, a labor pool will be needed to plant, cultivate, and harvest the trees. In order to accomplish this task, the welfare population in a specific area needs to be divided into three groups. These relatively homogeneous groups will be rotated through three tasks. The first task is to provide labor for planting, cultivating and harvesting the trees. The second task is to provide day care services and supporting services for the other two groups. The third and most important task is to develop a more intelligent, educated, and motivated group of citizens.

Hopefully, through a strong education of the basics, some participants will be motivated to learn more about their task. Those who are motivated and who desire more should be given the opportunity to pursue growth. The result will be that some participants will eventually get off Welfare and find a job in the private sector. When this attrition rate happens, the groups will shrink, and over a period of years, as each successive stand of trees matures and is harvested, the need for a large workforce for planting and cultivating the trees will diminish. The initial labor requirements will be high as acres upon acres of trees need to be planted and cultivated. After the third year of growth, fewer man hours will be needed per stand of trees until the sixth or seventh year when the trees are harvested.

As each group rotates on a weekly basis through their three separate tasks, their preschool children will be in day care. To help with daycare of their school-aged children, school should be in session year round with extended hours. With this system, separate daycare facilities will not be needed for children attending school, since their school days will be as long as a work day. With both the parent and child in a learning environment, hopefully we will end up with a class of citizens who will want to contribute to society instead of being a drain on it. Even if that goal is not reached, at least we will have a labor source to care for these energy farms.

These energy farms will be tree farms grown specifically for biomass that can either be converted into electricity, ethanol fuel, or even wood pulp if there is a paper plant nearby to utilize the pulp. Regardless of the end product, tree farms will require a pool of unskilled labor to plant and cultivate them during the first three years of growth.

If tree farms are designed for electrical production, the trees will need to be harvested whole and loaded onto trucks and hauled to the electrical power plant where they will be stacked and dried before being burned for heat in the whole tree energy system. Each step of the way, whether it be planting, cultivating, cutting, loading, delivering, or unloading, people will be needed to perform these tasks. These tasks do not require a college education or specialized skills. Some training will be required to run the harvesting equipment and a Class One license will be required to drive the semi-tractor trailer trucks if the trucks are driven on the public highways. If the trucks are driven on "farmland," no special driver's license is required to operate these vehicles. At the power plant, knowing how to operate a crane will be necessary for unloading and stacking of trees.

For the most part, planting and cultivating could be done with unskilled labor and would represent about one half the cost of producing this energy crop if the labor was supplied through the open market system. If huge tractors were used to cultivate the rows of trees—instead of workers with hoes or weedeaters—less labor would be needed. Since the labor would be provided by welfare recipients, and their labor is already "paid for," a study would need to be done to determine if the capital costs of buying and maintaining the tractor would be greater than the capital costs of buying and maintaining weedeaters or hoes. A big factor in this equation is the question: How much land do they have available to them, and is their labor source too big or too small to handle the cultivation? Regardless of which method is chosen, the goal of this program is to produce a crop that can be used for electrical production that the state or county Government can run in an attempt to make Welfare pay for itself.

In order for this work system to be cost effective, the production costs must be kept down and at the same time the price that they receive for the electricity must be high enough to defray their capital and operating costs. Since their facility would qualify under the 1992 Energy Policy Act as a closed loop biomass energy system, they could receive an additional 1.5¢ per kwh (adjusted for inflation) through the Department of Energy's Renewable Energy Production Credit. If the utility companies pay the total avoided costs for this electricity (which would include sulfur dioxide emission credits), these Government power plants would stand a good chance of at least breaking even. If this workfare program pays for itself, and doesn't make a profit, everyone wins. Our environment will be cleaner (less sulfur dioxide emissions emitted), welfare costs would be reduced substantially, the biomass industry and the rest of the economy would be stimulated, and welfare recipients would no longer be a burden to our society. Nor will they be putting additional pressures on the existing market of low paying jobs.

Similar benefits will be obtained if the tree farms are harvested for ethanol production. Depending on market prices for dilute ethanol, the welfare workers cultivate trees as they would if they were producing trees for whole tree energy production. The difference will be in the handling of the trees after they are harvested. In order for trees to be prepared for ethanol production, they need to be chipped before being hauled away to the ethanol plant. Using concentrated acid hydrolysis, the wood chips can be converted into sugars that would then be used to produce dilute ethanol through various proprietary methods. At this time, the cost of producing ethanol with these methods has been estimated to be equal or less than the cost of producing dilute ethanol from corn. Once dilute ethanol is produced, it can be sold to an ethanol producer who would then dewater it to produce fuel grade ethanol.

If there is no local outlet for the dilute ethanol, the trees can be harvested for paper pulp, if there is a paper plant nearby. Cultivation and harvesting techniques would be the same for ethanol production with one modification: debarking the tree before chipping, which is easily done with no additional handling of the tree.

Regardless of the eventual use of trees, they can provide an avenue to transform welfare recipients into workfare recipients while stimulating the economy and improving the quality of the air we breathe. It will also produce real products that are valuable to us and from which our Governments can earn real dollars to help defray the cost of Welfare.

SEVEN

INCOME GENERATION

P rofits can be derived from three operating infrastructures that exist at the city or county level: the garbage collection system, the sewage system, and the city or county prison system. Through recycling and energy conversion of waste materials, income can be generated for counties or cities that own the garbage and sewage treatment plants.

Additional income sources can be generated from landfill methane and tire recycling. These two potential profit centers are dependent upon ownership of the non-functional landfill and local regulations governing the disposal of tires.

Every state across this nation can generate money from land and human resources available to them. Every state has highways, state-owned land, welfare recipients, and state prisoners. By employing all of the land in conjunction with people who are a financial burden to our society, states will be capable of generating a valuable product while optimizing an underutilized human resource. By employing welfare recipients and prisoners, electrical energy and ethanol can be produced and sold on the open market or used in-house for electrical and fuel needs.

When electrical energy is produced using a closed loop biomass system, the Department of Energy's Renewable Electric Production Incentive gives qualifying states a 1.5¢ cash payment (adjusted for inflation) for every kilowatt hour of electricity produced. This cash payment would be in addition to the prevailing wholesale rate paid by the surrounding electrical company. According to the 1992 Energy Policy Act, states would be considered as a qualifying facility.

The 1992 Energy Policy Act also plays an important role in the use of alternative fuels in the transportation sector. There are additional state laws and incentives that promote the use of alternative fuels. This information is listed state by state in a Department of Energy report called "State Alternative Fuel Laws & Incentives." This report is available from the National Alternative Fuels Hotline at (800) 423-1DOE. The report number is DOE/CH100093-319.

One example of the laws that can be found in this report is Act 927 of Louisiana, instituted in 1990. Act 927 states that up to 80% of all state vehicles must be converted to operate on alternative fuels by 1998. Since alternative fuels are to be used in state vehicles, it will be important to use an engine and vehicle design that burns alternative fuels efficiently since many of the alternative fuels have about one half the energy value of a gallon of gasoline. The turbine-powered electric hybrid vehicles would be a prime candidate for the use of alternative fuels since they can burn a variety of fuels very efficiently and their commercialization is supported by the 1992 Energy Policy Act.

The 1988 Alternative Motor Fuels Act can also help the commercialization and implementation of alternative fuel vehicles by providing Federal funds for the purchase of and installation of alternative-fueled vehicles. The 1988 Alternative Motor Fuel Act is governed by how much money Congress allocates to this piece of legislation. In addition to the 1988 Alternative Motor Fuel Act, the 1990 Clean Air Act has mandates within it for the use of alternative fuels in fleet vehicles.

Since there are so many pieces of legislation promoting the use of alternative fuels such as ethanol, it would make sense to use the fuel that is produced by the state to promote the commercialization of alternative-fueled vehicles and reduce trade deficits and foreign dependency of imported oil. By using this fuel, the state can displace millions of gallons of gasoline. Of course, there is the economical side of producing the ethanol at approximately 70¢ per gallon. This figure of 70¢ is the equivalent of a $1.20 for a gallon of gasoline, assuming that ethanol has approximately 60% of the energy content of gasoline. In order to produce ethanol at this price, either the feedstock, the process, the labor, or transportation costs need to be below market. Electrical production faces the same cost problems as the production of ethanol. This is because biomass has only about half the energy value of fossil fuels.

Since labor constitutes one of the largest costs in producing trees for energy, reducing labor costs will be essential in producing a cost effective feedstock for either ethanol or electrical production. Since each state has an abundant source of welfare recipients, prisoners, and land, optimizing these resources to produce ethanol and electricity is a better alternative than keeping these people locked up in prisons or letting welfare recipients sponge off hard working Americans who pay taxes to support both systems.

Biomass Farms

Biomass farms are capable of generating income for local, state, and Federal Governments. Biomass farms can develop crops that would be used for electrical generation, ethanol, paper pulp production, or biodiesel. These crops could include switch grass, trees, or oil plants (switch grass is commonly known as prairie grass). Trees could include hybrid poplars, cotton tails, or even a clone of the Chinese paulownia tree that grows to a height of 20 feet in its first year. Oil plants are those such as sunflower, soy, and rape seed. This biomass can be farmed on any army base, freeway buffer zone, prison land, and on any Government-owned land that is suitable for the production of trees, switch grass, or oil plants. These farms can be cultivated by prisoners, welfare recipients, or military personnel.

If prisoners are utilized to cultivate a crop, their labor could be used creatively. Prisoners can cultivate hundreds of thousands of miles of highways. Currently, states control over 104,000 miles of highway, while cities and counties control over 680,000 miles.[54] Along highways, there is a greenbelt or buffer zone that separates the physical road from the adjoining property. Soil conditions, climate, water availability, and the size of the buffer would determine the type of crop to be cultivated. If tree groves were to be grown along highways, their constant care for the first three years would be essential. Weed abatement is one of the most important aspects of tree farming to insure that trees survive. Prisoners could be given weed-eaters or a hoe to knock down the weeds during those first three years. Harvesting the crop would not happen until the sixth or seventh year. If, on the other hand, switch grass is grown on these buffer zones, very little care is needed.

Switch grass is drought tolerant and can be harvested once a year. After it is harvested, the soil needs no other attention and doesn't need to be tilled until the tenth year.

If we opt for the oils produced by soy beans or rape seeds, traditional farming techniques will need to be employed, otherwise it wouldn't be profitable. Since it is an agricultural product, it requires all the cultiva-

[54] Statistical Abstract Of The United States, 1994, p. 642

tion and caring as if it were a regular farm: suitable land, irrigation, and climate. Tractors, not manpower, are better suited for the production of this crop. Since tree harvesting and the farming of oil plants require heavy equipment, this work would also be better suited for welfare recipients or the military, since they would pose no security threat.

Regardless of who harvests the crop, the biomass has the following potential uses. If trees are grown, they can be converted to ethanol, burned whole to produce electricity, or used as feedstock for paper pulp. If switch grass is grown, it would be used solely as feedstock for ethanol production. If oil bearing plants are grown, the oil can be sold on the open market or used internally by Government agencies as biodiesel.

If trees are used as feedstock for ethanol production, dilute or fuel grade ethanol can be the end product. Dilute ethanol normally contains a high percentage of water. Extracting all of the water from dilute ethanol results in fuel grade ethanol. However, this water extraction process is very expensive and is one of the main reasons why ethanol costs substantially more than gasoline to produce. If fuel grade ethanol is produced, it can be sold on the open market to be used in the production of ETBE, a gasoline additive that improves the octane rating and its burning characteristics. If dilute ethanol is the primary goal, it can be used as fuel in a Direct Fuel Cell to produce electricity. Electrical production costs will be competitive with other means of generation since the efficiency of the fuel to energy conversion process is very high. Efficiencies greater than 50% can be achieved with the Direct Fuel Cell. Only half of the energy potential is lost in the electrochemical process. This is very good news considering 75% or more of the potential energy of other fuels can be lost in other forms of electrical generation.

Regardless of whether fuel grade or dilute ethanol is produced, the production and harvesting of the feedstock will require the same amount of effort. Trees will need to be planted, cultivated, and harvested. The harvesting methods will be the same and will require a fell buncher, a log grapple, and a whole tree chipper. A fell buncher is a machine that can hold and cut a tree up to 18 inches in diameter. One such machine is the Morbark's 18 inch Fell Buncher Shear or the 18 inch Rapid Buncher Disc Saw. The first uses hydraulics to shear the tree, while the other uses a carbide blade to cut a tree in less than a second. Once either of the machines has the tree or trees, it can place it or them on the ground in bunches, just like a bunch of carrots. With three to six trees to a bunch, a log grapple picks up these bunches by the trunk end and drags them to the chipper. This chipper has a boom with a grapple at its end to pick up the trees and feed them into the chipper. The Morbark's Models 20, 22RXL, 23, or 27 has this feature in addition to the ability to debark the tree before chipping it. It can debark and chip a whole tree in seconds and send a stream of chips shooting into the back of a truck. Once a truck is loaded, it can be hauled off to an ethanol facility where it is ready for the next step in ethanol production.

Ethanol production from wood chips requires an additional step called concentrated acid hydrolysis. This process takes wood fibers and converts them into sugars which can then be distilled into ethanol. There are many companies entering the marketplace that have the ability to convert wood fibers into usable sugars. Once sugars are obtained, it can be converted into ethanol. Some are closer to commercialization than others, but the technology exists. With just a little more time and money, these processes will be able to produce ethanol economically.

Cost will always be one of the biggest factors in determining what to do with the trees. Since the harvesting costs for Whole Tree Combustor technology is substantially less than ethanol production, electrical generation can be another avenue for income generation. How much revenue can be generated from the tree will help determine whether electrical generation is the desired market for those trees. In Whole Tree Combustor technology, chipping the tree is not required. Eliminating this step can reduce costs substantially. The whole trees are hauled directly to the power plant where they are stacked and dried for a month. By reducing the water content of the trees to about 20%, they will burn much hotter and more efficiently, thereby keeping cost of production low. This makes them competitive with coal-fired power plants. Since trees have very little nitrogen and sulfur, their sulfur and nitrogen emissions will not require expensive exhaust treatments. This would keep Whole Tree Combustor technology cost competitive with dirtier and cheaper coal.

If these groves of trees are in a market where electricity is extremely cheap, the trees can be used as feedstock for paper production. The planting, cultivating, and harvesting costs will be identical to feedstock generation for ethanol production. Since Morbark's chippers debark the trees before chipping them, the wood chips are ideal for paper pulp production. If paper prices remain as high as they have been, paper pulp production could become an avenue for income generation.

On marginal lands where large tree groves are not practical, additional income can be generated from switch grass. Switch grass is a hearty, drought tolerant plant that can be harvested once a year. The land doesn't need tilling, except maybe once every ten years. Switch grass would only be grown for ethanol production. Standard straw harvesting techniques can be employed to harvest the grass. Since switch grass is a cellulosic product, concentrated acid hydrolysis or similar technology will be needed to convert this material into sugars for ethanol production. Again, the ethanol can either be dilute or fuel grade, depending on costs and market conditions.

Market conditions for electricity, ethanol, or biodiesel are dependent upon location. If you are in an area where there is cheap and abundant hydroelectric power, it doesn't make sense to generate electricity. If, on the other hand, your area has an abundance of rich farm land that could produce oil plants such as sunflower, rape seed, or soy, it would make sense to utilize the land to produce those crops.

Besides market prices and costs, other factors such as tax codes and incentives will help determine how the land and biomass will be used to generate income for the various governmental agencies.

When governmental agencies are involved, the Department of Energy Renewable Energy Production Incentive will be an added inducement for these agencies to use the biomass to produce electricity. Whether it be Whole Tree Combustor technology or dilute ethanol and the Direct Fuel Cell, both technologies would qualify city, county, and state Governments for a cash payment from the Department of Energy. This cash payment would be 1.5¢ per kwh (adjusted for inflation) and would be in addition to the income they generate from the sale of the electricity.

Interpretation of the 1992 Energy Policy Act states that a municipality is considered a qualifying facility. As a qualifying facility, another source of income would come from Title IV of the 1990 Clean Air Act, assuming that the surrounding utility would be willing to pay for the total avoided cost. This means the utility would pay a corresponding amount to the municipality for the sulfur dioxide emission credit it would normally pay if the utility company was generating the electricity from coal.

If the production of electricity is not high on the priority list, but fuel ethanol and/or biodiesel is, these fuels can either be sold on the open market or be used internally by the Government agency. If the fuel is used internally on alternative-fueled vehicles, it will help develop the alternative fuel industry. In doing so, this will help publicize the 1988 Alternative Motor Fuel Act which was designed to help develop the alternative motor fuel industry. Unfortunately, you probably haven't heard much about this act since its effectiveness and publicity is governed by budget constraints.

At a time when Government is trying to reduce it expenditures, many politicians are either completely unaware of or choose to ignore the significance of developing the alternative fuels market. Some of them may even be receiving PAC money from lobbyists to promote the usage of gasoline and diesel. As an example, President Clinton signed into law in 1995 the raising of the speed limit. By increasing the speed limit, all of us use more gasoline and diesel. This would not be a problem if we had a hybrid vehicle that achieved 80 mpg and or had an infrastructure of alternative fuels. Through development of the alternative fuel market, trade deficits can be reduced and local economies can flourish, putting people back to work—people who will end up paying taxes back to the Government. This market, of course, is dependent upon costs. Until just recently, many of the technologies had not been available to effectively develop the alternative fuels market.

Assisting in the development of the alternative fuels market to generate income for the Government will require some creative joint ventures between Welfare, Government agencies, and Prison Industry Authorities. Since prisoners, welfare recipients, and military personnel are already receiving a check for their time, using them in this fashion will only make their expense more justifiable. Since the biomass industry is in its infancy, subsidizing it with labor will give the industry time to become more proficient in the production of energy. When this eventually happens, Government agencies that employ these technologies will be much further ahead in generating incomes and balancing their budgets.

Garbage Profit Centers

As of 1994, forty-four states have either announced or have legislated goals for waste diversion or recycling. As a result of this legislation, nearly seven thousand local Governments have curbside collection of recyclable materials and three thousand have composting programs for yard waste.[55] Some states wish to reduce their garbage stream by only 20%, but in the case of Rhode Island, 70% diversion of their garbage stream through recycling and composting is the target. Fifteen out of the forty-four states have goals of reducing their waste by 50% or greater, including the two most populous states: California and New York. As landfill facilities begin to close resulting in higher disposal fees, more states will eventually initiate more aggressive recycling and waste reduction programs. Some states may come to the conclusion that the recycling industry makes good economic sense as it creates employment and generates tax revenues. When states realize this benefit, a more aggressive stance on recycling will result.

---

[55] CRS Issue Brief: Solid Waste Issues, By James E. McCarthy, Environment & Natural Resources Policy Division, Page CRS-1

Statewide Solid Waste Recycling/Reduction Goals				
State	**Goal(%)**	**Recycling/ Deadline**	**Waste Diversion[1]**	**Reduction[2]**
Alabama	25	—	X	
Arkansas	40	2000	X	
California	50	2000	X	
Colorado	50 [3]	2000	X	
Connecticut	40	2000	X	
Delaware	21	2000	X	
Dist. Of Columbia	45	1995	X	
Florida	30	1995	N/A	N/A
Georgia	25	1996		X
Hawaii	50	2000	X	
Idaho	25	1995	X	
Illinois	25	2000	X	
Indiana	50	2000		X
Iowa	50	2000		X
Kentucky	25	1997		X
Louisiana	25	1992	X	
Maine	50	1994	X	
Maryland	20 [4]	1994	X	
Massachusetts	46 [5]	2000	X	
Michigan	50 [6]	2005	X	
Minnesota	30-45 [7]	1996	X	
Mississippi	25	1996		X
Missouri	40	1998		X
Montana	25	1996		X
Nebraska	50	2002		X
Nevada	25	1994	X	
New Hampshire	40	2000		X
New Jersey	60	1995	X	
New Mexico	50	2000	X	
New York	50 [8]	2000	X	
North Carolina	40	2001		X
North Dakota	40	2000		X
Ohio	25	1994	X	
Oregon	50	2000	X	
Pennsylvania	25	1997	X	
Rhode Island	70 [9]	—	X	
South Carolina	30	1997	X	
South Dakota	50	2001		X
Tennessee	25	1996		X
Texas	40	1994		X

State	Goal(%)	Recycling/ Deadline	Waste Diversion[1]	Reduction[2]
Vermont	40 [8]	2000	X	
Virginia	25	1995	X	
Washington	50	1995	X	
West Virginia	50	2010	N/A	N/A

N/A = Not available, because goals are subject to interpretation
[1]Generally includes recycling, composting, and source reduction; [2]Reduction in volume from disposal facilities, usually from a baseline year; [3]Goal announced by Governor in 1993, not legislated; [4]15% goal for counties under 100,000; 20% goal for counties over 100,000; [5]Source reduction is planned to offset any growth in per capita generation of MSW; [6]25% recycling, 10% composting, 10% source reduction, 5% reuse; [7]45% goal in the seven county, Twin Cities area; 30% in greater Minnesota; [8]Goal was developed pursuant to the state capital Solid Waste Management Plan; [9]Processing for recycling

Source: BioCycle May 1995, page 32

In order for each state to meet its goals of waste diversion, each state has determined what they will or will not take at their landfill facilities. Items banned include vehicle batteries, tires, yard materials, motor oil, and white goods. Car batteries are very toxic to our environment and contain lead and sulfuric acid. Traditionally, most of us recycle car batteries when we buy replacement batteries and most of them do get recycled. Automobile tires present a real problem for the landfill facility since they take hundreds of years to decompose and have a tendency to work themselves up through the layers of garbage when buried. Yard material such as grass clippings, branches, and such are better utilized if they are mulched or used for energy generation. Motor oil is extremely hazardous to our ground water. One quart of oil can contaminate thousands of gallons of water, making it unsuitable to drink. Recycled motor oil has been tested and the tester claims that the oil is as good as virgin oil. White goods are items such as refrigerators, dishwashers, ovens and any other major appliances. These items take up a tremendous amount of space, but most are made of metal and can be recycled. Refrigerators present a special problem in that they contain CFCs which damage the ozone. These items are big and bulky and require a tremendous amount of labor to break them down into their components so they can be recycled.

Disposal Bans For Selected Waste Materials

State	Vehicle Batteries	Tires	Yard Materials	Motor Oil	White Goods	Others
Alabama	X			X		
Arizona	X	X				
Arkansas	X	X	X			
California	X	X		X	X	
Connecticut			X[1]			X[2]
Delaware		X				
DC			X[3]			
Florida	X	X	X	X	X	X[4]
Georgia	X	X	X			
Hawaii	X	X[5]	X[6]		X	X[7]
Idaho	X	X				
Illinois	X	X[5]	X		X[8]	
Indiana	X	X[5]	X[9]			
Iowa	X	X[5]	X	X		X[10]
Kansas	X	X[5]				
Kentucky	X	X[5]				
Louisiana	X	X			X	
Maine	X					
Maryland		X	X			
Massachusetts	X	X	X		X	X[11]
Michigan	X		X			
Minnesota	X	X	X	X	X	X[12]
Mississippi	X					
Missouri	X	X[5]	X	X	X	X[13]
Nebraska	X	X	X	X	X	X[13]
Nevada				X		
New Hampshire	X		X			X[2]
New Jersey	X		X[14]			X[2]
New Mexico	X			X		
New York	X	X[5]				
North Carolina	X	X	X	X	X	X[15]
North Dakota	X			X	X	
Ohio	X	X	X			
Oklahoma		X[5]				
Oregon	X	X		X	X	X[7]
Pennsylvania	X		X[16]			
Rhode Island	X					
South Carolina	X	X	X	X	X	
South Dakota	X	X	X	X	X	X[17]

State	Vehicle Batteries	Tires	Yard Materials	Motor Oil	White Goods	Others
Tennessee	X	X		X		
Texas	X	X		X		
Utah	X	X				
Vermont	X	X		X	X	X[18]
Virginia	X					
Washington	X			X		
West Virginia	X	X	X			
Wisconsin	X	X	X	X	X	X[17]
Wyoming	X					

[1]Grass clippings; [2]Mercury batteries; [3]There are no landfills in District of Columbia, but residents are not allowed to dispose of yard trimmings in Municipal Solid Waste; [4]Disposal ban on demolition debris, devices containing mercury banned from incinerators; [5]Whole tires; [6]Landfills must divert 75% of commercial and 50% of residential green waste, or face a ban; [7]Scrap automobiles; [8]White goods containing CFC gases, mercury switches and PCBs; [9]Landfills recovering methane gas exempted; [10]Nondegradable grocery bags, carbonated beverage containers, and liquor bottles with deposits; [11]Glass and metal containers, recyclable paper and single polymer plastics; [12]NiCad batteries, telephone books, and sources of mercury, motor vehicle fluids and filters; [13]Small quantities of hazardous wastes; [14]Leaves; [15]Antifreeze, aluminum and steel cans; [16]Leaves & brush; [17]Office and computer paper, newsprint, corrugated and paperboard; glass, plastic, steel and aluminum containers; [18]Various dry cell and NiCad batteries, paint.

Source: BioCycle, May 1995, page 33

As more materials are redirected away from landfills and into recycling, market development has become an important aspect of the waste reduction process. To aid in this development, incentives and programs have come about to help drive the recycling industry. Grants, tax incentives, loans, market development zones, Government agencies, and special task forces are the tools used today to develop the recycling market. Typically, grants come from the Federal Government. As an example, the Environmental Protection Agency has the "Jobs Through Recycling" program that gives grant money to the states for economic development. To help the recycling industry grow and overcome marginal profit situations, tax incentives that lessens the recyclers' tax liabilities are used to help recycling industries overcome those lean years when costs exceed revenues. Loans are being offered by some states. The money is financed through fees such as the Advanced Disposal Fee, a fee collected from the wholesaler for products that do not contain recycled content. Millions of dollars are collected, giving the state a pool of money to loan at below market rates.

Market development zones are special zones designed to help economically depressed areas. States that participate in this type of program offer low interest rates for recycling industries who locate their business in economically depressed areas. Special Task forces that interact with Federal Government agencies help firms to overcome bureaucratic and technical hurdles.

State	Tax Incentive	Grants	Loans	Market Zones[1]	Commerce/ Economic Development[2]	Market Development Council	Task Force
Incentives And Programs For State Market/Economic Development In The Recycling Industry							
Alabama		X					X
Arizona	X	X			X		X
Arkansas	X						X
California	X	X	X	X			
Colorado	X		X		X		
Connecticut							X[3]
DC							
Delaware	X				X		
Florida[4]	X				X		X
Georgia							X
Hawaii		X					
Idaho							
Illinois	X	X	X	X[5]			
Indiana	X		X		X		
Iowa	X	X					
Kansas	X				X		
Kentucky	X				X		X
Louisiana	X				X		
Maine	X						
Maryland	X	X	X		X		X
Massachusetts			X				
Michigan		X	X		X		
Minnesota	X	X	X				X
Mississippi		X			X		X
Missouri		X			X		X
Montana	X						
Nebraska							
Nevada	X						

State	Tax Incentive	Grants	Loans	Market Zones[1]	Commerce/ Economic Development[2]	Market Development Council Task Force
New Hampshire			X	X[6]		
New Jersey	X	X	X			
New Mexico	X					
New York	X	X			X	
North Carolina	X				X	X
North Dakota	X					
Ohio		X			X[7]	X[7]
Oklahoma	X					
Oregon	X	X	X			X
Pennsylvania	X	X			X[8]	X
Rhode Island						
South Carolina						X
Tennessee						X
Texas	X			X	X	X
Vermont		X	X			
Virginia	X					X
Washington		X[9]			X	X[10]
West Virginia	X[11]					
Wisconsin	X	X	X			X
Wyoming					X	

[1]Zones dedicated to recycling market development; [2]Agency involved in recycling market development; [3]Not officially sanctioned; [4]Program for grants and/or loans is being developed; [5]Program will target economically depressed areas, not zones per se; [6]Tax Exempt bonds; [7]Legislation passed in 1994; [8]Department of Commerce represented on market development task force; [9]Technical assistant grants designed to benefit industry as a whole, even though individual businesses sometimes get direct help; [10]Policy Advisory Board within state Clean Washington Center; [11]Waiver of solid waste fees for businesses that recycle 70% of their waste.

Source: BioCycle, May 1994, page 31

Some cities and counties are directly responsible for garbage collection while other cities or counties subcontract this responsibility. Many cities and counties may do this simply because they do not own the landfills or mass burn facilities. In fact, according to the Environmental Protection Agency, 78% of the MSW landfills and 51% of waste-to-energy facilities are owned by local Governments.[56] Depending on the contracts that cities or counties have with the collection service, income genera-

---

[56] Congressional Research Service, "Solid Waste Issues," By James E. McCarthy, Environment and Natural Resources Policy Division, page CRS-8

tion may or may not be a possibility. For example, Folsom City has a joint venture with the California Prison Industry Authority. The city owns the refuse even after it has been sorted. Once the material is sorted, the recyclable material can be sold to processors. If the garbage is owned by a city or county, the city or county has an avenue available to them to generate income through recycling and energy conversion of the waste materials. Recycling materials is straightforward but not profitable under current market conditions. It has been estimated that it costs $50 a ton to sort recyclables and for every ton sorted, only $30 a ton in revenues is received. This disparity obviously makes recycling unprofitable. To make recycling and energy conversion of waste materials profitable, the garbage collection fees will need to be increased, or the cost of labor needs to be decreased.

To drive down the cost of labor, creative joint ventures can be actualized by linking either Welfare or prison systems. Since these two systems have a pool of labor that has been "paid" for, generating income for the system will help defray operating costs.

The California Prison Industry Authority (PIA) and the City of Folsom have created a joint venture whereby the prisoners of the City's "Community Correctional Facility" (CCF) provide the labor pool to sort through the municipal garbage, recovering all recyclables and compostables. For this service, the City pays PIA a per-ton processing fee and the City keeps the proceeds from the sale of recyclables. The City collects all of the waste from its customers as it normally does and then trucks it to an inmate-built material recovery facility next to the prison where the garbage is sorted by the prisoners. There are approximately one hundred prisoners working eight hour shifts to sort the one hundred tons per day of garbage. These prisoners are minimum custody offenders who have violated their parole and earn an average of 50¢ per hour wage with a day off their prison term for every day they work. The prisoners sort out all of the recyclables including appliances which are disassembled. The remainder of the unrecyclable material is being composted or landfilled. Besides generating income for the City, and helping defray the costs of incarceration of the prisoners, there are additional benefits such as work skills, responsibility, and work ethics taught to the prisoners. The program helps meet and exceed the State's mandate to reduce the garbage being buried in landfills and the program stabilizes landfill costs by extending lives of existing facilities.

To help make the economics of this program work out, the city charges its customers for garbage service. This fee is enough to cover the costs associated with garbage collection, sorting costs, and landfilling. Since the basic cost of operations are being covered by customers' garbage fees, the city obtains a profit when it sells the recyclables and composted materials.

Additional revenues can be generated when a city installs equipment to convert the unrecyclable materials into energy. At this time, there are various technologies that can perform this task. The first includes additional sorting of the garbage into suitable feedstock for ethanol production. Their second method of creating energy is to maintain their current level of sorting and use gasification technology to produce a combustible gas. Once a combustible gas is produced it can be used as fuel to run generators or fuel to be used in turbine-powered hybrid vehicles. This gasification technology can be supplied by Thermogenics or Proler International. If a municipality chooses to use Proler International's gasification process, Proler will own the gas and the municipality will not benefit from the usage of that gas.

If a city decides to produce ethanol, it would make better economic sense to have gasification equipment on site. Since distillation requires heat, the waste heat from gasification and electrical production can be used in the distillation process. Turning waste into ethanol requires sorting and chopping of the feedstocks. Additional preparation would include concentrated acid hydrolysis that would convert the cellulosic materials into sugars to be distilled into ethanol. Once ethanol is produced it needs to be dewatered if it will be used as fuel grade ethanol. Otherwise, the dilute ethanol can run directly into a Direct Fuel Cell provided by Energy Research Corporation to produce electrical energy. Electricity can be produced from dilute ethanol for about 6¢ per kilowatt hour assuming the cost of producing the dilute ethanol is comparable to corn-based ethanol. The residual material from ethanol production can be gasified to produce additional gas for electrical production or fuel for turbine-powered hybrid vehicles.

Electrical production, or "methane" gas for fuel, can be directly produced if the unrecyclable material is chopped and fed into a gasifier supplied by Thermogenics. The advantage of gasifying the unrecyclable material directly is there is no additional capital expense for ethanol equipment. Labor will be about the same since every piece of garbage will be handled and sorted for recyclables. There will be waste involved since heat generated from gasification and electrical production will not be used and will have to be vented into the atmosphere. Since the gasification process itself does not emit any air pollutants, the only pollution will come from burning the gas from the gasifier in either internal combustion engines or turbines. At this time, using the gas in a fuel cell is not recommended since the gas has not been tested to determine if it has any contaminants that may render the fuel cell inoperable. But once the gas is cleaned sufficiently for fuel cell usage, increased efficiencies can be obtained with lower pollution, which would mean more revenues with the same fuel costs.

Lower pollution can also be achieved if the unrecyclables are gasified and the syngas is used to produce plastics. This technology can be supplied by Proler International, but unfortunately there are two caveats. The first problem is not a large one if the given community with this facility can generate at least 50 tons of unrecyclable garbage per day. The other obstacle requires an industrial facility nearby so that the syngas could be piped to the facility and converted into feedstocks for energy, plastics, or other products.

In the first scenario, where ethanol and electricity are produced, several tax laws come into play that would give additional income to the municipality or the private party in the joint venture. If ethanol is produced for the purpose of electrical generation through a fuel cell, the city could apply for the Department Of Energy's Renewable Energy Production Incentive. This would give the city an additional 1.5¢ per kilowatt hour (adjusted for inflation) of electricity produced. This payment would also apply to electricity generated through methane gas produced by gasification of garbage. If the facility decided to sell waste heat and feedstocks to an independent ethanol producer, the ethanol producer can qualify under Internal Revenue Code §40 which would give the independent alcohol producer a 60¢ per gallon credit so long as the ethanol is 190 proof. Depending on the size of the facility, the ethanol producer can also qualify for a 10¢ per gallon credit if the facility produces less than 30 million gallons a year. Under this provision, the first 15 million gallons will qualify for the credit.

In the second scenario, where the unrecyclables are gasified, the municipality can apply for the Department Of Energy's Renewable Energy Production Incentive of 1.5¢ per kilowatt hour (adjusted for inflation) of electricity produced. The municipality will also benefit if the garbage is gasified for fuel for hybrid vehicles. Depending upon funding from Congress and whether or not the gas produced from garbage can be qualified as natural gas, the 1988 Alternative Motor Fuel Act provides funding for vehicles capable of using the natural gas as fuel.

In the third scenario where the municipality pays Proler International to take the refuse, the municipality will not qualify for any additional benefits. It will benefit only by paying less than it would for landfilling its unrecyclable material. Proler International will benefit from Internal Revenue Code §29, assuming this code gets extended by Congress and the President.

The economic feasibility of these three scenarios will depend upon many variables. Those variables include the price of electricity, ethanol, technologies, payback period, financing, tipping fees, and how much money is required to ship the garbage out of the area.

Depending on the area, timing, and the state of the economy, these variables can fluctuate. At the time of this writing, tipping fees and garbage exports are a known variable that can be a determining factor in deciding to install or implement one of the three scenarios. Implementing one of these scenarios in states such as New Jersey or Vermont makes sense, considering their average tipping fee is $75.00 per ton for landfill. On the other end of the scale, New Mexico's average tipping fee is $8.00 a ton, while Nevada and Wyoming only charge $10.00 a ton for landfilling. In these states, the costs associated with implementing any of these scenarios may not make it economically feasible in the near future until landfill sites run out.

	LANDFILLS			INCINERATORS		
State	**Number**	**Average Tipping Fee ($ ton)**	**Remaining Capacity (years)**	**Number**	**Average Tipping Fee ($ ton)**	**Daily Capacity (tons/day)**
Alabama	27	25	10	1	39	700
Alaska	740	40	N/A	3	80	200
Arizona	72	25	N/A	0	—	—
Arkansas	86	20	20	4	20	N/A
California	255	28.50	13-18	3	27.50	2,700
Colorado	64	12	N/A	1	N/A	N/A
Connecticut	6	60	N/A	5	73	N/A
Delaware	3	58.50	20	0	—	—
DC	0	—	—	0	—	—
Florida	105	41.86	N/A	13	60	19,000
Georgia	104	30 [2]	9	1	N/A	500
Hawaii	9	45	8	1	46	N/A
Idaho	39	N/A	N/A	0	—	—
Illinois	58	32.50	8	1	N/A	618
Indiana	50	25	14	1	25	2,175
Iowa	63	35	N/A	1	30	N/A
Kansas	60	25	N/A	0	—	—
Kentucky	29	30	14	0	—	—
Louisiana	23	19.70	10	0	N/A	N/A
Maine	14	45	5	5	38	N/A
Maryland	22	47	10	4	37.50	4,000
Massachusetts	108	55	N/A	9	50	9,300
Michigan	60	N/A	13	5	N/A	N/A
Minnesota	28	52	12	12	63.50	4,900
Mississippi	17	22	N/A	1	22	150

Landfill and Incinerator Capacity and Cost

State	LANDFILLS Number	Average Tipping Fee ($ ton)	Remaining Capacity (years)	INCINERATORS Number	Average Tipping Fee ($ ton)	Daily Capacity (tons/day)
Missouri	32	25.90	8	0	—	—
Montana	35	22.50	20	1	N/A	60
Nebraska	25	25	N/A	0	—	—
Nevada	28	10	N/A	0	—	—
New Hampshire	29	50	N/A	12	45	800
New Jersey	14	75	N/A	6	90	5,965
New Mexico	90	8	50	0	—	—
New York	64	70	9	11	65	10,350
North Carolina	65	24	N/A	2	29.50	N/A
North Dakota	16	25	12	0	—	—
Ohio	81	27	8	11	44	N/A
Oklahoma	40	20	35	2	43	N/A
Oregon	67	23	40	2	65	600
Pennsylvania	51	46	12	7	54	9,000
Rhode Island	5	32	20	0	—	—
South Carolina	34	23.15	20	2	51.50	800
South Dakota	20	25	N/A	0	—	—
Tennessee	110	20	25	2	45	N/A
Texas	192	19.50	20	8	N/A	N/A
Utah	79	18	20	1	60	300
Vermont	9	75 [2]	3	2	60	N/A
Virginia[2]	254	25	N/A	10	35	7,000
Washington	24	N/A	49	6	N/A	N/A
West Virginia	22	37	N/A	0	—	—
Wisconsin	53	30	9	2	32.50	N/A
Wyoming	77	10	100	0	—	—
Total	**3,558**			**158**		

N/A=not available
[1]The District of Columbia uses a landfill and incinerator outside its borders; [2]From previous "State of Garbage in America" survey
Source: BioCycle, April 1995, page 63

As the above table reveals, garbage disposal prices vary widely. Prices are even higher when municipalities decide to burn garbage, although there are exceptions to this situation in the states of Arkansas, Indiana, and Mississippi. In these three states, the average price of landfill is equal to the average price of incineration. In the case of California, Iowa, New York, and Vermont, the average price of incineration is actually less. Even though the average incineration cost is less than or equal to landfill prices in these seven states, real costs are not reflected because the external cost of air pollution is not accounted for. Raw garbage, which is unsorted, is being burned in these facilities. Dangerous metals such as cadmium and mercury from common products such as batteries and fluorescent tubes are burned in these facilities and their toxic emissions are being released into the atmosphere.

The air quality and efficiency of these facilities will be improved greatly if these mass burn facilities were to create joint ventures with either Welfare or Prison Industry Authorities to presort the garbage for recyclables and "hazardous" materials. By eliminating these hazardous materials from the burning cycle, emissions from these facilities would be much cleaner. Furthermore, they operate more efficiently by presorting the garbage and using the flue gas to "dry" the sorted garbage on racks. In doing so, the garbage will burn hotter and produce more energy with less garbage and emissions.

The next table indicates which states export and/or import garbage. The totals do not match exactly and not all states are represented. This table is at best an estimate of what happens between the major exporters and importers of garbage.

In the chart you will notice that Ontario, Canada, is listed. Even though it is not a state, it does export its garbage to Michigan, New York, Ohio, and Pennsylvania. However, the amount they have been shipping has come down since the tipping fees in their province were cut by 50%. Fortunately, the rest of the states have been transporting less garbage throughout the nation. Even so, millions of tons of garbage are still shipped throughout the United States. Unnecessary transportation and fuel costs are incurred simply because tipping fees are high and the options presented in this chapter are not being implemented.

Any facility will find it more economical to create a joint venture to sort through the garbage for recyclables with people from Welfare or a Prison Industry Authority. By eliminating 50% or 60% of the garbage through recycling, they would have less garbage to ship out of the area. Total elimination of garbage exportation will be achieved if gasification and/or ethanol production technologies are employed on the remaining garbage. If building separate facilities for recycling and energy generation for each municipality is too costly, one large facility can be shared by several cities. If enough volume is processed and placed near an industrial facility, the unrecyclable garbage can be gasified by Proler International. The feedstocks could be used to produce steam, electrical power, plastics, and other products.

By following one of these scenarios, the garbage problem will disappear, our trade deficit problem with OPEC will ease, costs will be reduced, and income will be generated for municipalities.

By employing prisoners or welfare recipients to sort the garbage, their respective systems will receive money, thereby defraying their operating costs. By putting prisoners or welfare people to work, it will teach them responsibility, give them a sense of accomplishment, and hopefully encourage them not to stay in their respective systems. It would also create new industries and stimulate the economy.

Exports and Imports of Municipal Solid Waste, 1993 (in tons)		
State	**Quantity Exported**	**Quantity Imported**
California	60,000	
Connecticut		775,000
Delaware	e178,985	
District of Columbia	c565,034	
Idaho	25,000	
Illinois	b1,000,000	i1,030,000
Indiana	f85,109	821,600
Iowa	b270,000	
Kansas		700,000
Kentucky	b252,719	k212,000
Louisiana		l5,652
Maine	41,700	142,640
Maryland	b197,790	55,000
Massachusetts	b400,000	700,000
Michigan	b67,000	N/A
Minnesota	200,000	
Missouri	970,000	30,000
Montana		12,500
Nebraska		i78,000
Nevada		i62,700
New Hampshire	g34,593	520,445
New Jersey	a1,578,230	
New Mexico		i209,500
New York	3,900,000	<200,000
North Carolina	96,000	
North Dakota	g9,000	i40,000
Ohio	340,573	1,670,914
Oregon	5,000	800,877
Pennsylvania	b800,000	h3,847,000
Rhode Island	b550,000	
South Carolina		96,000
Tennessee		l51,149
Texas	b230,000	
Utah		16,674
Virginia	b30,000	1,500,000
Washington	710,515	26,993
West Virginia	b120,000	525,000
Wisconsin	g30,000	359,213
Ontario, Canada	d250,000	

ªNew Jersey is one of the few States to distinguish MSW from other waste shipped to MSW disposal facilities. The State reports exports of 1,578,230 tons of MSW in 1993, but it also exported 932,024 tons of other waste to out-of-state MSW landfills.; ᵇCRS estimate based on partial information.; ᶜA landfill does not exist within the District, but the District owns land in Lorton, Virginia, on which both a landfill and a waste-to-energy facility operate. The District of Columbia Department of Public Works does not consider waste sent to these facilities to be out-of-state waste shipments since the disposal facilities are on land owned by the District.; ᵈCRS estimate based on partial information. Ontario also exports substantial quantities of construction and demolition waste, not estimated here.; ᵉFirst processed as refuse-derived fuel.; ᶠAs reported by Indiana. Two receiving states, Illinois and Ohio, report receiving more than three times as much waste from Indiana as Indiana reports in exports.; ᵍ1992 data ; ʰIn addition, Pennsylvania received 1,060,000 tons of other waste (sewage sludge, medical waste, ash, construction/demolition waste, or asbestos) from out-of-state for disposal at MSW landfills in 1993.; ⁱCRS estimate.; ʲ1991 data.; ᵏ1994, estimated by CRS, based on state data for first three quarters of the year.; ʲJuly 1992 - June 1993.; ᵐAs reported by North Carolina, July 1992 - June 1993.

"Imports" are defined as waste originally from out-of-state, including waste from other states and from other countries.

The above data is based on telephone interviews with and data provided by State program officials to Congressional Research Service (CRS). States not listed in this table were not able to provide data, but generally concluded that only small amounts of Municipal Solid Waste (MSW), if any, left their States for disposal. Most concluded that they did not receive major quantities of MSW from out-of-state. Because Michigan believes it is a major importer, it is listed in the table even though CRS was unable to estimate the amount of waste it receives.

Source: Congressional Research Service Report for Congress (95-570 ENR), May 5, 1995

Costs will always be a factor in determining if these technologies will work in any given situation. In areas where disposal costs are very high, employing a combination of technologies is very feasible. The opposite is true in an area where tipping fees and the price of electricity is very low. Each case will need to be reviewed on a site by site basis to determine if any of these solutions will work for the municipality.

To help make marginal facilities become a reality, or simply more profitable, these waste-to-energy facilities can be located on landfill sites that are required to install and maintain land fill gas extraction and control equipment. Amendments to the 1990 Clean Air Act mandates landfills to reduce emissions of methane (a potent greenhouse gas), non-methane organic compounds (contributes to tropospheric ozone), and toxic compounds which are hazardous to human health. It has been estimated that a cubic foot of methane gas is approximately twenty-five times worse than carbon dioxide in the sense that a cubic foot of methane gas can retain as much heat in the atmosphere as 25 cubic feet of carbon dioxide. For this reason, landfill facilities are required to control these emissions by several methods:

1.   Use the gas for fuel in boilers and brick or cement kilns.

2. Use the gas as fuel in engines that will generate electricity.
3. Upgrade the gas to pipeline quality or produce vehicular fuel.
4. Flare off the gas.

Since the quality of gas that is extracted from the landfill may be marginal, the capital expense of installing and operating land fill gas extraction and control equipment can be expensive. As the price for electricity may be low in certain areas, sharing the site will benefit both the landfill and the recycling and waste-to-energy facility. If the recycling and waste-to-energy facility is located on a landfill, their rent costs for land will be very low. Rent collected by the landfill could help subsidize the landfill facility, perhaps making it profitable.

The recycling and waste-to-energy facility benefits through this joint venture by having additional gas capacity at minimal cost. The gas would come from the landfill without the need to process additional garbage. If an internal combustion engine is used for electrical generation, landfill gas can be used directly without any prior cleanup. If a fuel cell is used to generate electricity, the landfill gas will have to be cleaned to prevent the contaminates from destroying the fuel cell. Otherwise, an internal combustion engine or turbine can be used with no gas cleanup. If the garbage is liquefied into dilute ethanol or used to make fuel grade ethanol, gasification equipment will probably be needed to eliminate the residue from ethanol production. If both gasification and liquefaction equipment are present, it may make sense to use a combination of different electrical power generation equipment on this facility.

Tire Recycling

Income generation from tire recycling is most suitable for local Government agencies that control the destination of discarded tires. Since we generate approximately two hundred forty million tires per year, and have roughly three to five billion tires stockpiled throughout the United States, we have a steady source of materials that can be used to generate income for local Governments.

Local Governments can profit from this untapped resource if they employ the TRTM-60 tire recycling plant. This plant is capable of recycling ten thousand tires a day into their basic components: oil, carbon black, and steel. These are basic components that can be sold back to the oil companies, tire manufacturers, and steel recyclers. If the plant is operating at full capacity, it will produce approximately 250 barrels of fuel grade oil, 30,000 pounds of steel, and 50,000 pounds of carbon black per day. On an annual basis, this translates into $1,650,000 for the oil,

$2,475,000 for the carbon black, and $297,000 for the steel wire. This adds up to $4.4 million a year but does not include the tipping fees, which can enhance the revenue stream considerably. Tipping fees vary from state to state and many states have enacted legislation providing tire disposal businesses the ability to charge for discarded tires. Depending upon your state and the legislation that exists or can be created, local Governments may be able to take advantage of this resource.

It will take a substantial amount of investment to make this plant a reality, but the payback period is short, depending on other costs and royalties. The plant itself would cost $5 million. Land, buildings, storage units, and other optional equipment drive the price up even more. The royalties are 7.5% of the revenues generated by the plant for the life of the plant. This calculates out to approximately $330,000 a year. For this royalty, the company provides technical support and maintenance of the central processing unit during the lifetime of the machine. Since royalties, employee salaries and other costs erode the approximately $4.4 million in revenues, it might take several years to recoup the investment. Depending upon land and other costs associated with building the plant, this time period might be longer. On the upside, the payback period is short and employee salaries will be small. If the plant operated three shifts in a twenty-four hour day, it will only require about sixteen people to run those three shifts.

Although initial costs are high, the long term benefits to the local Government that installs this plant will be substantial. Operational costs are low and depending on how the plant was financed, annual revenues can be substantial. So long as we have cars, we will always have discarded tires to provide a source of revenue.

Sewage Plants

Every time you flush the toilet, you are sending potentially valuable energy down the drain. Human waste contains a tremendous amount of energy that our bodies have not assimilated. This potential energy ends up in our sewage system where anaerobic digestors create methane gas and sewage sludge, both a wasted energy source. Many facilities today use the methane gas to heat the anaerobic digestors and the residual unused gas is flared off. The sewage sludge is then either hauled away to landfill facilities or used to irrigate fields. If the sludge is landfilled, it can cost up to $100 a wet ton to dispose of this material. If the sludge is used to irrigate a field, money and energy are being spent just for transportation costs. Regardless of how most municipalities handle their sludge problem, they are spending money on the disposal of the sludge without receiving anything in return. In either case, the energy potential from the gas or the sludge is not fully utilized.

Full utilization of this energy could bring additional revenue to municipalities that choose to employ technologies capable of converting this potential energy into electrical energy. This can be accomplished with two different existing technologies, each with different treatment paths. The first system involves cogeneration while the second method involves hydroponics.

The first method is highly suitable for existing sewage plants. The methane gas that is derived from anaerobic digestion is not used to heat the anaerobic digestors, but is used to power gas turbines that generate electricity and heat which is used to create steam. The steam is used for three purposes. First, it is used to create more electricity, second, it is used to heat the anaerobic digestors, and third, it is used to dry the sludge. Once the sludge is dry enough, it is burned to produce more steam that helps drive the turbine generators.

The second method is geared towards new sewage plants rather than retrofits. The sewage first passes through a filter in which anaerobic bacteria cling to tiny particles of diatomaceous earth. The bacteria converts the sewage into carbon dioxide and methane gas. The methane gas can be fed directly into a Direct Fuel Cell where electricity is created. The carbon dioxide gas can either be collected and sold or channeled into a tent that covers the hydroponics garden to assist the plants growth. The plants are periodically harvested for their biomass content which can be converted into dilute ethanol that will be fed back into the Direct Fuel Cell to create more electricity and revenue.

Additional revenue can be earned by the municipalities if the Renewable Energy Production Incentive is applied to this situation. Since both methods of electrical generation involve biomass, these facilities would qualify for an additional 1.5¢ per kilowatt hour, adjusted for inflation.

Another source of income would result from Title IV of the 1990 Clean Air Act, assuming the surrounding utility is willing to pay for the entire avoided cost, which would include the sulfur dioxide emission credits.

U.S. Government Online

Our Government is big and diverse. We have hundreds, if not thousands, of Government programs that can help our economy grow and prosper, but very few people are aware of them and few know how to access the programs that can help a budding business. Our Government services need to be downsized and streamlined. Duplication needs to be eliminated, and an emphasis in helping the entrepreneur become successful should be the priority. Without the entrepreneur, small business development and job creation are unlikely in our current economy.

We do need some form of Government assistance. In the past, monetary or tax policies have assisted the entrepreneur, but with the ever increasing national debt, tax cuts without debt reduction is not feasible, practical or politically popular. Since our debt is above $5 trillion, Government downsizing coupled with increased tax revenues is the only way we will eliminate the annual deficit and the national debt.

In order to increase tax revenues without raising tax rates for current taxpayers, we need to put more people to work. To accomplish this goal, small businesses and entrepreneurs need more tools that will assist them in becoming better business people and more competitive in this global economy. To facilitate that goal, a new service called U.S. Government Online needs to become a reality and an integral part of our Government.

U.S. Government Online is an idea for an online service available for a fee to anyone with a computer and modem. Just like the other online services such as Entrepreneur Online, Prodigy, CompuServe, and America Online, this service will be unique in that it will provide the United States Government with a revenue base while helping entrepreneurs become more effective in our economy and providing the average citizen with a way of understanding and participating in our Government. U.S. Government Online should become an extension of National Technical Information Service (NTIS). Since NTIS exists within the Technology Administration of the U.S. Department of Commerce and is a self-supporting agency that sells information to the public, an online service is the next logical evolution for this agency. This agency can advertise in the same fashion that the other online services do, by offering a free diskette which includes free time to learn and discover the services that are available. By employing this method of marketing, consumers will have very little to risk and will gain much in the area of learning how Government can serve them.

In order for this online service to be helpful to the average citizen, the interface needs to be easy to use and eye pleasing. To accomplish this task, the service needs to be arranged logically. It must be designed to assist users in completing their goals with the least amount of time and frustration. To ensure the end user gets a product that is useful and easy to navigate through, outside consultants, entrepreneurs, and maybe one or more of the online services should design the system. Once the system is put into place, day to day management of the system should be performed by one of the current online services. In this fashion, the Federal Government would simultaneously earn revenues while downsizing and helping private enterprise grow.

To help private enterprise grow and prosper in this global market, NTIS and the Department of Commerce Trade Promotion Coordinating Committee's nineteen agencies should be integrated and brought online first. Currently, the Trade Promotion Coordinating Committee's nineteen agencies can be reached by contacting one of the U.S. Export Assistance Centers (created by the 1992 Export Enhancement Act) that are scattered throughout the United States. Unfortunately, there are very few of them and their future may be limited due to budget constraints. By bringing these nineteen agencies and NTIS online first, a foundation will be provided from which the online system can grow and assist the average citizen in helping the economy. As new services are added and more users sign on, the interface will have to be updated.

As the interface is refined and new modules are added, more revenue can be generated for the Federal Government. This revenue can come from an online retail outlet for goods or services that will assist the entrepreneur and any end user in their goals. Software, books, seminars, or even booking a campsite at one of the National parks can be the type of products and services offered. As the online system grows and becomes more useful to the entrepreneur, the economy will flourish and stimulate innovation. An example of how innovation can help our economy flourish in our country, there is a list of needed products that require inventive effort. This list is currently available only by mail:

U.S. Small Business Administration
Office of Innovation
Research & Technology
SBIR
1441 L Street, NW
Washington, DC 20416

If this list were to be publicized through an online communications system, maybe some online users with specific knowledge can develop some of these products that would satisfy a need and help stimulate the economy.

Another way the economy can benefit is knowing how your Congressman/Congresswoman votes. This information is currently available through a database called Project Vote Smart. Project Vote Smart is a free service for anyone who wants to use it. The goal of this database is to turn the table on politicians. The information within this database can help voters decide more prudently about their elected officials. Information such as biographical history, voting records, campaign finances, campaign promises, and performance evaluations can be obtained from this database. If we know that our elected officials are voting for items that raise Government spending, destroys jobs, and negatively affects the environment, we have the power to correct this situation at voting time. We can vote these people out of office and replace them with people who understand that we pay their salaries and they have to answer to us. For more information, contact:

Project Vote Smart
129 NW Fourth Street, #204
Corvallis, OR 97330
Tel: 503-754-2746
Tel: 1-800-622-SMART
Fax: 503-754-2747
URL: http://www.vote.smart.org

To help promote the idea of U.S. Government Online, you have two options. Your first option is to contact your Congressman/Congresswoman by fax or letter. Your other option is to contact SBA Online (http://www.sba.gov). At SBA Online, you have the ability to contact over one hundred fifty Federal Government bulletin boards where you can offer suggestions about how Government can improve its service to citizens.

As you may know, there are many online sites and services available, but they are not centralized or standardized. By bringing all of these systems under one interface, America can move forward and prosper.

EIGHT

ECONOMIC COMPETITION & STIMULATION

The goal of this chapter is to introduce ideas for change that will ultimately help lower your personal income taxes. This can be accomplished by stimulating the economy that will add new tax payers to the system. New legislation needs to be added to the books and old legislation needs to be removed.

Internal Revenue Service

Most of us, except Internal Revenue Service employees, tax attorneys, tax preparation software companies, tax preparation services, and accountants would like to see this arm of the Government eliminated. If it will not disappear altogether, we would at least prefer to see it shrink. The Internal Revenue Service and its supporting infrastructure is a very large part of our economy. Billions of dollars a year are spent by private citizens and corporations complying with tax codes. Eliminating the Internal Revenue Service would destroy many lives and careers. Therefore, it is important to make evolutionary changes in this industry that will allow these workers to make a smooth transition from tax compliance to other occupations. Simplification of the tax codes would eliminate many people from this industry but could slow down any positive growth that would result from the simplification process.

To insure that the economy moves forward in a positive manner, the changes proposed to the tax system need to maintain some form of complexity so that the entire industry will not be destroyed overnight. The complexity of the tax code should remain with corporate taxes, not with personal taxes.

Personal Income Tax

Proposed Income Tax Systems

Middle class America is paying a disproportionate share of income taxes while the very rich are paying little or no taxes at all. There are tax havens and deductions for the very rich who know how to use the system. Exacerbating the problem, corporations pay very little or no taxes, and foreign corporations even pay less. Sometimes corporations do not have to pay taxes for years because they have tax havens, depreciation, depletion allowances, and their net operating losses to offset any income they have. When the rich and the corporations avoid paying their fair share of taxes, the tax load is transferred directly to middle class citizens who do not get a break.

The only citizens getting breaks in the system are the very rich who have the money to hire accountants and attorneys to wade through the more than two thousand eight hundred pages of laws and the more than eight thousand pages of IRS regulations. Since the system is so large and complex, Americans spend billions of hours filling out tax forms. Not only does it take time, but nearly $65 billion is spent annually by individuals to complete their tax returns.

Americans are fed up with the tax system. We feel that we are being taxed to death. We have income taxes, payroll taxes, sales taxes, gasoline taxes, excise taxes, and property taxes, just to mention the most visible. To make matters worse, President Clinton raised the tax rate in 1993. This raise made the tax system worse than what it was by punishing those who try to get ahead by working hard.

Our current system has many flaws. For example, we are double taxed. Savings and inheritance taxes are a form of double taxation. We get taxed when we earn the money and we get taxed again when we save it or try to pass it on to our heirs. We also get punished for having an entrepreneurial spirit. Capital gains punishes those who take risks in building businesses and later selling them for a profit. Capital gains punishes those who also hold assets for long periods of time and then sell them at a profit. Our current tax system encourages instant gratification and punishes delayed gratification. This exemplifies how our business education system has impacted our tax system. Business schools across the nation teach students to maximize profits in the short run while long run planning appears absent from the system. This neglect for long range planning is the reason deficits are rampant, the national debt is out of hand, and we have a regressive tax system that discourages hard work and saving. This problem will only get worse when short run solutions such as tax simplification are introduced. As an example, the National Sales Tax is simple, but impacts low income people the most. When every product is taxed at a proposed 20%, everyone will experience inflation at the stores.

Before we make any wholesale changes to the tax system, we will need to understand the ramifications of the changes being proposed. Our tax system is a multi-billion dollar industry supported by the Federal Government that spends nearly $14 billion a year in administration of the tax laws. Private individuals and industry spend billions more every year just to comply with tax regulations. We need to remember that, although we may view the IRS and accountants as necessary evils, the current tax system creates employment for thousands of people who have lives just like you and me. The wholesale changes suggested by some Politicians could be disastrous for the people who depend on the current tax system for their livelihood.

FLAT TAX BENEFITS

The flat tax proposed by Representative Dick Armey is appealing because the system is very simple. There is one tax rate for both individuals and companies. It will start out at 20% and will eventually be reduced to 17%. Businesses will pay a flat tax on any positive income. Corporations, partnerships, professional, farm, rental profits, and royalties are included as business income. Positive income is determined by subtracting expenses from revenues. These expenses include the cost of goods and services sold, capital equipment, structures, land, and wages and pension contributions paid to employees. If subtracting these expenses from revenue generates a positive number, then a flat 17% tax is paid to the Government.

Under the new proposed flat tax system, Subchapter S corporations will be a thing of the past. Under the new system, small business owners will have to pay themselves a salary that will be accounted for as an expense on the business. The remaining profits of the corporation will be taxed and the owner of the business will have to fill out the appropriate tax forms. Since the owner of the business receives a paycheck, this income will have to be declared on their personal income tax and taxes will have to be paid on that income.

Once the owner of the business receives this personal income, it becomes taxable at the flat rate of 17%. The tax rate applies to all personal income without regard to deductions, exemptions, or exclusions. Income can be adjusted with one type of allowance for dependents and marital status. These allowances are subtracted from the income and the balance is taxed at a flat 17%.

With such simplification, each of us will no longer need expensive tax accountants to help us fill out tax forms. Hours and money will be saved that can be used for more enjoyable endeavors. Businesses and corporations will also save time and money by not having to hire expensive accountants to assist them in filling out their tax forms. Since savings will not be taxed under this system, our country's savings rate should improve.

CONSUMPTION TAX BENEFITS

The Consumption Tax system proposed by Representative Bill Archer of Texas has many advantages. Without an income tax system capable of growing in size or complexity, neither individuals nor businesses will be required to fill out tax forms. This saves both individuals and businesses time and money that can be used more productively. When companies across the nation are not required to spend billions of dollars to comply with tax codes, their products will be more competitive in the global market. This helps exports compete in foreign markets and reduces imports when domestically produced goods cost less. Since this tax system places the burden of taxation upon consumption, it will have a positive effect on savings.

As savings increase, more money will remain in the banking system, making it cheaper for individuals and businesses to borrow money, which in turn helps the economy grow. This tax system will also tax the underground economy. People who currently get paid cash for goods or services who do not report this income are considered part of the underground economy. This includes a wide range of people from drug dealers to participants at flea markets who do not report their cash sales. Since most everyone buys goods and services from businesses that report sales taxes, those who currently are avoiding their fair share of income taxes will be paying their share of taxes when they consume goods and services from reputable businesses.

U.S.A. TAX SYSTEM BENEFITS

The U.S.A. tax system benefits the money supply and the business community by encouraging individuals to save and invest. This is accomplished by allowing individuals to deduct all of what that person saves or invests from their gross income. From this adjusted gross income figure, the remaining is taxed at a progressive rate, thus encouraging saving and investing. Furthermore, businesses benefit by not being taxed on income derived from exports, thus making their company more competitive in the global market.

FLAT TAX CONSIDERATIONS

The flat tax proposed by Representative Dick Armey is modeled after a flat tax developed by two economists, Robert Hall and Alvin Rabushka, from the Hoover Institution at Stanford University. This system does not tax savings or inheritance. It starts with your wages and pensions and subtracts your personal allowances. If you are married filing jointly, you can deduct $26,200. If you are single, you are allowed $13,100, and if you are single head of household, you can deduct $17,200 from your income. Each dependent that you have is worth $5,300. These allowances are subtracted from your income. If there is anything left, the balance is taxed at a flat 17%. For example, a family of four earning $36,800 would pay no income tax. A different family of four earning $50,000 would pay $2,244 or 4.5% of their gross income, while another family of four earning $200,000 would pay $27,744 which is about 14% of their gross wages.

Eliminating the existing tax system and replacing it with the Flat tax that can be filed on a post card would destroy the entire industry and the livelihood of those who depend on it for an income. The Federal Government would save billions of dollars by eliminating the Internal Revenue Service, but this savings would be offset by unemployment expenditures. More unemployment will result from massive layoffs in the supporting infrastructure. Tax accountants, attorneys, and preparers will be directly affected as will software companies that produce tax software. They would no longer be needed. Massive layoffs within this industry will occur overnight without the economy's ability to absorb these people. The Government would have to pay more money in unemployment benefits than they do now. Worse, these people will not have the skills or knowledge readily transferable to other occupations. As this group of people earns less money, their spending ability will go down and the effects will ripple throughout the economy, with devastating results.

One of the biggest negative results of the flat tax will be the devastation of the housing market. Our current tax system allows for interest deductions on income taxes that makes some peoples' homes affordable. Eliminating this tax deduction would place many people in a financial bind. These people might have to sell their homes or give them back to the banks to prevent a negative credit rating. If thousands (perhaps millions) of people found themselves in this dilemma, the housing market would collapse and banks would be saddled with unwanted real estate. People will owe more money on their homes than they could sell them for, similar to what has already happened in the state of California. Prices could deflate anywhere from 10% to 30% and the home building industry could go into a slump from which it might never fully recover.

Governments might also fail to recover from a drastic change in the tax codes. Tax free bonds that finance projects will no longer have any tax advantage under the new flat tax. If taxpayers are not given preferential tax treatment for Government bonds, these investors will invest their money in other instruments that will give them higher yields. For instance, stocks, which are already over-inflated, will be chased by more dollars. This will result in more inflation in these instruments. The bond market could suffer substantially unless bonds offer higher yields, but this would cost those Governments more in operating costs to service the interest on those bonds. As more expense is incurred to service the interest on those bonds, less money will be available for the general fund to operate the day to day activities of the Government. This will translate into fewer services, fewer employees, shorter hours, or all of the above. With fewer employees earning less money, the group will be less able to contribute to the economic health of its community.

The community as a whole would not be improved by providing allowances for dependents. Similar to the case of the Welfare system giving more money for additional children, providing tax allowances for children will not produce better parents or children. This monetary reward for childbearing promotes the baby-making process but it doesn't generate better parents with emotionally healthy children. Anyone can have children. However, to raise healthy and emotionally balanced children, emotional maturity, self esteem, communication, love, patience, and common sense are required.

Providing a healthy economic system where a parent can learn, work hard, and earn a better salary would go farther toward achieving family values. Providing an environment where conscientious adults can become good role models would be more productive than providing allowances for children. Of course, the parents must take the time to raise their children in order to instill good values in them. Parents with little time and a lot of guilt who resort to giving their children cash in lieu of love and time find themselves with children who are manipulative, demanding, and disrespectful. This is the same type of problem we have with welfare recipients who feel that the system owes them a living. If we want to prevent this from happening to future generations of children, we need to instill a set of values that will foster good work ethics that result in citizens who are willing to contribute to the betterment of our communities.

The economic health of the community might suffer more than it does today if there are no provisions for alimony or child support. If spouses have no incentives to send alimony or child support, many single parents may find themselves financially in need of assistance. Some of these parents may only need food stamps while others may need assistance from Welfare. Others may seek out charitable organizations for assistance. If this happens, both charities and Welfare will become overburdened. Since this new tax system doesn't allow for charitable deductions, our welfare roles may swell and many charities may have to turn people away due to insufficient funding. Once this happens, our Government will become more responsible for funding these charities.

Funding for economic stimulation and growth will become a major issue under this new Flat tax proposal. We have special tax provisions that help the economy reduce our dependency on foreign imported oil and fossil fuels for electric generation. Under existing tax laws, the fuel alcohol and biomass industry are given tax advantages to encourage the development of those industries. Without these provisions, our trade deficits will deepen. This will require us to sell off our country a piece at a time in order to keep the oil flowing. This is a ridiculous price to pay for tax simplification. Without tax incentives for the biomass industry, the electric power industry will continue to consolidate to reduce costs and drive out any form of competition. As this happens, these existing power plants will continue to use fossil fuels, which will always be cheaper, which in turn translates into a continued usage of fuel that will result in air and water pollution through sulfur dioxide emissions. If it is important to improve our environment, we will need to reconsider the new flat tax.

CONSUMPTION TAX CONSIDERATIONS

The Consumption Tax proposed by Representative Bill Archer is a simple National Sales Tax that will replace individual, corporate, business, gift and estate taxes, and be in addition to any sales tax that already exists. Some proponents of the National Sales Tax propose up to a 17% National Sales Tax plus any local sales tax. This will translate into a combined sales tax of up to a whopping 25% in some areas. Imagine everything that is consumed costing an additional 25%!

If this high sales tax is implemented, discretionary expenditures that were barely consumed previous to a National Sales Tax would probably disappear. If more products and services disappear from lack of consumption, unemployment will rise. People who were previously employed in either the production of, the sale of, or service of any of these products and services would no longer be needed.

Tax professionals and Internal Revenue Service employees will no longer be needed as a result of the National Sales Tax. The Federal Government could save $14 billion a year by eliminating the IRS, but it would still have to pay unemployment benefits. In addition, these people who become unemployed would also contribute fewer tax dollars to the system. Besides Federal employees, private industry that depends upon the complicated tax system will suffer equally. At best, these professionals will no longer earn as much. At worst, they will be forced out of business. As they join the ranks of the unemployed, they will not be able to spend as much nor contribute to the tax system. By drawing unemployment benefits, they would become a compounded burden to the tax system.

The problem is further compounded when tax free bonds no longer have their tax free status under this new system. Investors will be looking for the highest return possible if the combined sales tax rate is 25%. If the investor decides to invest in Government bonds that yield lower returns, the investor will lower his standard of living by doing so. To keep the investors' standard of living high, it will be necessary for the investor to look at other instruments or else Government bonds will have to offer more attractive rates of return. If Governments offered competitive rates of return on their bonds, then Government operating costs will also become higher, making less Government service available to the masses and the poor.

Low income people will also suffer substantially from this new National Sales Tax. Since low income people have so little money to begin with, their spendable income won't even go as far as it does with our existing tax system. When food is taxed at this new high rate, families that can barely feed their children will become hard pressed. What previously cost them $100 will cost them $125. This increase in cost will push marginally low income people down into poverty levels where they would become a burden to our system. Another group of people who might get pushed into poverty are the single parents who depend upon alimony and child support. Since there are no incentives for spouses to send this support under this tax system, many single parents who were previously supported by their ex-spouse may become a burden on our society.

Still another group of low income people who will be directly impacted by this new tax system are those dependent upon charity. Soup kitchens, food banks and other charity organizations will probably see a decline in donations. If donations are no longer tax deductible, the person or corporation that chooses to make donations for tax reasons will have less incentives to donate. As less money is donated for worthy causes, the sick, elderly, poor, and the handicapped will have to fend for themselves. If charities are to survive, our Government will have to pick up the slack directly.

The economic system will also be burdened when the housing market begins to collapse as a result of the new tax system. Mortgage interest deductions will be a thing of the past and will force many families who could barely afford their homes with the mortgage interest deduction to sell or give up their homes when this deduction disappears. As thousands (if not millions) of homes are dumped on the market, home prices will drop like a rock. People will end up owing more money on a home than they can recoup by selling it. With depressed prices, the housing industry will be in a slump for years to come. It will take years and inflation to bring prices back up to current levels. In the mean time, the construction industry will go into a tailspin and the effects will be felt throughout the entire economy.

Another casualty of the consumption tax will occur with commercial property. There are literally millions of landlords who own apartments, homes, warehouses, office buildings, strip centers, malls, storage centers, and other commercial properties that will no longer provide the landlord with any tax benefits. Under the new tax law, no depreciation, interest, or expenses can be deducted from the revenues. To make matters worse, maintenance of the buildings will cost landlords tax money since improvements will be taxed. If the landlord purchases paint, a new faucet, or a door knob, he will be taxed. The landlord will get no tax benefits by improving the properties. Some landlords will realize it is important to maintain their properties and protect their investments. Others who bought the property for a tax write-off will realize their investment is costing them more money than they are receiving and may try to sell it or let the bank foreclose. If landlords choose to let the banks foreclose, a whole new banking crisis will begin. If landlords try to sell the property for what it's really worth without any tax incentives, the price may be lower than what is owed, and landlords may eventually choose to let banks foreclose. Either way, banks are going to be in big trouble if this tax system is ever implemented. Once banks get into trouble, the Government must step in and bail them out with taxpayer dollars. What may look good initially can change with a deeper look. The obvious flaws in this system can cause our economy to regress.

Not only will the economy regress, but the environment and our health will take a back seat to profits. The electric power industry, without biomass energy tax credits, will force the demise of renewable energy. Renewable energy technology is not cost competitive with fossil fuels unless the industry has these tax credits. Without the development of the renewable energy industry, the electric power industry will continue to use coal. Even if these power plants switch to lower sulfur coal, tons of sulfur dioxide would be emitted into the atmosphere every day. Sulfur dioxide, when combined with water, turns into sulfuric acid. Both items are extremely hazardous to the environment and our health. It causes water pollution, air pollution, kills plants, destroys ecosystems, ruins buildings and causes respiratory problems. All this will happen by eliminating corporate taxes and tax incentives for biomass energy.

When tax incentives for alternative fuels are eliminated, alcohol will no longer be cost competitive with methanol produced MTBE. Since methanol can be produced from natural gas and natural gas is a product of oil exploration, the alcohol industry will disappear. Without competition from the alcohol industry, the alleged negative side effects of MTBE will go unchecked and the oil companies will gain control of the reformulated gasoline market and become richer. Oil companies will also shut the doors on any new developments in the alternative fuel industry. When we eventually run out of oil, the oil companies will most likely liquefy natural gas into methanol to use as an automotive fuel. When this happens, oil companies will maintain their monopolistic control of the automotive fuels market.

This scenario will happen if the National Sales Tax becomes law and eliminates any form of competition through tax incentives. Without competition, oil companies will achieve their short run goals of maximizing profits in the short run and their long term goal of monopolistic control of the market. Through their selfishness, they will hurt our economy by totally ignoring the negative ramifications of importing oil. As our trade deficits get out of hand, we have to sell off our country in order to pay for those deficits. Whether it be bonds, real estate, companies or stock, the OPEC nations are gaining control of our country.

Before deciding whether we should implement this consumption tax, we need to ask ourselves some very big questions: How much pollution are we willing to accept? When will we stop importing oil? How much ownership of the United States are we willing to give up? How much are we willing to pay for the next generation of fuel when we run out of oil? These are realistic questions that need to be addressed when we start considering the elimination of corporate taxes and tax incentives. If we are prepared to accept these possible scenarios for the sake of simplicity, we should not blame politicians for creating this tax system when the environment and our economic stability becomes worse.

U.S.A. TAX SYSTEM CONSIDERATIONS

The core of the Unlimited Savings Allowance (U.S.A.) Tax System is about business investment and the elimination of taxation on personal savings. Under this new system, personal income tax and business tax have two distinct tax structures.

The individual tax system provides an Earned Income Tax Credit for the working poor and defines personal income much as it does today. The difference lies in the Unlimited Savings Allowance. Everyone who decides to save or invest in stocks or bonds, or invests their own money for start up capital in their own business can deduct this amount from their income. This system also allows for other deductions which include:

1. Higher Education: A tax deduction for remedial education for children under the age of eighteen and tuition paid for higher education.
2. Home Mortgage: This deduction would work the same as it does under our current law.
3. Charitable Contribution Deduction: This deduction would work the same as it does under our current law.
4. Alimony Paid Deduction: This deduction would work the same as it does under our current law.

Once these deductions are subtracted from the gross income, the balance is taxed at progressive rates. Considering that two-thirds of our economy is based on consumption and this tax system is designed to encourage saving by penalizing spending through progressive tax rates, this system may defeat itself. While the savings rate would improve and more manufacturing and retail capacity brought on line, people might find spending painful knowing their taxes could be a lot lower if they saved their money. If people are being punished for spending (which is the basis of our economy) by progressive tax rates, it can substantially curb spending and cause the economy to stagnate and regress.

In the business world, all businesses would be taxed the same. It wouldn't matter if the business is a one-man shop or a fortune 500 company. Starting with gross sales, businesses would deduct expenses from the gross sales just as they do today. One big difference with this tax system is how the full cost of investments in new plant and equipment can be expensed in the year they are acquired. If the acquisition is made with cash, the accounting for the new equipment is very simple and the entire amount can be expensed. However, if the business borrows money to make the acquisition under this new tax system, the borrowed money must first be considered income. Any down payment or installment payments can be written off for the first year. For each subsequent year until the loan is paid off, the loan payments are expensed and deducted from the gross sales. Once these deductions are subtracted from gross sales, the balance is taxed at a low, flat rate.

Under this new system, the depreciation expense is entirely eliminated. Businesses will be able to replace equipment on an annual basis regardless of the condition of the equipment. In high tech industries such as the computer industry, this allowance can be useful in helping companies stay ahead of their competitors by having the latest equipment. On the downside, it can be abused. Imagine if new cars could be replaced on an annual basis for key employees of any company. The cars can be bought with company cash and written off the books entirely in the first year. In subsequent years, the same can be done and the one-year-old vehicle can be brought home for personal use. The same scheme can be done with computers and no one would be the wiser. Abuses like this could go on and on while the company reduces its tax liability to zero, and the tax liability would be shifted from the business sector to individuals.

Individuals would also suffer when certain tax provisions in the alcohol fuel market disappear. Without tax credits for ethanol, the industry and all the competition that currently exists in the reformulated gasoline market would disappear and more power will be given to the oil companies.

COMBINED PERSONAL INCOME/NATIONAL SALES TAX SYSTEM

As you have seen, there are many benefits and downfalls to each of the tax systems being proposed. Implementing a good tax system will play an integral part in solving our economic problems, but it is only a part of the answer. Awareness, education, intelligent buying decisions, right-sizing, assistance, and even subsidies will be necessary to bring our economy into balance. Using a simplified tax system without any equalizing provisions can result in economic chaos and monopolies. Simplification is very appealing, but our economic and social problems are very complex. Taking an eclectic and evolutionary approach in designing a tax system is my method. The new tax system will be a combination of the National Sales Tax along with the Flat, and Unlimited Savings Allowance tax systems.

Our personal income tax system should be one that encourages savings, investing and spending while maintaining fair treatment of everyone. It should be a blend of the three tax systems that are being proposed by Congressman Archer, Armey, Nunn, and Domenici. It should entail lower and flat tax rates used in conjunction with additional modifications and provisions. Income will be defined much as it is today with some provisions, adjustments, and deductions for:

1. Unlimited Savings Allowance
2. Higher Education
3. Charitable Contributions
4. Alimony & Child Support
5. Family Counseling
6. Health Insurance
7. Automotive Depreciation
8. Major Appliance Depreciation
9. Housing Depreciation
10. Home Mortgage Deduction for Historical Structures

Definitions & Conditions of New Tax System

Unlimited Savings Allowance Deduction

Any money that is deposited into a savings account, used to buy bonds or stocks, or saved and eventually used as start-up capital for one's own small business can be deducted from gross income.

Higher Education Deduction

Any remedial or higher education expenses can be deducted from one's gross income.

Charitable Contributions Deduction

Charitable deductions allowed today under current tax laws would apply under this system.

Alimony & Child Support Deduction

Parents paying alimony and child support can deduct these expenses from their income taxes much as they do today under the current system.

Family Counseling Deduction

Any family or individual counseling costs can be deducted from gross income.

Health Insurance Premiums Deduction

Any health care premiums spent by the taxpayer will be tax deductible.

Automotive Depreciation Deduction

Depending on the American made content value of an automobile, that content value can be depreciated over a five year period on a straight line depreciation basis. The higher the American made content of the vehicle, the greater the tax advantage. This would require the dealer who sold the product to send an additional form to the Internal Revenue Service indicating the purchaser's Social Security number and the product's related information. This form could be pre-printed and only require Social Security information and the retailer's Federal ID number. The manufacturer could print up this information and include it with the products. This way, the Internal Revenue Service can verify if the deductions taken are valid.

Major Appliance Depreciation Deduction

Depending on the American made content value of major appliances, those appliances can be depreciated over a five year period on a straight line depreciation basis. If the appliance has 50% American value and the product cost $1,000, the tax payer is allowed 50% x $1,000 ÷ 5 = $100 per year depreciation for a period of five years. The higher the American made content value, the greater the tax advantage. The definition of major appliance would include heating and cooling equipment, ovens, dishwashers, refrigerators, washers, and dryers. This would require the dealer who sold the product to send in an additional form to the Internal Revenue Service indicating the purchaser's Social Security number and the products related information. This form could be pre-printed and only require the Social Security information and the retailers Federal ID number. The manufacturer could print up this information and include it with the products. This way, the Internal Revenue Service can verify if the deductions taken are valid.

Major Consumer Electronics

Consumer electronics that would qualify for depreciation expense include computers, printers, televisions, video players and recorders. Depreciation expense is dependent upon the American made content value as it applies to major appliance depreciation deduction.

Property Tax Deduction

Property Taxes that are currently deducted today would be treated as the same under this new system.

Housing Depreciation Deduction

Houses will be depreciated over a fifty year life span. Existing homes will be treated differently from new homes. New homes will be depreciated based on their new home price less the land value. This remaining value will be depreciated over a fifty year period. The depreciation amount will not change over the life of the building and any new owners will assume the depreciation schedule until they sell that home or the fifty year period is up. Existing structures that are less than fifty years old will have their depreciation basis calculated on replacement cost less land value. That figure is divided by fifty years and if the house is twenty-five years old, the annual depreciation expense can be taken for another twenty-five years.

Historical Structures Deduction

Using existing rules to determine what buildings are qualified as historical structures will give the person who owns such a structure mortgage interest deduction.

Social Security Recipients

Under this proposed tax system, Social Security recipients will be treated like any other taxpayer who receives income. A married couple can receive a base income of $20,000 (arbitrary) tax free while a single person would be allowed a base income of $17,500 (arbitrary) tax free. Social Security benefits and the new Medicare premium payments that the elderly will receive will also be included as income. Of course, insurance premiums are tax deductible, which essentially makes their medical benefits "free." Under this new system, the Federal Government will get out of health care. Instead, the Government will send each person who qualifies for Medicare a premium voucher so that the individual can shop for his or her own health care. This provision will require all of the insurance companies to cooperate with this plan. If this plan is instituted, fraud will be reduced and the high cost of insuring the elderly will be spread amongst all age groups who are insured. It may mean slightly higher premiums for younger people, but it will help reduce fraud and lower the cost of caring for the elderly by spreading the high cost of health care amongst all citizens of the United States.

Welfare Recipients

Welfare recipients will also be treated as if they are average citizens, with the exception that their "pay" will be coming from the Government. This "pay" will be in the form of payment credits to cover such items such as phone, utilities, rent, health insurance, food, and cash for general spending. They will be able to spend their credits with a debit card system. All credits will be considered as income and their health care premium payments are deductible from their income taxes just like everyone else under this tax system. If these welfare recipients are ambitious and find time to work a part time job and their forty hours per week for Welfare, this part time revenue will be included as income. They will be taxed as everyone else is, once they reach their ceiling limit of $25,000 (arbitrary) for head of household or a family of four or more. If welfare recipients manage to find a forty-hour a week job in the private sector, but make less than what they received from the Government in terms of cash and benefits, the Government will make up the difference first with daycare, second with health insurance premiums, and third with food credits. All of these credits will be considered income. Their full time private sector income plus any Government assistance will not exceed what they previously were "earning" from the Government. Parents who receive daycare credits will only be able to use them by having their children watched by other welfare recipients in the system. Health care premium credits are to be used to shop for private health care coverage in the private sector just like all of us do.

Income

Income would be defined much as it is today. Child support, alimony, interest income, and the gains from the sale of assets would be counted as income, but inheritances and gifts would not be subject to tax. When stocks and bonds are sold, or when savings are withdrawn for any reason, those proceeds will be counted as income in the year they were received or withdrawn. A family of four or more and head of household will have a base of nontaxable income of $25,000. A married couple's base of non taxable income will be $20,000. A single person's base will be $17,500.00. These numbers may need adjustment; a more precise set of numbers for income ranges will need to be calculated using numbers provided by the Congressional Budget Office.

Tax Rate

Since the new tax system is a combination of three tax systems, two separate tax rates will have to be calculated in order to derive enough tax revenues to reduce the Government debt.

The National Sales Tax should be kept low so it won't discourage spending and consumption. The net amount of tax collected should be roughly equal to the amount of Social Security taxes that are collected at the present. At the end of 1994, the Government collected $461.5 billion from the Social Security system.[57] By using a low tax rate on every product and service sold (except homes and rent), the tax liability will be shared more equally by everyone, especially those who earned more than $62,700 (as of 1996) and avoided paying Social Security taxes on any income above this figure, and it will allow the income tax rate to be lower than what it is today.

The flat tax rate on income could be as low as 10%, but a more precise tax rate needs to be calculated. With a lower income tax rate, more disposable income will be available for everyone to either spend, save, or invest. If people spend more, more taxes will be generated through the National Sales Tax. If more is invested or saved, the economy can grow by having an increased money supply and lower borrowing costs, thus putting more people to work who will pay more taxes.

Regardless of what numbers are chosen, the goal is to generate at least the same amount of tax revenues we do today with the same amount of taxpayers. As more people are put back to work, deficits will disappear faster as more tax revenues are generated.

---

[57] Congressional Budget office, *The Economic and Budget Outlook: Fiscal Years 1996-2000*, January 1995, p. 94

Benefits

Fairness

The new tax system, which really is a blend of the old and the new, will result in everyone paying their fair share. To help achieve this goal, a National Sales Tax will require everyone to pay a sales tax on every product and service that is sold to them, with the exception of their homes or the rent they pay for housing. By using the National Sales Tax to replace income from Social Security taxes, the tax burden will no longer be born by the middle class. As you learned in Chapter 4, Social Security taxes are being used as income taxes and people who earn above $62,700 (as of 1996) do not pay any Social Security taxes on income above that figure. Since Social Security taxes are being used as income taxes, privatizing Social Security and replacing the lost income with a National Sales Tax will distribute the tax liability and will therefore be shared by everyone who is a consumer. Tax evaders will no longer be able to avoid paying tax since everyone is a consumer. The regressivity of a National Sales Tax to low income people will be offset by a rebate (that needs to be calculated) and its low tax rate. This will not impact the elderly or the poor greatly since they will receive a rebate for an approximate amount of money they will spend on sales tax. The rebate would count as income on their tax returns and it will essentially be a wash. Since low income people will be treated like everyone else in the income tax system except for this rebate, the amount of rebate will have to be calculated and would vary with the different levels of poverty. The system will be fair and will encourage people to save. It will also encourage them to work hard.

Since everyone will be treated the same in regards to income and income tax (except for the rebate), people who wish to work harder to earn more so they can save and invest will not be penalized the way they are today. The new income tax system will allow for unlimited savings which will eliminate the double taxation on savings, and more importantly, it will encourage people to save as much as they can afford since the amount they save or invest is deducted from their taxable income.

Taxable income can be further reduced through use of the depreciation expense on automobiles, appliances, major consumer electronics, and homes. With this system of depreciation, practically everyone who can afford to buy a new oven will be able to receive a tax break. The higher the American made content, the greater the tax break. Tax breaks will be available to practically everyone who works and earns a living.

Economic Stimulation

The economy will be stimulated by having provisions for depreciation on homes, cars, major consumer electronics, and major appliances. With time, these items eventually wear out and become liabilities to the owners. By allowing taxpayers to depreciate the value of these assets, people will be encouraged to replace them as these items live out their useful lives. As more cars, refrigerators, washers and dryers are replaced in a shorter period of time, more people will be employed in producing these goods. Once a home depreciates to zero, the land will still have value, but will be unencumbered by the bank. This will allow the developer to step in and redevelop entire neighborhoods, putting more people back to work.

More people will also be put back to work if American consumers change their buying habits and start buying automobiles and computers that have a higher American made content value. If this happened, companies with less American made content value will start to lose market share. In order to remain competitive, these manufacturers will start using more American made components and this will result in employing more American workers. As more American jobs are created and welfare recipients become better candidates for jobs, more people will be put to work and the economy will be further stimulated as more people earn higher incomes, which will in turn create a greater capacity to save. As people save more, more money will be available to loan out for further economic stimulation.

With a higher national savings rate, the money supply will grow, and borrowing will become cheaper for both the Government and individuals. As money becomes cheaper, there will be a greater demand for homes and automobile loans.

Underground Economy

By implementing a National Sales Tax, the underground economy will end up paying taxes regardless of its current ability to avoid paying taxes. Since everyone is a consumer who buys major products from tax paying reputable establishments, taxes will be collected from everyone who consumes goods and services in our economy.

Environmental

The environment will benefit from this new tax law when older and less energy efficient appliances, homes, and cars are replaced with newer more efficient models. Electric appliances that get their power from fossil fuel power plants will require less electricity to run. As less electricity is produced, less pollution will enter the atmosphere. The same will be true as older homes and cars are replaced with more energy efficient models. As these items consume less energy, there will be less air pollution.

Stabilization Of Industry

By changing the tax system slowly, the tax industry will not have to go through a major disruption. Normal attrition rates in the tax industry should accommodate and lessen the demand for tax professionals. Tax professionals will not have to worry about changing their lifestyles overnight because the personal income tax system will be a little simpler and the corporate tax system will remain pretty much intact. As our trade and fiscal deficits start to disappear, both corporate and personal income taxes can be further simplified. Corporate taxes should disappear when monopolies, trade and fiscal deficits eventually disappear. In the meantime, tax professionals will be needed to interpret the different tax codes in the alcohol and biomass industries which will help spur along competition in the oil and electric power industries.

Government Bonds

Income from tax free Government bonds will be treated as tax free and income will be determined under the new proposed tax system the same as it is today. These bonds will be better able to compete with other investment instruments that offer better returns because the income will be considered tax free. By insuring that bonds remain competitive against other investment instruments in this highly profitable and volatile financial market, funding for Government projects will not dry up and will insure that progress at all levels of Government will continue.

Government Interest Expense

Housing interest deduction has put unnecessary strain on the available money supply. When everyone refinances their home to lower their payments and to get the biggest tax deduction possible, money that could be available for other lending becomes limited and/or more expensive. By eliminating the interest deduction on homes except for historical structures, and replacing it with depreciation expense, more money will be available (and cheaper) which will make Government borrowing cheaper. When the Government can borrow money cheaper than it does today, it will pay less in interest. This will help lower the deficit faster, balance the budget, and it could reduce taxes for everyone.

Trade Deficits

When less efficient automobiles are replaced with more fuel efficient ones, less imported oil will be needed and smaller trade deficits with the OPEC nations can occur. Trade deficits with Japan and Germany will also be improved if American buying habits begin to change. If more Americans consume goods that have higher American made content in order to receive a higher depreciation deduction, Japanese and German car manufacturers may start to lose market share to vehicles with higher American made content value. If German and Japanese car manufacturers increase the American made components in their vehicles to regain market share, fewer imported parts will be used and the trade deficits with these countries will be improved.

Saving & Investing

This proposed income tax system will not penalize savings or investing as does the current tax system. Since all savings and investments will be subtracted from one's earnings, the adjusted gross income will not tax the money placed in savings or investments. Interest and dividends will be considered income, but won't be taxed if the dividend and interest is reinvested. Gains from the sale of stocks will be counted as income, but if those gains are reinvested in other instruments, the net effect is no tax due on those returns. In other words, as long as the dividends, interest and capital gains are reinvested, there will be no tax due on those gains. The more one saves and reinvests, the larger the money supply will grow. This will assist our economy's growth and expansion. If we want people to work hard and save, we must change this unfair and stupid system that punishes good behavior. Otherwise, our economy will be stunted.

Inflation

Low inflation will be a reflection of how well our manufacturers and retailers are able to supply us with goods and services by producing them at the lowest cost possible. One major factor that will reflect their ability to perform this task well is related to their cost of borrowing money for expansion and improvements in manufacturing, distribution, and sales. Since this tax system encourages investing in stocks and savings, companies will have several avenues in which to inexpensively finance their expansion and improvement plans. As manufacturing and distribution cost goes down for all companies across the United States, inflation will remain low.

Inflation will also be kept low when our import costs are less by having a strong dollar overseas. Our low inflation rate has been greatly attributed to the fact that we have been importing low cost imports into America. If we want to continue importing low cost goods, we need to have a strong dollar overseas. In 1995, the dollar was struggling against the Yen. Under normal market conditions, when the dollar is weak against foreign currencies, we buy fewer imports because they become more expensive. At the same time, other countries will start buying American made products because they are cheaper. Between consuming fewer imports and exporting more

American made goods, the trade deficits should disappear and eventually the dollar will strengthen against other foreign currencies.

This theory would have worked if we were able to substitute away from certain products as they become more expensive when the dollars value falls against other currencies. Unfortunately, there is no substitute for oil and the United States and the rest of the world is dependent on it. Since the rest of the world is incurring huge trade deficits for imported oil, they have few dollars to spend on luxuries such as American made products.

Despite the weak dollar in August 1995, our trade deficits were not disappearing. In theory, natural market forces would have eventually eliminated trade deficits because our products would have been cheaper to foreigners. Instead, the United States decided to prop up the price of the dollar against the Yen by buying the dollar with Government bonds. Not only did the United States buy dollars, Japan, Switzerland, and Germany got into the act to support the dollar. To help facilitate the market forces of the foreign exchange market, the proposed income tax system encourages people to purchase American made products which can be depreciated. As market forces change the composition of products produced by foreigners, trade deficits will eventually disappear which will help strengthen our dollar against foreign currencies. Imports will be cheaper, keeping inflation low.

Inflation can also be kept low when the dollar is strengthened by reduced Government debt. Since value is always based upon perception, the value of the dollar against other currencies will be based on how well the rest of the world perceives the strength of the United States in regards to its deficits and its ability to pay its debts. The stronger our economy and the less debt our Government incurs, the stronger the dollar will be against other currencies.

Take for example the Russian Ruble, which has little or no value against foreign currencies. The rest of the world perceives Russia as being unable to pay its bills and debts because the economy and Government is weak and volatile. Since there is no confidence in their economy or their Government, their currency is very weak against other foreign currencies.

We don't want to be perceived as a weak economy. This proposed tax system will go far toward fulfilling that and by reducing the deficit through stimulation of the economy and through depreciation allowances and savings. As the economy becomes stronger, our dollar will become stronger against other currencies. When the dollar gets stronger, imports will cost less, which helps hold down the rate of inflation.

Corporate Income Tax

Problem

The corporate income tax structure is very complex and offers benefits to many special interests, such as foreigners, oil companies, and even the environmentally friendly biomass industry. Because of its complexity and intricacies, many corporations can avoid paying income tax, which transfers the tax liability to all of us. Many corporations and some economists (including this author) will point out that a tax is like a tariff, and tariffs are inefficient. Tariffs raise prices of imported goods and allow less efficient American plants that are competing with foreign goods to enter the marketplace and produce products that will compete with foreign goods. By the same token, goods that are made by American corporations who pay corporate taxes have higher prices, which gives foreign imports an advantage over their American counterparts. For this reason, many American companies will do whatever is necessary to avoid paying income taxes just to remain globally competitive.

Considerations

There are many ways corporations can avoid paying taxes. Since our economy is structured around our tax codes, trying to change the system overnight would have disastrous consequences to our economic system. Some people will argue that corporations are not paying their fair share of taxes and should pay more. If corporations did pay more taxes than they do today, our individual tax liabilities would probably be substantially less. On the downside, corporations would probably change the way they do business in order to remain competitive in the global market. This might involve moving operations overseas and/or reducing the components or products that are made here in America. If this scenario happens on a large scale, there might be a substantial number of job layoffs that could negate the tax savings that would have come about by having corporations pay a bigger share of taxes. As people are laid off, the economy will begin to shrink, which will further the decline of our economic base.

Without tax incentives for certain industries, our economic base may further decline. Take for example the alcohol fuel market, which is heavily dependent on tax incentives and credits. If this industry did not receive any tax credits or incentives, it would dry up and disappear. If ethanol was no longer economically viable, the oil industry would take total control of the reformulated gasoline market and any competition that exists in the industry would disappear.

The reformulated gasoline market has two basic suppliers, the ethanol industry and the natural gas industry. Ethanol is made from corn which is the feedstock that is used in making ETBE, an additive used to make gasoline burn cleaner. MTBE, the other additive that makes gasoline burn cleaner is made from methanol. Today, most if not all of the methanol produced is made from natural gas. Natural gas is usually a byproduct of oil exploration and is abundant and cheap. Without competition from the alcohol industry, a monopoly situation would arise that could eventually put a stranglehold on our precarious economy.

Since there is always uncertainty in our economy, especially when the Federal deficit and national debt is out of hand, it becomes very important to insure that all industries across the nation remain healthy despite the deficit problem. Without healthy industries that employ American workers, the economy would sink into a recession that would worsen the annual deficit and defer balancing the budget.

If this scenario did come to pass, it would also further hamper the development of the biomass industry. The biomass industry has the potential to develop clean alternatives to gasoline and diesel while displacing some of our demand for imported oil. The biomass industry also has the capacity to displace dirty burning coal-fired power plants with cleaner alternatives. The 1988 Alternative Motor Fuel Act and the Department of Energy Renewable Energy Production Incentive are the vehicles that would help fund the development of these industries. The 1988 Alternative Motor Fuel Act would help develop clean fuels by providing funding for vehicles that burn clean fuels. Since alternative fuels are in their infancy, time and refinement of existing technologies is needed to make alternative fuels cost effective. The same situation exists within the biomass industry. There are existing and emerging technologies that will need time and refinement to make them more cost effective. Without tax credits and tax incentives to assist the development of these industries, our environment and future economy will suffer.

It is important to remember how the economic multiplier is a critical concept regarding policy towards tax incentives and credits in the biomass industry. When we import oil instead of developing the biomass industry, we export our capital abroad to pay for our trade deficits. We pay for our trade deficits with capital instruments such as real estate, companies, stocks, and Government bonds. If the money that is exported out of our country is used here to develop and expand the biomass industry, the economy will grow by the amount of money we keep here in the economy multiplied by the current multiplier factor. For simplicity's sake, if the multiplier factor is 1.5 and $50 billion is diverted back into our economy through the development of the biomass industry, the economy will grow by an additional $75 billion. This additional growth would be seen throughout the entire economy from manufacturing to retail.

Short Term Solution

Despite the many drawbacks to the current corporate tax system, there are benefits that keep competition alive in certain industries and that keep people employed here in America. While simplification is desirable, it can create more problems than it will solve in the short run.

The biomass industry is an example of how tax simplification will destroy an industry and give more power to an already too powerful oil industry. Small changes that yield big results are more important than big changes that yield disastrous results. The small changes that are being referred to in this book are the ones being proposed in the personal income tax system. At a time when corporate mergers and downsizing are being actively pursued by corporate America, eliminating the entire tax industry overnight would push the economy to its limits in its ability to absorb millions of unemployed people who may or may not be able to find new jobs depending on whether or not their skills and knowledge are transferable to other industries.

For these reasons, the best short term solution is to keep corporate taxes the same until the effects of the new proposed personal income tax system takes hold of the economy. Considering that the economy is very volatile, and downsizing and mergers are the focus of corporate America today, additional strains on the bleak job market are more than the economy can handle at the moment. Once U.S. Government Online is up and running and helping entrepreneurs export more and establish new businesses, then it will make sense to begin simplifying corporate tax codes. Until then, it is unwise to change too much too quickly.

Foreign Trade Zones

The 1934 Foreign Trade Zone Act can give the American economy a shot in the arm if more local economic development agencies, ports, or airport boards apply to the Foreign Trade Zones Board at the U.S. Department of Commerce. By obtaining the status of a Foreign Trade Zone, entrepreneurs become more competitive with imports. Goods assembled outside of a Foreign Trade Zone or Subzone made up of domestic and imported components have a disadvantage over imported complete kits (components that make up a finished good) and completed imports. Both complete kits and finished goods have lower tariffs than individual imported components. The entrepreneur who wishes to employ American suppliers and workers is placed at a disadvantage by this disparity.

The entrepreneur can regain an advantage and still employ American workers and suppliers by locating his assembly plant within a Foreign

Trade Zone or Subzone. The economy could benefit substantially if ex-military bases were classified as Foreign Trade Zones. These zones allow the entrepreneur to import separate components with little or no tariffs. Tariffs are paid when the finished goods are shipped out of the zone to the customers. This way, the manufacturer can build an inventory and defer the tariffs until the goods are actually sold. This deferment of tariffs can save the entrepreneur a significant amount of money since the money can be kept in income-producing instruments until the goods are sold and shipped out of the Foreign Trade Zone.

The economy can be made much stronger than it is today with more Americans working at better paying jobs if Foreign Trade Zones are coupled with new labeling laws and the depreciation expense is allowed under the proposed tax system outlined in this book. As people realize the advantage to purchasing depreciable products with higher American made components, and as more assembly plants locate their assembly facilities within these Foreign Trade Zones, the products could become cheaper while employing more American workers. As this happens, more people will be employed and the tax base will grow. This will further improve the condition of our economy and will reduce the deficit faster.

Ethanol Market Development

Our economy can benefit substantially by creating joint ventures between Government and farmers. This particular type of joint venture would stimulate the biomass industry. It would ease the problem of farm subsidies and reduce trade deficits that come about from importing oil. The farms would be used for biomass production and the states or counties could provide cheap labor to the farmers who would use them to cultivate the biomass crop. This situation would occur when states or counties do not have suitable or sufficient land themselves to be used for biomass production. Both farmers and Government would benefit from this arrangement. Governments would benefit by defraying their cost of keeping prisoners or people on Welfare and eliminating farm subsidies. Farmers would benefit the most by providing them with below market cost of labor. This labor would be instrumental in cultivating tree farms to provide the biomass for ethanol production. Lower feedstock costs would give the farmer better profits.

Additional profits could be made by the farmer if he decided to get into ethanol production as well. This farm would be a turnkey operation and would benefit the farmer possibly in three or four ways. The first benefit will come from Internal Revenue Code §40, which will give the producer of ethanol tax credits to offset tax liability. The other tax advantage would come through Internal Revenue Code §179A, which could give a maximum tax deduction of $50,000 for purchasing or retrofitting vehicles to run on ethanol. An additional $100,000 deduction can be obtained if the farmer became a fueling station for alternative-fueled vehicles.

The fourth way the farmer could profit from tax codes is if the farmer decided to produce electricity with the biomass that was produced. Under Internal Revenue Code §45, the producer of electricity from "closed-loop biomass" would receive an income tax credit of 1.5¢ per kilowatt hour (adjusted for inflation) of electricity. The farmer would have two viable options to produce this electricity. He could either produce dilute ethanol to run through a Direct Fuel Cell, or he could harvest the trees whole and burn them whole with Whole Tree Energy Technology (See Appendix C). Depending upon which situation is more economically feasible, the farmer would become a producer of electricity and get a tax break. These tax codes are complicated and should be reviewed by professionals. Assistance in these tax codes can be obtained in Appendix D.

These Internal Revenue Codes would help the farmer who would in turn help the biomass industry. This industry would be stimulated as more distillation equipment or electric power generation equipment is needed to produce the ethanol or electricity. The rest of the economy would benefit through the economic multiplier effect and trade deficits would start to disappear. With less money leaving the country to pay for these deficits, more money will be available to be multiplied out for growth in our economy. As our economy grows, more people, possibly welfare recipients, would find jobs and contribute to the tax system. If this happened, the budget could be balanced sooner.

GATT Reform

In order for our country and the rest of the world to prosper, the rules and results of world trade need to be more equitable. The latest version of GATT has taken us one step closer to free trade by reducing some very steep tariffs with different countries. If the entire world is to prosper from free trade, each trading country should not incur huge trade deficits with their trading partners. If they do, their currency and economy will become weaker which could result in world wide recessions that benefit no one.

To help facilitate free trade, and create an equilibrium in the trade balances, GATT needs to be revised to assist those countries who are always incurring trade deficits with the rest of the world. A country that incurs huge trade deficits must settle these deficits through their Capital Accounts. This would include the sale of real estate, companies, stock, and their Government bonds. If a country sells more bonds than any other type of capital assets, the ratio of its debt to its Gross National Product could be very high, which would result in a devalued currency. As an example, our country has incurred huge trade deficits for years. For a period of time, the American dollar was weak against the Japanese Yen. As a country's currency devalues, its demand for imports could drop off substantially, if what they import has an elastic demand. If what they import has an inelastic demand, such as gasoline, their demand might not drop significantly. This would result in higher fuel prices and inflation in their country since all imports will cost more.

If countries find themselves going into debt in order to purchase energy, they will have very little money left to spend on other imports that would help stimulate other countries' economies as well as their own. This combination would eventually lead to a downturn in their economy which will have a domino effect on world trade. Since many foreign countries are experiencing inflation with some form of recession, GATT needs to be revised to level out these discrepancies.

To help bring balance back into world trade, GATT needs to be reformed to include the following:

1. If a country incurs a trade surplus with another country, the surplus country's Government shall pay to the deficit occurring country's Government a tax equal to 5% (arbitrary) of the offending surplus amount.
2. The amount due will be calculated at the end of each quarter.
3. The funds are to be deposited with the World Bank by the end of the following quarter.
4. These funds are to be used first to pay down any outstanding debts with the World Bank, the International Monetary Fund (IMF), or other Government backed loans.
5. After debt settlement is made with the IMF, World Bank, or other Governments, the remaining proceeds will go to the deficit occurring country's Government.

If any country ends up having a trade surplus with another country, it benefits from this trade imbalance. Since trade deficits are financed through the Capital Accounts, the country with the surplus ends up with capital assets from the deficit country. These assets benefit the surplus country since they almost always incur a positive cash flow to the holder of those assets. As more income and assets are earned by the surplus country, the stronger their economy and country will become over time. The result of this is that more money is available for spending which in turn creates demand in their economy. This puts more people to work and allows the economy to expand and grow. Hence, the country becomes even stronger.

To counteract the negative effects of trade deficits, the surplus country's Government should deposit 5% (arbitrary) of the offending surplus into the World Bank where it will be held in escrow. If there is any outstanding debt with the World Bank, the International Monetary Fund, or with other Governments, those debts will be paid off first. The country that owes the debt will receive a discount for early payment, based upon present value of money. Any remaining proceeds will then be available to the deficit occurring country's Government. As the deficit country reduces its debt to the IMF, the World Bank, other countries, and at home, its currency will become stronger, which will make imports cheaper allowing them to import more and keep inflation low. Also, as their internal debt gets smaller, their interest rates should decline allowing further expansion and stimulation of their own economy. As their price of production decreases and their economy expands, they will be able to import more as well as compete more effectively in the global market which will help all countries who trade with them.

LABEL LAWS

Label laws were designed to help consumers make more intelligent buying choices. All of us by now have seen, read, and studied the labels that are on all of our food packaging. Armed with this information, consumers today are making better buying decisions regarding the food they are purchasing. This same reasoning will be applied to a new label that will help consumers make more intelligent buying decisions by providing information about the company and the product.

Company Facts

Today we have labels on our food products to tell us about calories, fat, cholesterol, sodium, total carbohydrates, protein content, and other miscellaneous information about the foods we buy. These labels help us determine whether or not we want to purchase and consume those products based on the information that is given to us. Using that same line of logic, I suggest that a new label informing the consumer about the company and the product be added to every product sold here in the United States.

This new label will give more detailed information about the company and the product, unlike the "Made in America" label that is defined in Section 5 of the Federal Trade Commission Act. Under the existing Act, "Made In America" means "all or virtually all parts are made in the United States and all or virtually all labor is performed in the United States." In 1994 two major manufacturers of footwear were disallowed by the FTC to continue using the "Made In America" label since a major portion of their products were assembled outside of the United States.[58]

---

[58] Figure from Fitzgerald, Nora. "Born in the U.S.A.," *World Trade*, December 1995, p. 52

In the case of automobiles, the new label would give information such as the name of the corporation, the corporation's country of origin, what percentage of the company has United States ownership, if any, how much value as a percentage is the product made with American parts and labor, where the engine and transmission originated, and how much annual depreciation allowance is available to the consumer.

Company And Product Facts	
Corporation	ACME Auto
Corporation Origin	Japan
% Of Corporation Owned By USA Company	25%
% Value Of U.S. Components & Labor	10%
Engine Origin	Japan
Transmission Origin	Japan
Annual Depreciation	$600.00

There are commercials today that indicate certain Japanese automobiles are made here in America, but those television ads do not tell the entire story. They do not tell us how much of the car is American labor or parts, in percentage terms. The existing law that is covered under Title 49 Code Of Federal Regulations Chapter V, Part 583: Automobile Parts Content Labeling, mandates that a label designated as "Parts Content Information" be available for all cars sold here in the United States. The label is small, confusing, and nondescript. The label that is diagrammed above should have the same importance as the mileage label that is plastered on every vehicle. It also gives the information more clearly and adds several pieces of information not currently on the existing label, which includes the corporation's name, the country where the corporation originates, percentage of the corporation owned by a USA company, and the annual depreciation allowance allowed for this vehicle which would be part of the new tax system designed within this book.

Other products that are depreciable under the new tax system would have similar labels, but would not include information on engine or transmission origins. All other products that are not depreciable would contain basic information such as the name of the corporation, the corporation's country of origin, percentage of the corporation owned by a USA company, percentage value of U.S. components and labor content.

Company And Product Facts	
Corporation	ACME Electronics
Corporation Origin	Japan
% Of Corporation Owned By USA Company	25%
% Value Of U.S. Components & Labor	10%

With this type of information available to the consumer, people who are "Made In America" conscious would be better able to make buying decisions based upon information supplied by the manufacturer. As more people purchase products with higher percentages of American content, companies who have lower American made content will start to lose market share, assuming product cost, value, and perceived quality are about equal. When companies begin to lose market share to their competitors based on value of American made content, these companies will begin to change their production to include more American made products and labor. As this happens, more American companies that make components for all types of products will have bigger demands and employ more Americans.

Pass Through Rebate Laws

The pass through rebate will be popular with most everyone except the oil companies. This law will use a subsidy to encourage demand for two specific products that will reduce our dependency on foreign oil and its related trade deficits costs. It will also stimulate the biomass industry by increasing the demand for domestically produced ethanol. The logic of this rebate law is based on the fact that we are currently importing more than 50% of our oil from other countries. It is far cheaper for our country and more beneficial to our economy to pass along a rebate than it is to finance trade deficits. This same type of reasoning has been used by the electric utility companies for customers who purchase energy efficient appliances. The utility companies reason that it is far cheaper to give a cash rebate to someone who buys an energy efficient appliance than it is to borrow money and build a new power plant.

The Pass Through Rebate Law could be a rebate of 3% (arbitrary) for what was spent purchasing on the qualifying fuel. The rebate amount will come directly from the Government to the oil companies and it will be financed through the Highway Trust Fund from increased taxes on gasoline and diesel. It will be the responsibility of the oil companies to pass the rebate on to the consumer. From a practical standpoint, only those consumers who use that oil companies credit card will receive the rebate. This type of rebate system already exists with some oil companies who give rebates to their customers on purchases of goods and services when they use the company's credit card. This plan would be similar, but the rebates would only be eligible for the A-21 fuel that is just coming onto the market.

By making the A-21 fuel qualify for a rebate, less money will be spent for fuel in all sectors of our economy. As more disposable income will be available to individuals and companies, money can be spent in other sectors of the economy that will further the growth and expansion of our economy.

NINE

WE WANT P.E.A.C.E.

P.E.A.C.E.

Let's work for P.E.A.C.E. (Progressive Entrepreneurs Actualizing Creative Enterprises) and not for big Government. We have a choice to either help entrepreneurs become successful or keep the status quo by financing irresponsible Government spending. We can either choose to help entrepreneurs make inroads into foreign markets or sit back and allow cheap foreign imports to destroy our economy. By helping inventors and entrepreneurs bring new technologies to market, we will drive our economy forward. If we choose to make them struggle, our economy will run out of gas. We can choose to have competition or we can let monopolies and oligopolies control product selection and prices. We can let welfare recipients and prisoners have a free ride, or choose to put them to work producing goods and services that our economy needs.

These are some of the choices presented in this book and that you as a voter have control over. Making P.E.A.C.E. will require cooperative politicians and a streamlined Government. Although these words are a contradiction of terms, P.E.A.C.E. can happen by choosing the right people for President, Congress, Governor, and other elected officials. Our level of success can only be commensurate with our efforts to vote in the right people. Without careful selection of elected officials, the economy will flounder, Government will continue to build debt, and your taxes will remain high for the foreseeable future, which could be a very long time.

To prevent this scenario from happening, U.S. Government Online needs to become a reality in order to assist the entrepreneur here at home and abroad. U.S. Government Online can provide the same function as Japan's Ministry of International Trade and Industry (MITI). This organization gathers and analyzes intelligence for their industrial conglomerates. Such a body could also provide information and intelligence about foreign banks and individuals regarding their creditworthiness and stability. It can assist the entrepreneur by informing him of the competition's technological developments, distribution channels, marketing tactics, financial information, and vulnerabilities. With this type of information in the hands of American entrepreneurs, we will be able to compete more effectively in the global market.

Since this type of information requires intelligence gathering skills and the cold war is all but a memory, the CIA would be highly suited for this type of role. By using the CIA to help the economy grow and prosper, the agency will not have to be dismantled or downsized. Besides, National Security is an issue that needs to be addressed. Our economy can be crippled without knowledge of subversives operating throughout the world. Take, for example, a scenario where the oil distribution system is destroyed by terrorists. If all the super tankers are destroyed simultaneously, every country that depends upon imported oil will be in great danger of economic collapse.

Oil independence is why the 1992 Energy Policy Act is an important piece of legislation. It has tougher standards for energy efficiency, encourages competition in electrical generation, has changes in the tax codes that encourage domestic energy production and conservation, and has incentives for alternative fuels.

Sections of the 1992 Energy Policy Act could be used as blueprints to help stimulate our economy. As you discovered in previous chapters, there are many emerging energy technologies that can add value to our economy. If we export less money out of our country for energy, then we will have more available to reinvest. As an example, we import over 50% of the oil we use. If we could keep that money here in the United States our economy would grow much faster. For example, we could have more money for the development of the biomass industry and how it relates to the alternative fuel and electric power industries.

The 1992 Energy Policy Act has many economic ramifications that will produce profound effects on the electric power industry. These can range from the development of biomass energy farms to waste-to-energy facilities. To help these industries develop, some mandates will need to be put into place. These mandates may cost a few extra pennies per kilowatt hour, but the benefits outweigh the costs. Those benefits would include:

1. Higher employment
2. More tax revenue for the Government
3. Lower cost for Welfare
4. Lower cost for prisoners
5. Lower taxes
6. Improved air and water quality

Mandates

If we want to reduce waste, pollution, and lessen the fiscal impact of using coal and imported oil, we need to put into place mandates regarding garbage management. This will include mandating all garbage to be sorted for recyclables and toxic materials before it is processed any further.

If the garbage is headed for a mass burn facility, and toxic materials are removed during the sorting process, air quality will be improved. If the garbage is normally landfilled, a mandate should be put in place requiring the garbage to be sorted first and then gasified. By mandating that a higher percentage of the garbage stream be reduced through recycling first, the elimination of hazardous materials second, and gasification third, our landfill space will be greatly extended. Recycling will profoundly reduce the total tonnage of garbage that eventually gets processed, and this reduction will become even greater when gasification technology or mass burn technology is employed. Through gasification or mass burn, solids can be cut to 10% of their previous volume. This will be achieved by mandating that all hazardous materials be pulled from the garbage stream.

By recycling a greater percentage of plastics, our need for imported oil will be reduced because oil is a raw material used in the production of plastics. Oil imports can be further reduced by employing Proler International's gasification technology next to petrochemical facilities. Garbage can be gasified into the raw material used in plastic production.

If there is a glut of plastics on the market, the gasified garbage can be used as either fuel to power Government-owned hybrid vehicles with turbine engines or as fuel in electric power production. By modifying the 1988 Alternative Motor Fuels Act to include syngas from gasified garbage as natural gas, the Federal Government can help finance and establish fleets of hybrid buses and trucks powered by this fuel. This would help further reduce our need for imported oil.

If gasified garbage is used as fuel to produce electricity, it will be important to make this technology cost effective. We can accomplish this by mandating all electrical power companies to purchase electricity produced from gasified garbage at total avoided costs. These total avoided costs would include the cost of the fuel, the cost of power plant capacity, and the sulfur dioxide emission credits. By insuring that these costs are covered in the purchase price of the electricity, garbage can be turned into electricity cleanly while reducing air and water pollution. Even though it may cost a few pennies more, all of us will be able to sleep better at night knowing that our air is becoming cleaner.

Air and water pollution can be further reduced when Government mandates the reuse of sewage sludge as fuel for electrical production. It will also be important to mandate that the price paid by power companies for the electricity produced by sewage sludge must include the cost of the fuel, power plant capacity, and sulfur dioxide emission credits if the power is produced by the sewage facility. If these costs are not covered, the sewage facilities cannot compete with power produced from natural gas or coal since natural gas and coal will almost always be cheaper than biofuels.

Mandating a price to cover the cost of production will insure that the sewage sludge will not fill up our landfills or pollute our waterways. If this mandate is not feasible for whatever reason, then we could mandate the use of gasification technology instead. As the deregulation of the electrical power industry continues, it is up to us as consumers to buy our electricity from companies that produce it cleanly. Eventually, the electrical power industry will accommodate this consumer demand.

ELECTRIC POWER INDUSTRY

The electric power industry, as we know it, will have to go through some dramatic changes in order to comply with the 1990 Clean Air Act. In 1995, Phase I of the acid rain reduction program of the 1990 Clean Air Act took effect, and in the year 2000, Phase II of the acid rain reduction program will require power plants to reduce their sulfur dioxide emissions 40% below what they were in the 1980s. To accomplish these goals, the 1990 Clean Air Act devised a credit system for polluting. Each power plant pays for emission allowance credits and is allowed to emit so many tons of sulfur dioxide emissions.

By placing the credits on the open market, supply and demand will determine the price of these credits and will transfer some of the cost of polluting to the polluter. It is this symbiotic relationship of buying and selling of these emission allowance credits that will allow for evolution. Unfortunately, the price that the polluter will pay for the credits will not cover the full cost of polluting. The air will still be dirty, all forms of life will still suffer from oxide emissions, and structures throughout the world will continue to deteriorate from falling acid rain. If the parties suffering damage from pollution were compensated fully, the cost of these credits would be much higher than they are today. In fact, the price would be prohibitive.

Since the 1990 Clean Air Act was designed to be practical, the cost of these emission allowance credits are much lower than the real cost of polluting that allows for evolution in the electric power industry. Examples of this evolution have led to the use of exhaust scrubbers and clean coal technologies. One example of this clean coal technology involves mixing automobile tires with coal while burning them at very high temperatures. Unfortunately, this technology is not 100% effective and is expensive. Other sulfur reducing technologies exist, but they too are not 100% effective and are costly.

In order to remove sulfur from coal, it has been estimated that it will cost the utility companies nearly $500 per ton.[59] As sulfur dioxide mitigation cost increases, resulting in higher electricity prices, competition from other technologies will enter the market and create a long term solution to the sulfur dioxide emission problem. This is not happening very quickly at this time because many power plants have been able to acquire lower sulfur coal which has dropped the price of emission credits and has prevented competing technologies from entering the marketplace.

As we get closer to the year 2000, and as the price of sulfur dioxide emission mitigation becomes increasingly more expensive, renewable and alternative energy industries such as biomass, wind, solar, water, and geothermal energy sources will enter the market. With the exception of biomass energy conversion, none of these industries create air pollution. With biomass, there will always be some pollution, but there is no net gain of carbon dioxide since the existing plants will absorb the carbon dioxide released during combustion. All of these alternative and renewable energy technologies can easily satisfy Phase II of the acid rain program of the 1990 Clean Air Act. Developing these technologies can help stimulate the economy if they get noticed, funded, and allowed to compete in the energy market. In order for this to happen, the Department of Energy and the electric power industry will need to change their attitude toward alternative and renewable energy. The Department Of Energy needs to validate other technologies, fund them, and give them a chance in the marketplace. The DOE prefers not to investigate or promote alternative energy sources other than their "sanctioned" list. As an example, Ocean Thermal Energy Conversion has not been readily re-

[59] Figure from Mayersohn, Norman S. "Borneo's Squeaky Clean Coal," *Popular Science*, April 1993, p. 82

ceived since it does not coincide with their agenda of developing a clean coal technology. The utility companies will need to realize the benefits of switching from coal to renewable and alternative fuel technologies. They need to pay the total avoided costs so that biomass technologies will survive. The end result will be cleaner air. In doing so, utility companies will realize certain benefits which would include:

1. Expensive clean coal technology will no longer be needed.
2. Expensive exhaust scrubbers will no longer be needed.
3. Expensive emission allowance credits costs could be reduced or eliminated.

Once power companies realize the benefits of switching to renewable and alternative energy technologies, cleaner air and cheaper electricity can be obtained. Otherwise, power companies will continue to use coal as their main fuel source. We need to vote for legislation that will ensure total avoided costs are covered. This will allow alternative energy sources to survive in the marketplace and compete effectively with the coal industry.

The coal industry is deeply entrenched in our economy. There are hundreds of electrical plants that use coal as fuel. Phase I of the 1990 Clean Air Act has made it difficult for coal-fired power plants to continue using coal unless sulfur dioxide emissions are reduced substantially. In the short run, some exhaust scrubbers are being used to clean up sulfur dioxide emissions, emission credits are being bought, and lower sulfur coal is being used in some power plants. Despite all of the additional expenses of using coal as a fuel, the Department of Energy is spending millions of our tax dollars (whether you like it or not) in the attempt to find some clean coal technology that will save the coal industry.

If the Department of Energy finds a clean coal technology that is cost effective, power plants across America will continue to use this fuel for the next several hundred years. If the Department of Energy fails to produce a clean coal technology by the year 2000, the 1990 Clean Air Act will either force more coal-fired power plants to shut their doors or continue to pay higher prices for emission credits. As the price of these credits becomes exorbitant, more power plants will be forced to change their fuel sources, or their technology, if they want to continue producing electricity. If these power companies do change their fuel source and technologies, the coal companies will lose a substantial amount of revenue or perhaps even become extinct. For this reason, it is in the best interest of the coal companies to spend some of their earnings to develop some form of clean coal technology that will save their industry from demise.

One technology that can save the coal industry is coal gasification. Coal gasification produces a syngas that can be used in a fuel cell to produce electricity, or it can be treated and condensed to produce methanol. Presently, coal gasification technology exists, but it is very expensive. However, once the price of producing syngas from coal is economically feasible, the coal companies can continue supplying electric power companies coal for several centuries. The coal companies also have the choice of becoming rivalries or associates with the oil companies. If methanol can be produced cheaply from coal, it could be the fuel of the future. This is assuming electric vehicles do not become practical in the near future or the price of producing methanol from natural gas becomes cheaper. Methanol is designated as a clean fuel by both the 1990 Clean Air Act and the 1992 Energy Policy Act. This fact would give the coal companies an arsenal of ammunition in their fight to make methanol the fuel of the future. If this happens and electric vehicles are still not practical, we will at least avoid spending our dollars abroad importing methanol from Canada and Saudi Arabia, thereby saving our foreign exchange dollars. Regardless of the changes that might occur in other industries, coal companies must realize their future is at stake. If coal companies want to continue to do business in the next century, they must start spending their earnings now to insure their future in the marketplace. If coal companies started investing huge sums of money in coal gasification, they would stimulate the economy as well as insure their future within it.

If coal companies do not reinvest in the economy to create a clean fuel, other technologies will enter the marketplace that may replace coal as the dominate fuel. One such technology that may be capable of competing is Electro-Farming (considering farm subsidies are on the way out). Electro-Farming utilizes existing and marginal farmland as a way of producing feedstocks that can be converted into fuel for electrical power generation. The power plant would consist of a Direct Fuel Cell (capable of using dilute ethanol and other gaseous fuels with no modifications), an ethanol facility, and an anaerobic digestor (optional if manure is present). This facility would use everything that is produced on the farm as fuel. It can use corn, crop residue, and even manure as feedstock for fuel that will run a Direct Fuel Cell.

Since the Direct Fuel Cell is very efficient (at least 50% or more), it would compete with older coal-fired power plants whose efficiency may be only 25%. These numbers are very important since biomass has only half the energy value of coal on a pound-for-pound basis. Since transportation costs are negligible on a farm, this will help Electro-Farming become more competitive against coal-fired power plants. As Electro-Farming becomes a reality, it will help stimulate the economy and reduce Government deficits by eliminating farm subsidies.

The economy will be stimulated when an increased demand for components to assemble an Electro-Farming power plant takes hold. Ethanol facilities, anaerobic digestors, fuel cells, and farm equipment will be needed to run the facility. Due to the economic multiplier, the investments made into equipment expense will be multiplied into the rest of the economy. This will create jobs, new sales, new profits, and new tax revenues for the Government.

These same types of benefits will result when the garbage industry changes its focus from refuse disposal to recycling and energy production. Since most garbage has energy value, a very high percentage of it can be converted into electrical energy. Garbage can be converted into a gas or into dilute ethanol, depending on the type of technology used. If dilute ethanol is produced, a Direct Fuel Cell would be the preferred method of using that fuel. If the garbage is gasified, and the syngas is suitably scrubbed, it too can run through a fuel cell. Otherwise, it can be burned in turbines or internal combustion engines to produce electricity. This electrical production can be further enhanced when landfill gas is used as fuel for electrical production. Land fill gas is a natural byproduct of land fills. As garbage starts to decompose, it emits a combustible gas suitable for fuel. It can be scrubbed and upgraded to pipeline quality and used to run automobile engines, or it could be burned in turbines without need for any scrubbing or upgrading. By employing these technologies, our economy can be stimulated and the Government will benefit through higher employment and tax revenues.

AUTOMOTIVE INDUSTRY

The automotive industry will make big strides in energy efficiency that will reduce oil consumption and help us save foreign exchange dollars. This is due to the fact that the Government has already signed Cooperative Research And Development Agreements (CRADA) with the big three automakers.

In December 1993, the DOE signed a "master" CRADA with the Big Three; the agreement covered a number of research efforts and received $16 million in Government funding in 1994. The idea behind the master CRADA is to provide "one stop shopping" for car companies, said Energy Secretary Hazel O'Leary. To find information on any specific discipline, an auto maker can now turn to a designated lab representative who refers the auto maker to labs with expertise in the field.

Argonne National Laboratory Argonne, IL	Flywheels, fuel cells, batteries, recycling, high temperature lubrication
Brookhaven National Engineering Laboratory Upton, NY	Natural Gas Storage
Idaho National Engineering Laboratory, Idaho Falls, ID	Gas turbines, laser beam welding techniques, finishing, assembly, and joining
Lawrence Berkeley Laboratory Berkeley, CA	Batteries, electrochromic switching devices, fuel cells
Lawrence Livermore National Laboratory, Livermore, CA	Flywheels, aerogel, ultracapacitors, batteries, high performance computer modeling, superplastic steel, composites, machine tooling
Los Alamos National Laboratory Los Alamos, NM	Fuel cells, plasma-source ion implantation for surface hardening, ultracapacitors, high performance computer modeling, combustion dynamics
National Renewable Energy Laboratory, Golden, CO	Alternative fuels, hybrid vehicles, batteries
Oak Ridge National Laboratory Oak Ridge, TN	Motors, generators, flywheels, ceramics and coatings for high temperature engines, rapid prototyping, composites
Pacific Northwest Laboratories Richland, WA	Superplastic forming of aluminum alloys, hydrocarbon traps for catalytic converters, advanced fuel-combustion systems, emissions sensors
Sandia National Laboratories Albuquerque, NM	High performance computer modeling, microelectronics, automated manufacturing, machine tooling, aluminum alloys, ultracapacitors, combustion dynamics

Recently President Clinton informed us of a new program to develop a "supercar" to get greater gas mileage—as much as three times what current autos now get. By using advanced technology already developed in advanced weapons research, this type of mileage would allow anyone to drive across the country on only a couple of tankfuls of gas!

If this fuel-efficient car is affordable to everyone, this technology will have a great impact on future gasoline consumption, not only in the U.S., but world-wide. The technology explosion of third-world countries, particularly in Asia, is expected to increase the number of gas-guzzling cars by hundreds of millions. If this prediction is true, we definitely need a fuel-efficient car or our oil resources will not be able to fulfill the world-wide need early in the next century.

If we expect the auto industry to help us reduce trade deficits with the OPEC nations, we will need to voice our opinions, needs, and desires to them. The saying "the customer is always right" is important to a sales-oriented organization such as the automobile industry. Perhaps they should take it to heart. If an automobile company does not respond to its customers needs and wants with satisfactory products, that company will lose its customers. This happened to Chrysler, Ford, and General Motors as a result of the 1973 oil crisis.

Up until 1973, the three big automakers made big gas guzzling vehicles that were not competitive with Japanese cars. As a result of their ineptitude, these three companies lost a tremendous amount of market share and revenue. Customers wanted fuel efficient vehicles and the big three couldn't deliver. Even today, these three companies are still feeling the backlash of their inability to produce a reliable fuel efficient vehicle in the early 1970's.

These auto companies now face another set of obstacles and goals if they are to survive in the upcoming century: the 1990 Clean Air Act and the 1992 Energy Policy Act, which mandates cleaner running cars with better fuel efficiency through alternative technologies. These alternative technologies include the use of alternative fuels and engine designs to accommodate the use of these alternative fuels.

At present, companies such as Ford are offering a flexible fuel vehicle that can run on gasoline or alcohol. General Motors has their electric Impact car which they have been demonstrating across the United States. Chrysler has been working on their Patriot race car, a turbine-powered hybrid vehicle. All three of these entries are trying to achieve better mileage with cleaner emissions. Unfortunately, the big three auto companies are headed in different directions that will fracture the market.

Without direction from their customers, this fracturing will continue to happen, or similar to the situation in 1973, the Japanese will beat us to the punch. To prevent this from happening again, the industry has to become more focused in trying to comply with the 1992 Energy Policy Act and the 1990 Clean Air Act. In the short run, the auto companies will continue using conventional internal combustion engines that will still make us dependent upon foreign imported oil, that is, unless Rudy Gunnerman's A-21 fuel becomes a reality in the marketplace.

Without a technological breakthrough with internal combustion engines and/or with gasoline, our country will still incur huge trade deficits with the OPEC nations. If this is the most likely scenario regarding gasoline, then we will need to focus our attention on alternative engine designs that will make us energy independent. There are two technologies that have very promising futures that can utilize the existing liquid fuel infrastructure. Those technologies are the fuel cell and the turbine engine. Both of these devices are capable of using a variety of liquid fuels that can be produced within the United States and save foreign exchange dollars. There are other fuels and technologies that are currently being developed and tested today, but do not adapt to the existing infrastructure as well as the turbine engine and the fuel cell. With this great diversification, we are only opening the door for the potential of substituting one import for another.

As an example of this import substitution, methanol is primarily produced and imported from Canada and Saudi Arabia. If methanol becomes the fuel of the future because big industry spent enough money developing the technology to make it cheaper, we would be stuck with another fuel that would do nothing for our trade deficits.

Another fuel that helps fracture the market is the compressed natural gas vehicle. This form of fuel has its place in fleet vehicles which have a prescribed driving range. Since an infrastructure does not exist to refuel these vehicles, they are not practical nor economically feasible for the average driver.

Another option includes electric vehicles. General Motors is interested in promoting this product to the extent that they have already spent approximately $500 million in the development and promotion of their electric vehicle, the Impact. The electric vehicle has its problems, especially its battery life which limits the driving distance between recharging. This obstacle can be overcome with different batteries and other technologies. By solving the driving distance problem, we would only create additional problems for our economy.

A wholesale change in the way we fuel and service our vehicles would be extremely disrupting to our economy. Service stations and the oil industry would be devastated if their industry became obsolete overnight. This disruption would be felt through the entire economy. Therefore, we must be cautious against instituting changes that are not evolutionary in nature and may cause chaos or the collapse of our economic system. Considering all of these factors, the best solution is to remain with a liquid fuel vehicle so that we can utilize the existing liquid fuel infrastructure.

To voice your opinion to the three auto companies you can call or write:

Ford Motor Company
Customer Service
Fairlane Business Park III
1555 Fairlane Drive
Allen Park, MI 48101
1-800-ALT-FUEL
Speak with
    Beth Ardisana
    Tom Artushin
    Tom Barker
    Al Updegrove

Chrysler Corporation
800 Chrysler Drive East
Auburn Hills, MI 48326-2757
Speak with:
    Fred Maloney   810-576-5472
    Eric Ridenour   810-576-8076

General Motors Corporation
Alternative Fuels Division
30500 Mound Road
Warren, MI 48090
Speak with:
    Gerald J Barnes,
    Manager, Alternative Fuels
                   313-556-7723
    Betsy Hemming   313-556-6990

To help develop a more fuel efficient vehicle, a cash prize should be awarded as was done with Whirlpool's award-winning refrigerator. They designed a refrigerator that was more energy efficient and is considered environmentally "safe" since it used hydrofluorocarbons. This design did not cost more to build and Whirlpool won millions of dollars in prize money awarded by the utility companies. If a sizeable pool of money was created with gasoline taxes, a huge prize could be raised. With hundreds of millions of dollars being offered as a cash prize, it wouldn't take long for the auto manufacturers to develop a car that could achieve 80 miles per gallon while reducing air pollution.

Hybrid Vehicle Exportation

If we can put a man on the moon, why can't we build a reliable hybrid automobile? If a reliable and affordably priced hybrid automobile can be manufactured and sufficient demand existed for such a vehicle, we could make great strides in reducing our trade deficits. It would appear that the oil and auto companies are hindering the development and commercialization of this technology because they have too much money tied up in existing technologies and tooling. Oil companies do not want to see this happen because it would cut into their revenues.

To prevent a major disruption in our economy, the next best thing to do is to export this technology to countries such as Thailand, Vietnam, Indonesia, and China. China could easily adapt to the hybrid vehicle because they have an underdeveloped supporting infrastructure and no great social attachment to the automobile as we do. On the plus side, such a vehicle would keep air pollution at manageable levels, stimulate the economy, keep inflation in check, help reduce trade deficits, and reduce the negative impact of trade deficits on our national annual deficit.

The hybrid vehicle is a very clean running and fuel efficient vehicle. If the vehicle burned locally produced ethanol instead of imported gasoline, air quality would be enhanced and China's trade situation would improve since they wouldn't have to import crude oil. By producing ethanol from waste products that normally end up in the waste stream, methane gas from the normal decomposition process will be eliminated and overall air quality improved.

Local production of ethanol fuels can stimulate the local economies as well. Since labor is cheap in these countries, and the raw material for the fuel would come from waste material, production costs would be competitive with gasoline. Since gasoline would not be imported, these countries would save their foreign exchange dollars to be used for development of their economy and infrastructure instead of energy. Therefore, the hybrid vehicle would help keep inflation in check while stimulating America's and China's economy.

Economic stimulation will also occur here in the United States with the sale of hybrid vehicles to developing nations. As more vehicles are sold overseas, more people will be put back to work building these cars. More steel, rubber, plastics, electronics, turbine engines, etc., will be needed to produce these cars. With new money being injected into our economy from overseas, the economic multiplier will take effect and real growth will occur. This growth can cause inflation, but if all of the other policies laid out in this book are put into place, inflation should not happen. A slow adoption of this vehicle into our society will also help the inflation picture. When an automobile can run on the cheapest fuel available, operating costs will be low. This will be especially true when the vehicle gets 80 miles per gallon or more. If enough people in America were to start buying these vehicles and the oil companies were to develop alternative markets for petrochemicals, the demand for fuel would decline and prices might drop or remain stable.

As the demand for gasoline drops, so will our trade deficit with the OPEC nations. If we could consume 50% less oil, our trade deficit with the OPEC nations would disappear. If this doesn't happen, we can make up the trade deficit by selling more automobiles to other countries and thereby offset our trade deficit by the amount taken in from that source. As we reduce our trade deficit with the rest of the world, fewer bonds will be sold and less interest will be paid on those bonds. By reducing interest costs, our annual deficit will improve and the need to cut essential Government services such as Medicare or Social Security will not be required.

ALTERNATIVE FUELS

Ever since the inception of the 1990 Clean Air Act and the 1992 Energy Policy Act, our country has gone off in many different directions in an attempt to satisfy both of these acts. The 1990 Clean Air Act's main purpose is to clean up our air, while the primary purpose of the 1992 Energy Policy Act is to reduce our dependency on imported oil. The common denominator between these two acts is alternative fuels. Alternative fuels, as defined within these acts, include methanol, ethanol, other alcohols, reformulated gasoline, reformulated diesel, natural gas, liquefied petroleum gas or propane, hydrogen, electricity, fuels derived from biomass, and liquid fuels derived from coal. At this writing, Rudy Gunnerman's A-21 fuel has not been classified as an alternative fuel since approximately half of it is made up of water and is not made up from one of the fuels defined by either act (see Appendix C). Regardless of whether this fuel is classified as an alternative fuel, common sense and market demands will help determine what the future fuel will be.

Common sense would tell us to use a fuel that can readily adapt to the existing fuel production, delivery, and consumption infrastructures with the least amount of modification. Considering that our fuel delivery system is set up to handle liquid fuels that are dispensed through storage tanks and pumps, gaseous fuels that are pressurized would not take advantage of our existing infrastructure and therefore would not be a good choice. Fuels in this category would include natural gas, propane, liquefied natural gas or hydrogen. The best use for these fuels would be in niche markets where fleets have to comply with the 1992 Energy Policy Act now and can afford the engine modifications and the special refueling capabilities.

Another fuel that is not practical at this time is electricity because electric vehicles do not have sufficient traveling range. The economy is not capable of handling this change at this time because the oil companies and their supporting infrastructure represent a big part of our economy. If the economy were growing and creating new industries on a daily basis, then it might be possible to radically change the oil and automotive industries to accommodate futuristic technologies. Unfortunately, the economy is barely growing and major changes in the oil industry will not occur overnight. For this reason, it is better to make slow evolutionary changes that will not upset the apple cart.

These evolutionary changes need to accommodate the existing infrastructure and engine designs. These changes can include the use of the A-21 fuel, reformulated gasolines and blends that use ethanol as a component, and biodiesels when waste elimination is desired over the lower costs of fossil fuels. Before these types of fuels can enter the market place, the oil companies will want to insure their profitability by either expanding their markets and/or increasing production of gasoline and diesel. This happened in December of 1995 when President Clinton signed the law raising the 55 mph speed limit. During that time, Rudy Gunnerman was working with the Department of Energy to get his fuel qualified as an alternative fuel and was also negotiating with major oil companies to distribute his product. Since the oil companies realized his fuel would reduce their revenues and profits, they probably figured they could keep their profits up by increasing the amount of gasoline and diesel produced. Raising speed limits across America would serve this purpose. So every time we race across our freeways and waste gasoline, we are giving the oil companies more money and power.

Considering the oil companies are very powerful and are a formidable component of our economy, it is better to work with them than to try and overcome them. Helping them develop and expand their markets while weaning our economy away from gasoline is the best way to come out on top. Through product substitution and alliances, oil companies can remain economically vibrant while helping us satisfy the 1990 Clean Air Act, the 1992 Energy Policy Act, and our demands for cleaner fuels that are more benign to the environment.

With our help, oil companies can become a major supplier of raw materials for building components. Since plastic can be made from the same molecules as gasoline, substituting plastic for gasoline production will help oil companies keep their revenues high while we wean ourselves away from gasoline. As building codes and tax laws are changed to accommodate the use of more plastic in construction products, the demand for plastic will increase as prices for plastic drop. This will be especially true if tax codes are changed to accommodate depreciation expenses to make it practical to tear down our old and dilapidated housing stock and replace it with homes primarily built with plastic. Since garbage and plastic can be gasified to produce the raw materials for plastic production, we will need the oil companies' facilities to turn this syngas into feedstocks for plastic production.

Oil companies will also be needed when the billions of tires stockpiled across America are converted back into fuel grade oil through the TRTM-60 process. This oil is suitable for fuel or plastic production. Again, the oil companies will be needed to convert this oil into products that we need. Their involvement in the process will generate revenues for them while expanding their markets.

Despite these possibilities, the oil companies are taking a defensive stance regarding their revenues. It's only natural for them to do this since it appears that every alternative fuel industry would like to see them out of business. For example, the ethanol industry is a very large nemesis to the oil companies. Ethanol is mostly used as a feedstock to produce ETBE, an additive that helps gasoline burn more efficiently. Another additive that is used for the same purpose is MTBE, made from methanol. Oil companies prefer to use MTBE over ETBE, despite complaints from consumers who feel sick from gasoline that has been treated with MTBE. This preference by the oil companies seems suspicious considering ethanol is produced locally from corn. On the other hand, methanol is imported from Canada and Saudi Arabia and is made from natural gas and is a product of oil exploration.

Since methanol is being imported from Saudi Arabia and Canada, it appears that the oil companies are only interested in their own well being without regards to the negative consequences of incurring trade deficits. If the coal industry could produce methanol more cheaply from coal than from natural gas, they would be very strong advocates of MTBE over ETBE and might even enter the alternative fuels market. Since oil companies wish to maintain control of the reformulated gasoline market and keep their profits high, they brainwash us into believing that their products are the only ones suitable for our engines.

This arrogant and selfish approach to the market has created resentment among consumers and their competitors in the reformulated gasoline markets. This resentment is what makes people hate the oil companies. People would love to see them suffer, even though it would be disastrous for the economy. This resentment is understandable to anyone who suffered through the 1973 oil crisis. If you experienced that period waiting in line for gasoline, you hated the oil companies for creating a shortage just to raise prices. You resented them and wished someone would have destroyed their power and their industry. Since it's not practical to destroy the oil companies, it's more valuable to show them a better way of helping themselves and the economy evolve, a way that will employ Americans and keep our dollars here in America.

OIL EVOLUTION

The oil companies have us over a barrel because most of our cars run on gasoline. They can be converted to run on other fuels, but the conversion process is expensive and there are inherent problems with alternative fuels. Alternative fuels have less energy per gallon compared to gasoline and they are more expensive. This means that should you adopt an alternative fuel, your driving range would be substantially shorter and it will cost you more. Compounding the problem is the practical issue of finding the fuel. Every gasoline station across America handles gasoline and sometimes diesel. Trying to find ethanol, gasohol, methanol, or liquefied natural gas at a service station is almost impossible. Oil companies will continue to produce gasoline so long as there is insufficient demand for alternative-fueled vehicles. So long as this exists, we will continue to see the negative effects of pollution, energy dependency, and trade deficits.

Air and water pollution is a direct result of our consumption of oil. No one needs or wants to see another oil spill like the Valdez in Alaska. Yet there are two other forms of oil pollution we rarely talk about. The first comes from backyard mechanics who are irresponsible about their oil changes. The other form of oil pollution results from no point pollution that comes from everyone's cars. That slow oil leak or drip that makes an oil smudge in your driveway is far more hazardous to our environment than the Valdez oil spill. Millions of cars pollute our water supplies by dripping small amounts of oil across our highways.

To make matters worse, many of us now have our motor oil changed in these quick oil change shops that recommend oil changes more frequently than the manufacturer suggests. This increased consumption of oil keeps our country dependent upon imported oil. This dependency could be greatly reduced if more people and Government agencies started using the TF Purifiner™ On-board Oil Purification System. By extending the intervals between oil changes on a vehicle, millions—if not billions—of gallons of oil can be saved. This action will help reduce costs, trade deficits, and lessen our dependency upon imported oil.

Does anyone want to see a repeat of the 1973 oil crisis? Who wants to fight over gasoline? Do we need to have another Gulf War? There are many hidden costs associated with gasoline, but they do not show up in the price we pay for it at the pump. When our Government sent troops to the Persian Gulf, the oil companies didn't remunerate the Government for its expenses, but everyone pays for it through their tax dollars.

The price we pay for fossil fuels does not reflect the real price to society since this industry is being heavily subsidized by our tax dollars. These subsidies come in the form of depletion allowances and the protection costs that our Government supplies through its military maneuvers. Even though this money is being spent for the protection of oil, it is not counted as part of the cost. In fact, some traditional economists will argue that the reason why alternative fuels are not economically viable is because fossil fuels are too cheap. So long as our Government continues to subsidize the oil industry in this manner, our trade deficits will continue to get larger.

The trade deficit grows larger because direct costs associated with oil production here in the United States are greater than the oil production costs in OPEC nations. OPEC nations have vast pools of oil that readily flow to the surface, while oil reserves here in the United States require more energy to pump it out of the ground. This additional cost of pumping is the reason why we are importing more oil than we are producing domestically. As we import more oil, and spend more abroad to pay for these imports, our economic base erodes.

To prevent the erosion of our economic strength, American consumers will need to speak out in favor of alternative technologies that will keep oil companies in the black while at the same time strengthen our economy. These alternatives include product substitution, recycling technologies, and energy farming of waste feedstocks.

Product substitution can occur at two different levels in the refinery process. The heptane molecule which is used for gasoline production can be refined to produce plastics. If, for example, building codes are instituted to mandate the use of Wallframe™ Systems and similar products in the construction industry, the need for polystyrene will increase dramatically. To offset this increased demand for the heptane molecule, oil companies can choose several avenues without affecting their profitability. Their options include using Rudy Gunnerman's A-21 fuel, or stepping up the production of biofuels to replace fuels that would be displaced through the increased demand for polystyrene. If Rudy Gunnerman's A-21 fuel becomes commercialized quickly, oil companies can make more money with less raw material costs.

By using naphtha and water to produce a cleaner burning fuel, wholesale cost per gallon will be substantially less. Oil companies could charge a lot less, but that would be doubtful. If oil companies were to charge less, and if the Government offered a pass-through rebate to be administered by oil companies, consumers would benefit at several levels. Those benefits would include better emission levels, lower operating costs, and cash back on their purchases of A-21 fuel. The rebate would be funded by tax dollars derived from the sale of gasoline and diesel of drivers who haven't converted their vehicles to run on A-21 fuel. The tax would be collected and sent to the Treasury where the funds could be held in a trust account. Oil companies will have to request and prove to the Treasury that they indeed have rebated the amount in question for reimbursement. Any leftover amount could be saved and later used for a prize in the same way utility companies created a prize for refrigerator manufacturers to produce a superior refrigerator that was more energy efficient. The prize money could be used for either a fuel and/or engine design that substantially reduces our use of fuel. The rebate would be administered by the oil companies for purchases of A-21 made on gasoline credit card accounts. This will encourage everyone to use their respective gasoline or Mastercard at their service stations to receive the rebate. The more a consumer spends on this type of fuel, the greater the rebate. This rebate would stay in place until our trade deficits with OPEC disappear. Since A-21 fuel is comprised of nearly half water, we can cut down our imports by nearly half if most of us convert our vehicles to run on this fuel.

Trade deficits will be reduced further if more product substitutions occur in the liquid fuel market and feedstocks for that fuel are produced locally on farms. This could be done with wastes and with crops grown on marginal lands. By using concentrated acid hydrolysis and fermentation, crop waste and cellulosic crops grown for ethanol production can help reduce our trade deficits. This would happen if a greater percentage of our liquid fuel usage includes the use of ethanol. Some of it will be used with Rudy Gunnerman's A-21 fuel as an antifreeze or some of it can be used as the base fuel. In fact, Rudy Gunnerman's initial invention used ethanol and water as a fuel. He successfully made it work, but realized there wasn't sufficient ethanol production available to make a difference in trade deficits. If sufficient ethanol is produced and substituted in our fuel distribution systems, conventional internal combustion engines can burn this fuel with minor modifications. If this happened, we might be able to turn our trade deficits with OPEC into trade surpluses.

Lower trade deficits with OPEC can also occur if automobile manufacturers decide to build turbine-powered hybrid vehicles. By building turbine-powered hybrid vehicles that achieve 80 miles per gallon, our demand for fuel would go down substantially. Turbine-powered hybrid vehicles produce less emissions, use less fuel, and can use a variety of fuels. If Rudy Gunnerman's A-21 fuel is not readily commercialized, then having more fuel efficient vehicles will be very important in reducing our trade deficit. If everyone had a vehicle that could get 80 miles per gallon, the demand for imported oil would drop substantially, regardless of whether or not Rudy Gunnerman's A-21 fuel is commercialized. The mere fact that a vehicle could obtain such mileage would make a great difference in our demand for imported oil.

Another advantage of a turbine-powered hybrid vehicles is that the engine can run on practically any type of gaseous fuel. Locally produced ethanol, methanol, or biodiesel can run through this type of engine and perform very well. In order for oil companies to survive in this type of market place, they will need to either squash the biofuel industry or become the most efficient producer of these fuels. Since the oil industry is not an expert in biofuels, and it appears they have no interest in it as well, the oil industry will probably take the path of destroying the biofuel industry. As a consumer, you can change that situation by writing letters to the automobile and oil companies requesting these changes. Remember, the customer is always right, and we are the customers. Businesses who do not cater to their customers will eventually lose out in the long run. It is up to you to write to your Congressman/Congresswoman to ask for his/her help in advocating these technologies that will save foreign exchange dollars and ultimately your tax dollars.

Foreign exchange dollars can also be saved if the emerging rubber and plastic recycling industries gain a foothold in our economy. If these technologies gain acceptance and become commercialized, our demand for imported oil will decline. Both the consumer and the oil companies will benefit from these technologies. By using the TRTM-60 tire recycling process, fuel grade oil can be produced here locally from the ever increasing stockpile of worn out tires. It has been estimated that we have anywhere from three to five billion tires stored throughout the United States. Since the cost of processing each tire is only pennies per tire, the cost of the fuel grade oil will be very competitive with imported oil. This resource has great potential and will benefit the consumer as well. The consumer will know that the worn out tires will be recycled back to its components and will not scar our countryside with an ugly and potentially hazardous waste. The derived byproduct from the recycling process can be used to make more tires, fuel, or plastics. The carbon black can be used to make more tires, the steel from steel belted tires can be recycled into anything that requires steel. This recycling technology has a close cousin in the plastic industry.

Whether the TRTM-60 tire recycling process is used for plastics, or Proler International's gasification technology is used to recycle plastic, oil companies should not lose too much revenue from these technologies since their facilities will be needed. If anything, as the demand for plastic increases, oil companies may be able to make more money by processing all of the feedstocks that would be generated from recycled waste materials.

Oil can be sold back to the oil companies where it can be used to make fuel or more plastics. If gasification technology is used next to a petrochemical facility, more plastics can be made from all types of feedstocks. The oil companies win, the plastic companies win, the recycling companies win, and the consumer wins as well knowing that garbage, tires and plastics are being recycled and trade deficits are being affected.

Trade deficits can positively be affected if the oil industry gets into energy farming of waste feedstocks. Waste feedstocks can include municipal solid wastes, paper mill sludge, tires, garbage, crops grown for energy, and even crop residues. Since waste materials have a negative value, turning them into fuels will be a bonus for the holder and processor of these wastes. If the oil companies have the foresight to see the benefits in creating alliances with these waste facilities and ethanol producers, they will be able to purchase or produce fuel, plastic feedstocks, and ethanol at a lower cost than is produced today through conventional means. By creating alliances early in the game, they will be able to maintain control over the liquid fuels market and distribution system while playing the role of heroes in helping our country reduce trade deficits, create jobs, comply with the 1990 Clean Air Act and the 1992 Energy Policy Act, and at the same time satisfy the changing attitudes of the American consumer. All of this can be done with a substantial and favorable impact on economic growth, inflation, trade deficits, taxes, and Government debt.

Our economy can be stimulated without inflation while reducing trade deficits and the annual deficit by employing Rudy Gunnerman's A-21 fuel. By using naphtha and water to produce our fuel, we can cut our usage of oil to about half of that we currently use today. With fewer dollars being spent for fuel, inflation in the fuel sector will be negative and our individual savings will vary from person to person, depending on how much each of us spends on fuel today. As each person spends their savings in other sectors of the economy, stimulation and real growth will occur. This growth will not be dependent upon people changing their lifestyles or habits regarding their personal transportation. Once trade deficits start to disappear and interest rates drop, the amount of capital assets sold to foreigners will be less than it is now. This will help our Government because there will be less foreign ownership of companies and less real estate with preferential tax treatment. The picture gets better when fewer Government bonds are sold to foreigners and the interest payments on those bonds becomes a smaller percentage of the Government's budget. When all of this happens, more people will be working and more tax revenues will be collected to help drive down taxes and the deficit.

Debt reduction and economic stimulation will also occur when we consume less gasoline and substitute gasoline production for plastic production. If we can convince big industry to use more plastic, the price of plastic will drop as the supply of feedstocks increase and the total tonnage of plastic also increases. As an example, there would be more vinyl siding, vinyl windows, polystyrene wall panels, plastic lumber, fencing and on and on. Plastic can also replace conventional production materials that saves energy. As an example, lighter cars made from plastic components would be more fuel efficient. As plastic becomes cheaper and more profitable, more specialized products and companies will enter the market place employing more people to manufacture, sell and service their products. This surge in employment and plastic production will insure a need for oil companies so long as they are willing to evolve.

In order for the oil industry to survive and play the heroes in our changing economy, they will need to help create products and alliances that will put more people back to work. It will require an open mind on their part, along with economically feasible and viable technologies and industries to make it happen. Through product substitutions and expanding markets, the oil industry will be able to generate more revenue while reducing trade deficits with the OPEC nations. With foresight and planning, oil companies can live down their reputations for being greedy and environmentally unfriendly companies while moving forward to serve their customers by providing products and solutions that will be beneficial to the environment, economy, and our trade deficits.

Unfortunately, the oil companies haven't acquired this mindset yet and will continue to look for oil wherever they can find it. If the pumping price per barrel is cheaper in Saudi Arabia than it is in the United States, oil will continue to be imported. This is their short run solution to our insatiable demands for energy. The long run solutions outlined in this book take into account that the oil companies are a necessary and formidable part of our economy. It may be true that they are no different than spoiled children with too much power, but they are essential in the way our economy operates and functions. As it is in the case of spoiled children, we must educate them to see that there are alternatives that can create a win-win situation.

FOREIGN TRADE DEFICITS

When we incur trade deficits, we pay for them through the Capital Accounts. Stocks, bonds, real estate, and companies, are the type of assets sold to settle trade deficits. When a company is sold to foreign ownership, profits from that company are also exported out of the country. As more foreign owners accumulate earnings, they have a greater ability to buy up America, which in the long run erodes our tax base.

Another reason why our tax base is eroding is because foreigners have a better tax structure than their American counterparts. Foreigners pay less tax, which of course puts a greater burden on middle class America. This burden can be eased if GATT is changed to force all countries to pay a tax on any surplus they incur with any country. For the United States, this would help out a little or a lot, depending on the tax rate. In 1994, the United States had a $150 billion trade deficit with the rest of the world. If a 5% tax rate was enacted, the United States would receive $7.5

billion in taxes from the rest of the world. Most of it would come from Japan, Germany, China, and the OPEC nations.

If the tax rate is a lot higher than 5%, our trading partners will be inclined to find ways to help us develop markets for our products in their countries. As more equitable trade develops across the world, every country's economy will expand and more people will be able to work and enjoy a decent standard of living. As trade deficits around the world begin to disappear, every country will have a stronger economic base from which to build their society. Each country will have money to build schools, sewage plants, roads, airports, and other necessities of a modern industrial nation. This would help our trading partners such as Mexico. Their country, except for a few large cities, is very poor. Their country's infrastructure is antiquated and needs billions of dollars in improvements. Since they are constantly running trade deficits with the rest of the world, they don't have the capital to make improvements in their own country or to help their own people or economy.

Mexico has an upper class, a middle class, and very large poor population. Their economy is not strong enough to help the very poor and they also have an exceedingly corrupt Government. By having the surplus tax administered by the World Bank, it would at least keep the money out of the hands of corrupt officials. By having the World Bank administer the funds, the money could be used to pay back the United States, the World Bank, or the International Monetary Fund. As these debts begin to disappear, the world will have more confidence in their economy and their currency should appreciate. As this occurs, their buying power would improve and they will become better trading partners. Since Mexico benefits from NAFTA, they will be able to buy American products more cheaply. This would further stimulate our economy.

FOREIGN TRADE ZONES

Foreign Trade Zones will be instrumental in helping our economy turn the corner. By publicizing their use and instituting changes in the tax laws to reflect depreciation for automobiles and electronics, hopefully our foreign trading partners will decide to locate their assembly plants inside these Foreign Trade Zones. Since they are required to manipulate their product with American labor, foreign built cars and electronics will have at least some American labor and possibly some American made parts put into their products.

Because Americans have an insatiable desire for German automobiles and Japanese cars and electronics, we always incur huge trade deficits with these countries. Our trade deficits could improve substantially if these offending products had a higher American content value. If some

Japanese and German auto makers started to lose their market share to their competitors due to America's quest for tax write offs, then German and Japanese car makers would be induced to locate their assembly facilities within these Foreign Trade Zones in order to keep their tariffs low and regain their market share.

As the Germans and Japanese increase the American made content of their products, more American workers will be put back to work, further stimulating the economy. These manufacturing jobs will also help establish a base of blue collar jobs that our economy needs if we are going to take people off Welfare. As more welfare recipients move off of Government support, they too will become consumers who will need homes, cars, televisions, and the like. Their dollars will add to the economy and will be a source of tax revenue for Government that is not currently available on a broad scale today.

CODEX REVISIONS

To help us help ourselves, Codex needs to be publicized on the Internet or on Government Online to include a list of all known carcinogens and the countries that use them on their fruits and vegetables.

Through public knowledge and the boycotting of products from those countries that use carcinogenic insecticides, we will be able to make free trade more equitable. When countries use known carcinogenic pesticides to control otherwise uncontrollable insects, they are creating an imbalance in free trade. International trade exists because products and services can be produced more cheaply in other countries than in the U.S. If insect mitigation costs are kept low due to the usage of known carcinogenic insecticides, international trade is no longer free or equitable. External costs of pesticide use is not accounted for in the cost of the fruits and vegetables that we see at the store. If they were, imported produce would be priced higher than they are today and domestically produced fruits and vegetables would compete more effectively in the stores.

When grocery stores purchase produce from abroad with carcinogenic pesticides, the petrochemical manufacturers and the produce exporting country benefits greatly at our expense. Chemical companies can continue to sell their products abroad without suffering revenue losses. Unfortunately, these companies have no consciences and should be reprimanded with the loss of revenues. We can accomplish this by refusing to purchase produce from countries that use carcinogenic insecticides. When this happens, countries will be forced to find alternative means to mitigate insects in order to keep our markets open to them. If not, they will have to find other markets for their products that continue to be treated with carcinogenic insecticides.

CONSTRUCTION INDUSTRY

Home building is one way of employing millions of people who contribute to the growth of our economy. Unfortunately, home building tends to be a cyclical industry that depends upon interest rates and the state of the economy. The cyclical nature of home building can evolve if tax laws are changed to reflect depreciation expense instead of mortgage interest deduction. When we use mortgage interest deductions to reduce taxes, most of us subject ourselves to the highest mortgages that we can afford. This invariably places excess demand on the available money supply which eventually drives up the price of money. If depreciation was used for the main tax deduction, people will no longer be motivated to incur huge mortgages. This would result in a larger money supply for the economy and for each of us individually.

If we can avoid huge mortgages, we will have more net disposable income to spend on other items such as cars, appliances, and electronics (items that are depreciable under the proposed tax system) that will result in an improved standard of living and a healthier economy. As the economy gets stronger, money becomes more available and cheaper, which also helps the home building industry with new home construction.

As more new homes are built (using the building products suggested in this book), the lumber industry will experience changes that will help us reduce our foreign trade deficits while stimulating our economy. Even though less lumber will be used in new homes, the same amount of lumber can be harvested without losing jobs or revenues. The lumber that is not used could be exported to countries (such as Japan) that lack this natural resource to help us reduce our trade deficits.

As plastic replaces lumber in home construction, the oil industry will remain strong despite the increased use of alternative fuels. Most of the components that make up a house can be gasified and turned back into more plastic which will require the use of a petrochemical facility. This will be a source of revenue for the oil companies that will help keep their revenues flowing, despite the changes that will occur in their market. As more construction debris and garbage is gasified for the purpose of creating feedstocks for plastic, our demand for imported oil will lessen. As our trade deficits begin to improve, more money will stay here in America where it can used to help develop and stimulate our economy.

The steel industry will also see benefits from the change of tax laws and construction technology. As steel becomes a predominant building component, the demand for this resource will increase. Unfortunately, our nation's steel industry has been lagging behind the Japanese. At this time, America's biggest export to Japan is scrap steel. This can change if two major things happen here in the United States. First, the cost of borrowing money has to become cheaper. This can be accomplished by increased savings (changes in the tax system), a reduced demand for money from home mortgages (change in tax code), and reduced demand for money from the Government (lowered deficit). Second, the price of electricity needs to be reduced. Electric arc furnaces are far superior to traditional blast furnaces. They pollute less and are more energy efficient. If American steel companies are going to compete with Japanese steel companies on price, they will need the latest energy efficient technologies and cheap electricity to run their electric arc furnaces.

RECYCLING EVOLUTION

The recycling industry is still in its infancy. Many states across the country are making good progress toward eliminating the amount of garbage that is landfilled or burned, but millions of tons are still being handled in the traditional manner—burying it. If all of us put more effort into recycling at home and at work, garbage fees would be less and landfills would be greatly extended.

We can start by separating our garbage at home. By separating organic waste and recyclable waste from other household waste, we can lessen the load on landfills. We can also demand that our local governments model their garbage collection after Victoria, British Columbia, where residents are charged by the pound. Since their program began, there has been an estimated 60% *decrease* in household garbage.[60] If this is not feasible for our local garbage companies, we will need to write our state legislators and encourage them to implement programs similar to what is being done between the California State Prison Industry Authority and Folsom City.

Greater progress can be achieved if prisoners and/or welfare recipients were to become involved in garbage recycling. This activity will help defray the cost of keeping prisoners and welfare recipients on the "payroll." Revenues will be generated from the sale of recyclables. As other recyclables, such as steel and paper, are removed from the garbage stream, less mining and foresting will be needed to produce these raw materials. As more steel is exported overseas for processing, our trade deficits will begin to come down. The same is true for waste paper. At this time, most paper plants are not equipped to handle the volume of waste paper that is generated. A great deal of waste paper is exported overseas. As more of it is removed from the garbage stream, trade deficits will improve.

Trade deficits can also be improved if Proler International's gasification equipment is used on the waste material next to a petrochemical facility. The waste material can be gasified and turned into a syngas suit-

---

[60] Information from Kantra, Suzanne, "Trash By The Pound," *Popular Science*, May 1994, p. 57

able for plastic production. Any type of materials can be gasified into a usable product. Items usually considered unrecyclable, such as mixed construction debris and yard wastes can be gasified and made into plastics thereby increasing the amount of feedstocks available for fuel production. If this is done on a wide scale, we can greatly impact our need for imported oil and reduce our trade deficits.

Future savings in trade deficits might occur when it becomes feasible to mine existing garbage dumps. We could extract paper, steel, glass, aluminum, plastic, and the unrecyclable materials can be gasified to produce a syngas suitable for either plastic or energy production. This is possible because modern garbage dumps are designed to hold garbage for years without any decomposition.

It might be economically feasible to mine landfills if excavation costs are reduced by using efficient heavy machinery, conveyor belts, and low cost labor wearing protective clothing to sort through the excavated garbage. Mining landfills could also become feasible when raw material and tipping fees become exorbitant due to a diminishing supply of both raw materials and landfill space. When a combination of these factors occur, existing landfills will be mined resulting in the creation of jobs, tax revenues, and foreign exchange dollars.

Recycling Fee Law

A Recycling Fee law could be instituted to help the recycling industry. The recycling fee will be a non-refundable fee that will help lower your state and local taxes by providing the capital to build facilities for welfare or prison workers to recycle garbage. Tax savings will result when state and local Governments realize a profit by selling recycled materials. When state and local Governments make a profit, they will be less likely to raise taxes and in some cases, may even reduce taxes.

This fee is a non-refundable tax for some of the external costs of pollution related to the production and disposal of all of our goods. Since we have never really paid for most of our external costs, most of us may want to reject this tax. We may want to reject it simply because it is a tax, but more likely because most of us believe that there is such a thing as a free lunch. In reality, there is always an opportunity cost, and for years we have avoided it. The only time we have had to pay for externalities with tax dollars is for things such as the Love Canal, which was a Superfund site, or nuclear waste disposal and storage. Since these expenses are buried in the Government budget, we do not realize we are paying for them much less understand how much cheaper it will be for all of us—and much better for our environment—if we mitigate the pollution as we create it. By handling the problem a little at a time, we wouldn't end up with monsters such as the Love Canal, which ended up costing us billions of dollars to resolve.

This is a very simple law, much like what we are already accustomed to when we pay redemption value on soda cans and bottles. This recycling fee will become part of the final price of the product and will vary according to how many man hours it requires to completely disassemble the product into various types of materials. Each product sold will have a bar code indicating the amount to be charged for that product. A database of all products sold here in America will need to be constructed. As manufacturers update their products and improve their disassembly times, their bar codes can be updated and their taxes reduced. The funds will be collected by merchants and deposited with the state on a monthly basis and followed up with a quarterly deposit form. The state will then administer the money to the appropriate areas.

Part of the fee should be set aside in a trust fund to be used as a cash incentive or prize for developers of new technologies for recycling composite materials or the manufacturing of products that easily disassemble. A cash prize for recycling technologies will encourage inventors and manufacturers to develop better products.

This recycling fee law will save you money in the long run. This law will make businesses become more efficient, build better products that will last longer, create products that are easier to repair and easier to recycle.[61] As products become easier to disassemble into components, repairs will be more likely but long term cost of ownership will be less since you will not have to replace the item entirely until several years later.

As manufacturers develop better and easier products to recycle, their products will have a smaller recycling fee associated with their cost. If manufacturers are interested in maintaining market share, keeping recycling costs down for the consumer will be important. The total cost of the product plus its recycling cost and the quality of the product will determine the winner of the market share race. Of course, the real winner will be you, the consumer. You will have a superior product and an environmentally friendly one as well.

EDUCATION

Our educational system needs to overhauled. We need to get back to the basics of reading, writing, arithmetic, and economics. Schools should be taught year round with school hours extended. Each class should be at least 1-1/2 hours in length. This would provide the teacher a time to lecture, a time for class participation, and a time for students to accomplish part, if not all, of the homework assigned. This will allow students to

---

[61] Achieving this goal can be accomplished with the use of Design for Manufacture Software, by Boothroyd Dewhurst, Inc.

ask teachers for help when needed. By having longer days and an extended year, students will learn and retain more. This will also benefit the Welfare system and parents who have long days as a result of work and gridlock commuting. Children will be in school longer with supervision that will enable children to learn more and have structure in their lives. In addition to longer school hours, class size needs to be reduced to no more than twenty pupils per class.

Besides teaching the basics, students will need skills not traditionally taught in schools today, skills that will assist them in becoming productive and competent adults in this global market. To accomplish that goal, they will need to learn:

➤ Entrepreneurialship and Total Quality Management
➤ Communication and active listening skills
➤ Logic and problem solving skills
➤ Negotiation and sales skills
➤ Self esteem and time management skills

Teaching entrepreneurialship and Total Quality Management will be ineffective if students do not possess effective communication or active listening skills. Total Quality Management requires upper management to listen to their workers and communicate effectively with them. It works much better if both management and workers can communicate effectively with each other. Once communication and understanding is established between management and the workforce, logic and problem solving skills will be needed to implement the suggested improvements. Of course, a well produced product is useless unless it can be sold on the market for a profit. Hence, negotiation and sales skills will be essential for future entrepreneurs to succeed in this global market. Not all students will excel at entrepreneurialship or sales, but everyone needs effective communication, problem solving, negotiation, and time management skills, along with good self esteem. Without good self esteem, the average person is unhappy and lacks the self-respect which enables one to make good choices in their lives.

Unfortunately, our current educational system does not provide these skills and worse, intelligence is penalized. It is not the educational system itself, but students who penalize intelligence. When an average student feels threatened by an intelligent student, the average student usually resorts to name calling and bullying. Intelligent children are commonly referred to as geeks, dweebs, nerds, bookworms and other derogatory names. With this type of ostracism, it is no wonder that mediocrity is king in America. It is up to the teachers and parents to try to instill a different set of values regarding achievement. Without this change of attitude, our country will continue to slip behind in global competitiveness.

In order for us to become competitive in the global economy, we will have to have a better educated society. We will need to invest money into our young if we hope to improve our current standard of living. By the time the average person has acquired self esteem, communication, problem solving, time management, and negotiating skills, they are usually married adults saddled with other responsibilities that sap their creative energies. If average students can acquire these skills by the time they reach college, they will be emotionally adjusted and can devote more of their energies to creative endeavors, rather than wasting their time learning how to cope with the responsibility of being on their own.

Since our educational system hasn't taught our young the basics of education or good time management skills, our students rank near the bottom amongst the industrialized nations in science and math achievement, with thirteen year olds bettering only their Jordanian and Irish peers in a fifteen country international exam. A "disproportionately low" percentage of high school seniors have even rudimentary math and science problem solving skills, according to a report from the National Assessment of Educational Progress, a Federal program that continuously tracks what American students know in various subject areas. Worse yet, millions of adults are functionally illiterate.

These problems are a reflection of societal values. Our society places greater value on physical prowess than it does on academic achievement. Football players are paid millions of dollars a year, while educators are only paid moderate salaries. Funding for education seems to take a back seat to other issues.

To change our value system, the Federal Government needs to take the initiative by putting education first. Funding for schools should come from the Department of Education. If the Federal Government provided the funding for education on an equal basis, poor areas with very little property taxes will be able to provide students with comparable tools and teachers such as those enjoyed by an area with a higher tax base. Besides, genius comes from any walk of life, regardless of socio-economic status. Even if geniuses aren't developed in poor areas, a better educated class of citizens can contribute more to our society than a poorly educated one. If all of the funding for education is provided by the Federal Government, all counties and states can use the money previously allocated to education for either a tax cut or apply it to other areas that require additional funding. The Department of Education should be an information clearinghouse providing a database of proven instructional programs and curriculum. This information should be stored online as a part of U.S. Government Online.

Getting our legislators and the President to agree on this agenda will take time. For now there is an organization called Keep The Promise® that can help fill the gap. This campaign is dedicated to changing the educational system and to the proposition that the nation's children receive the education they deserve in order to keep our economy competitive in the world market. Keep The Promise® produces a booklet called *"Moving America To The Head Of The Class, 50 Simple Things You Can Do."* It lists fifty simple things that parents, employers, educators, and others can do to help children become better educated. This booklet can be obtained by calling 800-96-PROMISE.

WELFARE

Our national Welfare system will never go away. There will always be a segment of our society that will not be able to function within our economic system, or the system itself will not be able to absorb them. These people may come from all walks of life and may have experienced unusual circumstances that have placed them into their situations. Some welfare recipients will take responsibility for their lives and move out of the system and contribute to society while others will not. There will be yet another group who wishes to exit the Welfare system, but for the lack of skills or jobs, the private sector will not be able to absorb them.

Our system cannot absorb some of the people from Welfare because there will always be structural unemployment. Structural unemployment exists when regional job vacancies occur but do not coincide with the labor pool's availability, skill requirement, or location. Structural unemployment has grown worse due to our buying habits and the resulting exportation of jobs. Unfortunately, many of us perceive American made products as being inferior to foreign imports. This perception, whether real or not, has made it difficult for American manufacturers to compete with foreign companies.

In order to keep costs low, many American companies have moved their manufacturing plants to Mexico or offshore. As this happened, many of the newly unemployed factory workers had to take lower paying jobs in order to make ends meet. These workers end up competing for jobs that would normally go to the young and inexperienced labor force, such as welfare recipients. As a result of this competition for available jobs, many welfare recipients are unable to move themselves off the Welfare system. Since this structural unemployment will persist throughout our economy until buying patterns change, the Welfare system needs to be made more cost-effective, rather than placing time limits on people who have poor prospects in finding a job.

Welfare has made some changes over the years but has not achieved the goal of taking many off the system due to lack of funding. The 1988 Family Support Act required states to provide basic education, child care, health insurance, and training while recipients looked for work in the private sector. This act was called the JOBS training program (Job Opportunities and Basic Skills Training Program).

This type of welfare reform is very expensive since the recipient is not participating in providing day care and there is no guarantee they will find a job in the private sector. For this reason, funding for this program has been limited. Politicians realize that our economic base is eroding and there is structural unemployment in the system. By putting welfare recipients into the available workforce without changing our economic base, there will be additional pressures on the job market that will cause social unrest and possibly heightened racial tensions. To prevent this from happening in the short run, welfare reform must not add any additional pressures to the already bleak job market. In order for this to happen, welfare recipients can subsidize budding industries that cannot compete in the open market place due to high costs of labor. Since welfare recipients are being paid and are not doing anything to contribute to society, I suggest using their labor to rebuild our economic base. It is the least they can do, considering they are leaching off the work of hard working taxpaying citizens. Their labor can help subsidize two industries that need assistance: recycling industry and the biomass industry.

The recycling industry is not a cost effective industry. Garbage companies who engage in recycling measures do so at a loss. Costs have been estimated at $50 a ton to process the garbage for recyclable materials. For every ton processed, they can only receive $30 a ton in revenues. Since garbage is "free," most of the expense is attributed to labor and hauling costs. Since welfare recipients are receiving a check anyway, their labor might as well be used for some good. Because many of them have no skills or education, this work would be highly suited for their abilities. The use of their labor for this type of service would compete with the prison labor force that is available. If more prisoners are available for garbage processing, prisoners should be given this job first since they present a security risk in developing the biomass industry.

Our economic base can increase substantially if the biomass industry is able to flourish. New equipment and products brought to the market will lead to the expansion of our manufacturing base. As more jobs are created in the industrial sector, lower paying jobs will free up for the young, for the underprivileged, and for welfare workers. This process will occur over a period of years and this evolutionary process would absorb new workers entering the workforce.

In order to make this a smooth transition, the Welfare system must prepare the recipient for the real world. This can be accomplished by giving them responsibility, education, and a purpose. To facilitate this goal, the new Welfare system will have a daycare, education, and work program that will not only help the individual become a better person, but will provide an avenue for its recipients to pay back the system.

Recipients can help themselves and pay back the system by doing three things: subsidize the biomass industry, get better educated, and participate in supportive services for the other two groups. Each task will last one week and each group will participate in all three activities. There is no time limit on this program, since the goal is to produce citizens who are better educated and can contribute to society. By creating a cash crop, they can minimize their expenses and become self-supporting while developing the biomass industry.

Subsidizing the biomass industry today is essential if planning for the future is important to us. One day we will run out of fossil fuel and petro-chcmicals. The biomass industry can supply both fuel and chemicals through renewable resources, but at this time cannot compete with the price of fossil fuels. Fossil fuels are much cheaper for several reasons. First, the industry is subsidized by both the military and the tax system. Second, biomass fuels have only half the energy content for the same volume of fossil fuel, making it more expensive to transport and manufacture. Third, the technology is in its infancy and labor is still a large component in the cost of producing biomass fuels. Since time and labor are needed to evolve this industry into an energy efficient one, the Welfare system can help in both measures. It can provide a cheap labor source that is necessary to develop the biomass crop which could include switch grass or hardwood trees.

Switchgrass requires very little labor or attention. Switchgrass is prairie grass that used to cover the midwest plains when the buffalo roamed. This plant is hearty and drought resistant. A crop can be harvested once a year with soil tilling every ten years. The drawback for using this crop is the distance it must be hauled in order to process it into fuel. Transportation cost is one of the prohibiting factors keeping it out of the commercial market. Luckily, it does not require high labor costs like tree farms.

Tree farms can yield a higher tonnage of biomass per acre than switchgrass and trees have multiple uses, but these farms require more labor to bring them to fruition than switchgrass. First, it takes labor to plant and care for the trees. During the first three years of growth, weed abatement is necessary if the trees are to survive. Both tasks can be performed quite easily with little instruction by welfare recipients. Since this task can produce a cash crop for the Welfare system, performing it efficiently and cost effectively is essential if the system is ever to be self-sufficient. With effective management of people and resources, more money can be spent on daycare and education to give these recipients a way out of the system and a better life. In order for this to happen, they must have time to develop a career path and mental skills. To accomplish this goal, daycare must be provided.

Daycare will be the second task that every man and woman will be required to perform. By providing centralized daycare for a group of children, parents will be free to perform their required tasks. At first, professional supervision will be required until the welfare parent has the necessary skills to supervise the children. As more welfare recipients become proficient at this task, professional supervision will no longer be needed and the system will be able to run on its own. As this happens, more of the recipients will be able to contribute back to the system so each group will be able to perform the third task.

The third task is education. Without good grounding in the basics, welfare recipients will not be able to compete in the job market. The recipient's ability to fulfill an employer's expectations will depend upon their emotional stability. If these people are emotionally unstable and immature, they will not have the fortitude to hold down a job. For this reason, it will be important to teach them parenting skills, communication skills, and a method for gaining self esteem. In addition to this, they will need to be taught how to conduct themselves more responsibly, since their situation is partly due to their irresponsible actions. To help them understand this, they need to be taught home economics and budgeting. Interpretation and analysis of their welfare usage statements would hopefully drive this point home. Once these basics are mastered, their continued education will be essential if they ever expect to get off of Welfare. They will need a very strong understanding of reading, writing, and arithmetic. Of course, there will be some people who are not motivated to learn and get off the system. Trying to force these people to learn more than they desire will be a waste of time. Rather than waste time and money on people who are not motivated, we should do the next best thing, which is to let them serve the system through daycare and the development of the biomass industry.

By letting these people help develop the biomass industry, they will be helping themselves and the rest of us in the future. Some of them may even become experts in the industry. If that happens, the system will have come full circle.

BIOMASS INDUSTRY

The biomass industry is in its infancy. There are literally dozens, if not hundreds, of technologies that are competing in this sprouting but struggling industry. The basic drawback to this industry is cost. Pound per pound and dollar for dollar, fossil fuels have the biomass energy industry beat. It took nature millions of years to take biomass and fossilize it into coal. Millions of years were also needed to create pockets of crude oil. As a result of this densification process, fossil fuels will always have more energy pound for pound and be more economical under current market conditions. To overcome these market conditions, the biomass industry will need to be subsidized in the short run if some of these technologies are to compete with their fossil fuel counterparts. Unfortunately, in an economy that is heavily in debt, direct cash subsidies are not likely to appear unless the Government debt disappears overnight, or the general public pressures Congress to spend money on unproven technologies. Considering the current state of our economy and the general apathetic nature of our populace, neither of these scenarios seem likely. Fortunately, there are several Internal Revenue codes that give the biomass industry a shot in the arm. These advantages, coupled with "nearly free" labor and some promising technologies, will make certain aspects of the biomass energy industry viable and economical. Other biomass technologies will eventually find niche markets but on the whole, the biomass industry will probably never become mainstream unless all, or most, fossil fuels disappear, or we have another energy crisis or war over oil.

ENERGY TECHNOLOGIES

Developing countries need cheap electricity and fuel for their automobiles. If these countries have cheap and abundant coal or oil reserves, they will develop those sources of energy. If, on the other hand, emerging countries not blessed with these natural resources end up paying higher prices for electricity and gasoline, any foreign exchange earnings they have will be depleted. If the developing countries spend all of their foreign exchange earnings for energy, they will not become very active trading partners for goods or services that we produce here in the United States. In order to help these emerging nations become better trading partners, we need to help them develop a cost effective energy infrastructure that will free up their foreign exchange earnings. These earnings can be spent on goods and services, and this will benefit our country. In order to accomplish this task, we will need to export the most advanced and economically viable technologies that are available that can utilize each country's resources. Since every country produces garbage and sewage, these raw materials can be the feedstocks for their energy production. To facilitate their energy needs, anaerobic digestors designed for human and animal waste will need to be installed. Once the sewage is treated, the methane gas can run fuel cells that will generate electricity. The resulting sludge can be dried and burned to produce steam that will turn a turbine and generate more electricity. The excess heat from the steam production can be used to dry the sludge or help the anaerobic digestion process. Garbage can be gasified and the resulting syngas can be burned in turbines to produce power or be used as fuel for hybrid vehicles. These technologies can be found in Appendix C.

By exporting these technologies to emerging countries, their economies will be stimulated, our economy will be stimulated, and the demand and price for all forms of energy will stabilize.

EMPLOYMENT DEVELOPMENT DEPARTMENT

The Employment Development Department needs a better way of finding jobs for the unemployed. This can be accomplished by creating a database of jobs and resumes that list jobs by experience required and to search for candidates by the qualifications needed. Resumes will need to be scanned into a computer whereby a text search can be performed on the resume. A direct link into U.S. Government Online will also facilitate the employment process. An entrepreneur with the ability to search for candidates online will save time for both the entrepreneur and the unemployed person.

Another tool that will help an entrepreneur build an organization is Career Mosaic on the Internet. This database contains resumes of people who are currently employed. If entrepreneurs have both tools at their disposal, they will be able to find qualified people in a shorter amount of time. This will help the unemployed person get off unemployment. To further facilitate this process, on-site job training in the use of computers should be performed on a daily basis. Computers with up to date mainstream software should be offered to those who wish to learn to use this equipment. Video training tapes for software programs should be made available so that individuals can learn at their own pace.

TEN

DEFICITS & TAXES: CONCLUSION

America is pissed off. Everyone feels they are paying too many taxes—too many Federal, state, payroll, sales and property taxes. We are being taxed to death. Most of us feel helpless in this "taxing" situation. So what do we do? We cut off our nose to spite our face. Yes, tax revolt at the lowest levels is hurting us more than it is helping us. This tax revolt has manifested itself in the form of legislation like Proposition 13 in the state of California. Property taxes are essentially frozen until the sale of the property. When the sale happens, the new owner gets hammered with an outrageous tax bill. Legislation like Proposition 13 really hurts the local communities. Education, libraries, police, and fire services are directly affected by this type of legislation. As a result of low tax revenues, children are getting an inferior education and police protection is down. Meanwhile, criminals and prisoners are reaping the benefits from this type of legislation. Without adequate funding for police and prisons, criminals are not being caught or prosecuted. If they are caught and incarcerated, their stays are usually shortened due to budget constraints.

To reverse these scenarios, our local, state, and Federal Governments have to implement four major changes. First, Government must become more efficient with their expenditures. Second, Government must become profit driven to produce goods and services that generate revenue. Third, the Federal Government must make their accounting system accountable. Finally, the tax system needs to be revised.

If our Governments do not make these changes, more of us will get frustrated with the tax situation and revolt by implementing legislation that is similar to what already exists in California and Oregon, or worse, have our legislators implement some simplified tax system that would drive out competition in the oil industry and do nothing to help stimulate American industries that will help bring our trade deficits into a balance.

Our fiscal deficit is mostly made up of entitlements and mandatory spending. Our past legislators and Presidents are to blame for most of the annual deficit and the resulting national debt, which is at the $5 trillion mark. Deficits at all levels of Government have arisen from a welfare state that has gotten out of hand. We have too many freeloaders, prisoners, and expenditures that waste tax dollars. Money is being spent to coddle welfare recipients, illegal aliens, and prisoners who place a financial burden on our society. These people get housing, food, medical care, and money without earning it. In fact, medical care for low income people was one of the big items that had caused the budget stalemate between President Clinton and Congress. President Clinton wanted to make sure that this program got adequate funding, while the Republicans wanted to cut it. A better solution is to make welfare recipients, illegal aliens, and prisoners more cost effective.

In order to make these people more cost effective, they need to work at projects that will actually create something useful that has monetary value. A cash crop can be generated from biomass and garbage. This could include electricity generated from biomass, trees sold to paper mills for wood pulp, sale of recyclables generated from garbage, electricity generated from garbage, or methane gas or ethanol developed from garbage. By using welfare and prison labor to generate income for our Governments, expenses are minimized at the least and profits made in the best case scenario. Even though Governments would become profit-oriented, they still won't lose sight of the main purpose of helping people who need it. The difference with this new type of Government is *how* it would help its people. This new plan is designed to help the needy by teaching them how to be self-sufficient. As an old proverb goes: "If you give a man a fish, you only feed him for one night, but if you teach him to fish, you feed him for life." By incorporating education and training in the Welfare system, hopefully many of the recipients will eventually move off the roles of Welfare and contribute to society and help reduce Government debt.

Our $5 trillion national debt will continue to get bigger until the Government balances its budget. This growth of the debt will be dependent upon how accurate Congressional Budget Office numbers are in their budget projections. In the best case scenario, their numbers will be right on and the budget will be balanced in seven years. If the economy under performs, it will take longer to balance the budget and the national debt will continue to grow larger.

In Chapter 4, you learned that part of the national debt is caused by trust fund programs. For every dollar that enters the Treasury on behalf of trust fund programs, an equal dollar amount of debt is created and accounted for in the national debt. The national debt also increases as Congress decides how much future spending authority each trust fund program shall receive. Even though this debt is "not real" for the present, it will become real when our Government finally finances the spending authority.

For the approximately $1.2 trillion worth of Government-owned debt, most if not all of it, will have to be financed from borrowed money unless present and future Presidents and Congress can agree upon a plan to end the deficits, and bring Government into a surplus. Until that day happens, Government-owned debt on trust fund programs will be financed with borrowed money.

The problem with this system is that many of the trust fund programs generate very little revenue from its benefactors. The Civil Service Retirement trust fund program only generates a very small percentage of revenue from its benefactors while the Military Retirement trust fund program generates no income at all. The Social Security trust fund program subsidizes other trust fund programs that receive little or no income, such as the case with the Military and Civil Service Retirement trust fund programs.

Since the Government chooses to confuse us with the accounting of trust fund programs, the impending financial crisis for the Social Security program is being disguised with its future spending authority. At a glance, these trust fund programs would appear to have huge surpluses, but trust fund programs do not contain any real assets. Those "surpluses" are only future spending authorities which will have to be financed with borrowed money. This will raise the price of money which results in higher interest expense, not to mention the cost to other trust fund programs and declined benefits to recipients. This accounting nightmare is short-sighted and has placed the burden of our current and past legislators irresponsible spending behavior onto us and our children.

To help clear up *some* of this confusion, the General Accounting Office created a report called "Social Security Trust Fund Reserves" whereby they made recommendations that would depict more clearly the various important fiscal relationships within the budget, yet still show how they combine to show the Treasury's cash financing needs. In the report, it is suggested that the total budget could be subdivided into six different constituent parts that, taken together, would sum to an amount very like the total currently counted under Gramm-Rudman-Hollings.

The budget definition used under Gramm-Rudman-Hollings (or the unified budget definition used before 1986) highlights the net cash flow of the treasury but hides many other fiscal relationships. The report proposes that the budget presentation be modified to depict more clearly the various important fiscal relationships.

Under the proposal, the budget would be divided into capital and operating components. Each would then be further divided into trust fund, general (Federal or non-trust fund), and enterprise (the activities in which the Government is sponsoring a Government enterprise-e.g. the Tennessee Valley Authority). Each of these elements would have its own revenue, expenditure, and deficit subtotals.[62]

GAO Revised Budget Structure Illustrative Example for Fiscal Year 1987 ($ in billions)				
		ACCOUNTS		
Budget Component	**Total**	**General**	**Trusts**	**Enterprises**
Operating surplus/deficit (-)	**-96.2**	-136.1	68.0	-1.1
Capital Financing Requirements	**-54.2**	-57.7	3.7	-0.2
TOTAL FINANCING REQUIREMENTS	**-150.4**	**-220.8**	**71.7**	**-1.3**

In their example they estimated that the $150 billion deficit reported for fiscal year 1987 was actually composed of a deficit of $96 billion in operating accounts combined with $54 billion in capital expenses. Viewed differently, the $150 billion total deficit was the result of a $221 billion deficit in the general fund accounts, a $72 billion surplus in the trust fund accounts, and a $1 billion deficit in public enterprise accounts.

---

[62] General Accounting Office. *Social Security Trust Fund Reserves*, 1989, p. 40

The report goes on to further state that their approach offers the following advantages:

➤ Dividing the budget into separate trust fund, general fund, and enterprise fund accounts highlights the relationship between a growing deficit in the non-Social Security portion of the budget and the growing surpluses in Social Security. In so doing, it makes clear the extent to which the movement toward budget balance is being achieved at the expense of substantial future Government spending promises.

➤ Dividing the budget into capital and operating accounts emphasizes the extent to which Government borrowing can be viewed properly as a reduction in funds available for investment, versus being a means of financing Government capital expenditures.

➤ Summing each of the components to a total deficit similar in concept to the unified budget corresponds in concept to the aggregate cash flow of the Treasury. Such a correspondence between budget totals and cash flow helps assure honesty in budgeting. Cash needs cannot be hidden by redefinition of budget accounts.

They sum up by stating, "if done carefully, restatement of the budget into its various constituent subtotals can highlight important relationships hidden in current budget figures without obscuring important relationships that the budget totals now highlight."[63]

This change in the way the Government would report the deficit is in the right direction. It at least establishes important fiscal relationships that are currently hidden under the existing reporting methods. This change will not prevent the impending financial crisis that will occur with the Social Security trust fund program in the early part of the next century because the cash flow surpluses are being used to finance current consumption in other sectors of Government. When the cash flow surpluses are used in this manner, Social Security taxes are being disguised as another form of income tax.

Since our Social Security taxes are really another form of income tax, we should privatize Social Security. As the baby boomers start to retire around the year 2010, the "surpluses" reported in the Social Security trust fund program will have to be financed through borrowed money, Social Security taxes, income taxes, other trust fund cash flow surpluses, or through reduced benefits. Since revenues will always be less than the outlays in the Social Security trust fund program, the program is doomed to bankruptcy. Since the system is designed to fail and cannot be self-supporting, we should privatize Social Security and make it optional for those who are thirty and older, increase the retirement age, and reim-

---

[63] General Accounting Office. *Social Security Trust Fund Reserves,* 1989, pp. 40-41

burse all payments made into the Social Security system (plus interest) to each person who will invest their funds in a Government approved mutual fund. Even though the cash demands would be substantial, the demands would be far less than what they will be in the year 2010 and the subsequent years. Taking several years to reimburse everyone will be the best way to handle privatizing Social Security, but privatizing Social Security will work only if the economy is booming and the new tax system discussed in this book is implemented, which includes using the National Sales Tax as a method of replacing the revenues that would be lost due to privatization of Social Security.

Privatizing the retirement trust fund programs will be a big step toward preventing the impending financial crisis, but it won't prevent deficits from happening. The way to slow down increasing deficits is to privatize the entitlement programs, which include Medicare and Medicaid, through payment vouchers/credits that recipients would use to shop for private health care. From the table below you can see that entitlements and mandatory spending account for nearly half of the Government's budget from 1975 forward.

Outlays for Major Spending Categories Fiscal Years 1962-1994 (In Billions of Dollars)						
Year	Discretionary Spending	Entitlements and Other Mandatory Spending	Deposit Insurance	Net Interest	Offsetting Receipts	Total Outlays
1962	74.9	32.3	-0.4	6.9	-6.8	106.8
1963	78.3	33.6	-0.4	7.7	-7.9	111.3
1964	82.8	35.7	-0.4	8.2	-7.7	118.5
1965	81.8	36.1	-0.4	8.6	-7.9	118.2
1966	94.1	39.9	-0.5	9.4	-8.4	134.5
1967	110.4	47.4	-0.4	10.3	-10.2	157.5
1968	122.1	56.1	-0.5	11.1	-10.6	178.1
1969	121.4	61.2	-0.6	12.7	-11.0	183.6
1970	124.6	68.7	-0.5	14.4	-11.5	195.6
1971	127.1	82.7	-0.4	14.8	-14.1	210.2
1972	133.1	96.8	-0.6	15.5	-14.1	230.7
1973	135.0	112.2	-0.8	17.3	-18.0	245.7
1974	142.5	127.1	-0.6	21.4	-21.2	269.4
1975	162.5	**164.4**	0.5	23.2	-18.3	332.3

Year	Discretionary Spending	Entitlements and Other Mandatory Spending	Deposit Insurance	Net Interest	Offsetting Receipts	Total Outlays
1976	175.6	**189.7**	-0.6	26.7	-19.6	371.8
1977	197.1	**206.6**	-2.8	29.9	-21.5	409.2
1978	218.7	**228.4**	-1.0	35.5	-22.8	458.7
1979	240.0	**248.2**	-1.7	42.6	-25.6	503.5
1980	276.5	**291.5**	-0.4	52.5	-29.2	590.9
1981	308.2	**340.6**	-1.4	68.8	-37.9	678.2
1982	326.2	**372.7**	-2.1	85.0	-36.0	745.8
1983	353.4	**411.6**	-1.2	89.8	-45.3	808.4
1984	379.6	**406.3**	-0.8	111.1	-44.2	851.8
1985	416.2	**450.0**	-2.2	129.5	-47.1	946.4
1986	439.9	**459.7**	1.5	136.0	-45.9	990.3
1987	444.9	**470.2**	3.1	138.7	-53.0	1,003.9
1988	465.1	**494.2**	10.0	151.8	-57.0	1,064.1
1989	489.7	**526.2**	22.0	169.3	-63.9	1,143.2
1990	501.7	**567.4**	58.1	184.2	-58.8	1,252.7
1991	534.8	**634.2**	66.3	194.5	-106.0	1,323.8
1992	536.0	**711.7**	2.6	199.4	-68.8	1,380.9
1993	542.5	**762.1**	-28.0	198.8	-67.1	1,408.2
1994	545.3	**788.7**	-7.3	202.9	-69.1	1,460.6

Source: Congressional Budget Office

The problem of entitlement spending becomes clearer when you look at the projected deficits into the year 2000. In the following table, the deficit will reach $401 billion before any cash flow surpluses from trust fund programs are applied to the deficit. You will notice that the Military and Civilian Retirement trust fund programs actually have cash flow surpluses. This has resulted from unspent money and net transfers from the general fund. The Congressional Budget Office deceives us by counting interest on the Social Security trust fund as offsetting revenues to lower the deficit. Approximately half of the surpluses of Social Security are a result of counting their interest income as real income.

As you know from Chapter 4, the income derived from trust fund programs are paid with more special issue securities that have no real value. Not only does the Government use our Social Security taxes as income taxes, they are using worthless IOUs as income to help them balance the budget! This is ridiculous, considering one of the big battles between Congress and President Clinton over the budget was what set of numbers they were going to use to balance the budget. President Clinton finally gave in and agreed to use the numbers provided by the Congressional Budget Office which produced the report called *The Economic and Budget Outlook: Fiscal Years 1996-2000*. Since the numbers are erroneous, the budget will not really be balanced in the promised seven years because they are counting interest from trust fund programs as real income. Any boasting made by either party is based upon falsehoods and illusions.

CBO Projections of Trust Fund Surpluses (By Fiscal Year, In Billions of Dollars)						
	1995	**1996**	**1997**	**1998**	**1999**	**2000**
Social Security[a]	69	73	78	84	90	96
Medicare						
Hospital Insurance	3	-2	-7	-12	-19	-25
Supplementary Med. Ins.	-9	b	1	1	2	2
Subtotal Medicare	-5	-2	-6	-11	-17	-23
Military Retirement	5	4	4	2	1	b
Civilian Retirement[c]	29	31	32	33	34	36
Unemployment	8	7	5	4	3	3
Highway & Airport	-3	1	2	2	2	2
Other	4	4	4	4	4	4
Total Trust Fund Surplus[e]	107	118	119	119	116	117
Federal Funds Deficit[e]	**-283**	**-326**	**-343**	**-341**	**-369**	**-401**
Total Deficit	-176	-207	-224	-222	-253	-284
Memorandum:						
Net Transfers from Federal Funds to Trust Funds	203	2332	252	269	290	314

a. Old-Age and Survivors Insurance and Disability Insurance; b. Less than $500 million; c. Civil Service Retirement, Foreign Service Retirement, and several smaller funds.; d. Primarily Railroad Retirement, Employees' health insurance and life insurance, Hazardous Substance Superfund, and various veterans' insurance trust funds.; e. Assumes that discretionary spending reductions are made in non-trust-fund programs

Source: Congressional Budget Office

If the Government does manage to balance the budget in seven years, entitlement spending will have to suffer tremendously unless the economy is stimulated greatly. If it is not, Medicare, Medicaid and Social Security, will suffer profoundly. Even if the budget is balanced and no major cuts are made in Medicare and Medicaid, our Government will still face a financial disaster surrounding the trust fund programs. Future spending in Social Security, Medicare, and Medicaid will place huge demands on the Government in the upcoming years unless these programs are privatized. Other trust fund programs will also place big demands on the budget since they have no real assets or money to fund their spending.

Making the Government totally accountable for the trust fund programs will be a big job. It cannot be done at this time. If all the trust fund programs were funded with real assets, the entire national debt of $5 trillion would be publicly-owned debt. This means approximately $1.2 trillion worth of bonds will have to be sold to the public to finance all of the trust funds. In order to attract these funds, the Government will be forced to push up interest rates. Considering the state of the economy and the volatility of the financial markets, an additional $1.2 trillion worth of Government bonds would put the economy into a downward tail spin. The additional interest costs would be prohibitive unless the economy was first stimulated enough to generate additional tax revenues. Legislators would be hard pressed to make good decisions on an already shaky and erroneous budget. Implementing this plan will have to be done when replacement funds for Social Security are generated and/or when the budget is truly balanced (both are preferable).

If our leaders had any vision at all, they would realize that their plans are headed for a disaster that will cost all of us precious tax dollars and benefits. To circumvent this impending problem, privatizing these entitlement programs is the only way to provide our citizens with income and services without causing too much strain on the budget. Our legislators have warned us about the impending bankruptcy with regards to the Medicare trust fund program, but in reality it is already broke since the cash flow surpluses are being used to finance current consumption in non-trust fund activities. The surpluses that exist are just future spending authorities that will have to be financed with some form of future tax dollars.

Because of screwy Government accounting and the fact that trust fund revenues are being used as income taxes, the national debt could be close to $7 trillion ($2 trillion of it could be Government internal IOUs) by the time Government balances the budget.[64] Once a balanced budget is achieved, it will take the Government years and hundreds of billions of dollars a year in interest and principal expense to eliminate this $7 trillion national debt. The national debt will become astronomical if Government tries to fund every entitlement program.

---

[64] Congressional Budget Office. *The Economic And Budget Outlook: Fiscal Years 1996-2000*, 1995, Chapter Two, p. 51

Government rhetoric gets even more confusing when they refer to their Net Interest expense. The Congressional Budget Office feels that Net Interest expense is the most useful measurement of the Government's debt service cost. Included in the Net Interest expense is interest income they received from trust funds which gives the illusion that the Government is doing much better than it really is. Since the Government is using smoke and mirrors to hide the real story about the deficit and the national debt, their accounting system needs to be changed so that our legislators are held accountable for their reckless and irresponsible spending habits. To insure that our legislators are held accountable for their spending, we must not give them trust fund revenues to use as income taxes. We must replace the trust fund revenues with tax revenues derived from a tax system that promotes saving, investing, and spending.

By changing the personal income tax system outlined in this book, the economy will be stimulated, more people will be working, more taxes will be collected, investments will be up, and the savings rate will be improved. As the savings rate improves, businesses will be able to borrow money cheaper and expand their capacity and markets more easily. Since certain durable goods are allowed to be depreciated and deducted from one's income tax, this should encourage people to replace these durable goods more frequently thereby stimulating the economy. The tax rate on income will be flat and fairly low because additional income taxes will be collected from a National Sales Tax that will also have a low tax rate. The purpose of having a National Sales Tax is to collect taxes from the underground economy and from foreigners and very wealthy individuals who avoid paying any income taxes at all. Between the two tax systems, the tax burden should be more evenly distributed among the taxpayers.

Because more people will be paying taxes and the tax burden will be shared by everyone, there won't be a great need to drastically change the corporate tax system at this time. Besides, existing tax laws are needed to insure that certain industries remain competitive in the economy. Without competition, industry will be dominated by a few companies. Oil companies, along with Japanese automobile and electronic manufacturers, will eventually control our country if we do not insure competition from alternative fuels and American companies respectively. Even though the corporate tax system will remain fairly static, the change in the personal income tax system insures there will be competition from American car and electronic manufacturers. Competition in the fuel market will result from the existing tax codes that help the ethanol market, along with assistance from the 1988 Alternative Motor Fuel Act, the 1990 Clean Air Act, and the 1992 Energy Policy Act.

As you can tell, our economy is built around complex laws and regulations. Making sweeping changes in the corporate tax system at this time would destroy all the progress made in the alternative fuels market and the biomass industry. Until the day we have strong competition in the automotive fuel market and we eliminate our trade and fiscal deficits, corporate taxes should remain fairly static, allowing for minor adjustments.

One type of adjustment that should be done in the next few years is the elimination of capital gains. Capital gains are essentially the excess proceeds made from the sale or exchange of an asset. If entrepreneurs are penalized too heavily for their risk-taking behavior, it may eventually thwart the continued growth of our economy. Without economic growth, less people will be employed who can pay income taxes. If less tax revenues are generated from our economy, legislators may try to collect more tax revenues from corporations. This could further jeopardize their economic health and our economic growth. If corporations are not profitable, they will do whatever is necessary to become profitable. Unfortunately some of their methods of tax reduction are unscrupulous, which has negative consequences for the economy.

Take for example the usage of net operating losses by corporate raiders. The Simplicity Pattern Company came under attack by corporate raiders because it was a profitable business with huge cash reserves and pension funds. These raiders took over the company and eventually invaded the pension funds for nearly $11 million. Over a period of years and four owners, the cash reserves were used for ventures such as mining, oil and gas exploration, real estate, and sugar refineries. The raiders also took the Simplicity Pattern Company from a zero debt company to nearly $100 million in debt. This nearly bankrupt the company.

One raider, the Triton Group LTD had the company for three years. In that time the Simplicity Pattern Company made $100 million in profits. As a result of the net operating loss tax deduction (being able to take a previous year's losses and apply it to future tax liabilities), Triton paid no income taxes on profits because they had a tax loss of $200 million that could be carried forward.[65] The original intent of the law was to help start-up companies in the early years of losing money to be offset later, when they finally turn a profit in their operations.

In this situation, Triton took advantage of the tax code by applying their losses to the profits made at Simplicity. Due to poor management at Triton, money and resources were squandered that eventually cost the Government tax revenue. This procedure of acquiring companies for their tax benefits is irresponsible on behalf of those people who employ this method of tax reduction. Not only does Government lose tax revenues, many helpless victims lose their jobs and livelihood, all in the name of tax relief.

---

[65] Facts from Barlett, Donald L. and Steele, James B. *America: What Went Wrong?*, Andrews and McMeel, 1992, pp. 153-159

To offset the negative effects of using net operating losses by corporate raiders, this tax deduction needs to be modified (it would remain the same for any company that was not merged). This modification would include a maximum usage against profits, but with limited benefits. For example, if one of the companies (raiding company or takeover company) has a $100 million loss and the other company has a $100 million profit, the total amount of loss is used up in the first year. Modification of the tax code would be the percentage of the tax loss that could be written off. Arbitrarily, let's assume the percentage amount is 50%. In the first year, the total net operating loss is eliminated, but the corporation only receives $50 million in tax write-offs that yields a positive income for the corporation that they would have to pay taxes on.

By minimizing net operating losses on mergers and combining this change with the elimination of capital gains, the expectant results should negate each other. By discouraging wasteful use of capital and resources and rewarding genius, prudent money management and risk taking, corporations will get the message that it is more profitable to develop new products and companies than it is to raid an existing company for its tax benefits. As this attitude and belief filters throughout corporate America, those who have the capabilities to develop new products and start new companies will be rewarded instead of penalized. For those who have only larceny tendencies, they will not prosper under these new changes. Once corporate America is headed down the right path, more tax relief for everyone will be possible.

In order to reduce taxes for everyone, all Americans will have to spend their money more responsibly. This will involve people who have discretionary income to take the lead. If, for example, there are two electric saws for sale and both are of comparable quality, but the import is just $10 cheaper, the person who can afford to spend the extra $10 should do so because of the economic multiplier. Money spent on American made products will have a higher multiplier effect than if the money is spent on imported goods. If we want to help our economy build a strong economic tax base, we will have to begin purchasing more products that are made here in America.

Besides, as you learned from Chapter 5, trade deficits are settled with capital assets that include stocks, companies, real estate and even Government bonds. When we sell off our country a piece at a time to pay for our trade deficits, we lose in many ways. We first lose our tax base to foreigners who usually pay lower income taxes on the same amount of revenue than their American counterpart. Second, profits derived from foreign-owned companies are exported out the country, which eventually gives foreigners additional capital buildup that enables them to purchase more of America. Finally, some of our trade deficits are settled with

Government bonds. On one hand, selling Government bonds to foreigners brings cash into America to help finance the annual fiscal deficit. The downside of selling Government bonds to finance trade deficits is that tax dollars are subsidizing the cost of imports. Worse yet, the interest that is paid on those bonds to foreigners is done with our tax dollars. As this happens, the national debt gets larger while the President pats himself on the back for his alleged superior fiscal policies that lowered the deficit. What appears to be a good bargain at the store ends up being extremely high-priced when you consider the total cost to our economy, the deficit, the national debt, and taxes.

Deficits and taxes are also affected by all types of expenditures, including those for electrical energy, motor oil, fuels, tires, prisons, FEMA, and for military protection of oil. The deficit picture becomes worse when you factor in expenditures for Unemployment Insurance, Government pensions, Social Security, Medicare, Medicaid, and Welfare. None of these things will go away overnight, but we can make changes now that will affect the overall outcome of the deficit picture.

As you can see, our economic system is very complicated, and it will require a complex and comprehensive plan to eradicate the different problems that exist within Government and in the economy. Imagine being on a 747 that is experiencing technical difficulty. Unfortunately, the pilot and copilots are pigheaded and refuse to land the plane and make necessary repairs despite some very loud protests from some passengers. As each engine catches fire, explodes and falls off, the pilot announces that the plane is very capable and there is no need to worry. As the last engine catches fire, the pilot announces, "We have good news and bad news. The good news is that the airline has authorized a fare cut for those passengers who wish to fly with them on their next flight. The bad news is that the plane will crash and there won't be a next flight." Just like our economy, pigheaded leaders with eloquent rhetoric and control will crash our economy.

This book in itself will not solve our problems unless everyone decides that these solutions make sense and they are willing to help implement them into our system. This will require everyone who reads this to share this information with their friends, family, peers, and more importantly, with every member of Congress. Without the support of Congress, these ideas are wasted and the problems that face us will become larger and more unmanageable as we get closer to the year when baby boomers start to retire. If we wait too long to implement some of these solutions, their validity will expire and they may only have marginal benefits. Now is the time to pull together and solve our problems so we can head into the next century with momentum and a purpose that will keep our country strong and vital.

Without a plan that gives us momentum and a purpose, we will be faced with skyrocketing deficits and taxes that will kill our economy. During the month of September 1996, 540 copies of this manuscript were hand-delivered to Congress. Depending upon the time you read this, and the willingness of Congress to consider the problems and solutions outlined in this book, some or none of them may or may not be acted upon. If the problem of Social Security is being addressed seriously, we should encourage, support, and applaud our leaders for their courageous actions. On the other hand, if they only pay lip service to this problem, we should scold Congress and tell them: "It's Social Security, Stupid!" If you believe the problems and solutions outlined in this book warrant Congress' attention, and feel they should act upon these ideas, you should communicate to all of them with a letter or fax. To assist you in your communication with Congress, below is a form letter that you can use or modify to convey your support and enthusiasm of the solutions that will save our country from an economic meltdown.

John Q Voter
123 Any Street
Anytown, Any State, 12345

Dear Congressman/Congreswoman:

I am a Republican/Democrat who did/did not vote for you in the last election. I understand that, because of party affiliations and the persuasive powers of lobbyists, it is difficult to create and pass good legislation even when intentions are honorable.

Are you interested in my vote in the next election? Are you interested in having me spread the good word about your work to my constituents as well?

Do you want a long, successful, and popular political career? Are you interested in being perceived as a Congressman/Congresswoman who is intelligent, fair, fiscally responsible, ecologically-minded, and responsive to your voters' needs? Do you want to go down in the history books as one of the brave, progressive Congressman/Congresswoman with the foresight to help solve our country's problems?

If you answered yes to the above questions, then ask yourself the following:

- Are you willing to be open-minded about new ideas?
- Are you willing not to buckle under lobbyists pressures?
- Are you willing not to buckle under your political party affiliations?
- Are you willing to learn as much as possible about economics?
- Are you willing to read the book "OPERATION PROSPERITY," by Christopher C. Lai and encourage your constituents to do the same?

Please read the book "OPERATION PROSPERITY" by Christopher C. Lai. Please pay special attention to Chapter(s) _____ regarding _____. I would like to see you create legislation that is in favor of these items. Your vote and lobbying for these changes will help all of us create a "win-win" situation. As a taxpayer, I win by having lower taxes. As a politician, you win by having my vote, as well as being perceived by other voters as someone who is intelligent, fair, fiscally responsible, ecologically-minded, progressive, courageous, insightful, and responsive to his voters' needs.

You might be concerned about being ostracized by your peers if you take a new stance regarding an old problem. You also might be concerned about receiving less PAC money from lucrative industries that currently have a stranglehold on our economy. These are valid concerns for a politician, but ask yourself this question: Will your conscience bother you, when knowing you could have legislated and voted responsibly to fulfill your voters' needs, but you buckled under peer pressure and/or to special interests and their alluring PAC money? Consider which is the lesser of the two evils: Being perceived by your voting public as untrustworthy, unresponsive, selfish, spineless, and unworthy of being re-elected or being considered by your peers as an individual who has courage, foresight, intelligence, and fortitude, the qualities of a great person and a true leader.

As soon as you finish this letter, pick up a copy of "OPERATION PROSPERITY." Digest it and try to understand the author's logic. Encourage your peers to do the same. Remember that what comes around goes around. If you are helpful in making changes that will benefit me as a taxpayer, you will be remembered on voting day. Good things come to those who work hard and persevere. And I am asking you to do just that: work hard, persevere, and legislate responsibly.

Sincerely,

John Q Voter

P.S. If you fail to be courageous and own up to the problems that exist or fail to take a stand for positive change, in my eyes you will be joining a fraternity/sorority of Congressmen/Congresswomen who have the dubious distinction of being C.R.A.P.P.Y. politicians: Corrupt, Repugnant, Arrogant, Patronizing, Pompous, and Yellow-bellied.

If you are an avid communicator and wish to write letters to more than one Congressman/Congresswoman, listed below are several software programs that will assist you in accomplishing that task. I do not endorse these products, nor do these companies endorse me or this publication. I offer no warranties on the product or its suitability to the user.

Personal Advocate
Parsons Technology
One Hiawatha Drive
P.O. Box 100
Hiawatha, IA 52233-0100
Tel: 319-395-9626
Fax: 319-395-0217

Federal Soap Box
Soap Box Software, Inc.
2800 Woodlawn Drive
Suite 162
Honolulu HI 96822
1-800-989-7627

CRAPPY Politicians

Sometimes we invariably cut our nose off to spite our face. Eliminating good politicians is counterproductive. Even though they are few and far between, having experienced Congressmen/Congresswomen is important. They bring to the forum their knowledge and experience which enables them to get things done because they understand the process and know the right people. If they are corrupt or not qualified, get rid of them. Term limits are not the issue; having the right people in office is.

What we really want is good people in office and not C.R.A.P.P.Y. politicians, which stands for CORRUPT, REPUGNANT, ARROGANT, PATRONIZING, POMPOUS, and YELLOW-BELLIED. You know the type, the ones who take huge sums of money from special interests and legislate in their favor even though their supporting voters prefer that they didn't legislate in this fashion. These words are my favorite to describe the current batch of undesirable politicians. They may not describe your Congressman/Congresswoman to the tee, so for your convenience, I have compiled a list of adjectives to assist you in expressing your sentiments more clearly:

C	R	A	P
Callous	Racist	Abhorrent	Paradoxical
Cancerous	Raunchy	Abrasive	Parlous
Capricious	Recalcitrant	Absurd	Partitive
Caustic	Recreant	Abusive	Patronizing
Cheesy	Redundant	Accursed	Pathetic
Chicanerous	Reprehensible	Acrimonious	Pecable
Clamorous	Reproachful	Adulterous	Peccant
Clandestine	Repugnant	Alcoholic	Peculiar
Cocky	Repulsive	Ambiguous	Pernicious
Comatose	Ridiculous	Ambivalent	Pertinacious
Complacent	Rude	Antiquated	Perverse
Condescending	Ruthless	Apathetic	Perverted
Confused		Archaic	Pesky
Conniving		Arrogant	Pessimistic
Conspiratorial		Asinine	Pettish
Contemptuous		Assumptive	Petulant
Contentious		Astatic	Philistine
Contradictory		Atrocious	Phony
Corrupt		Avaricious	Piggish
Crabby		Averse	Pigheaded
Crooked			Pimping
Crude			Pinheaded
Cruel			Pitiable
Crummy			Pitiless
Crusty			Portentous
Cunning			Preposterous
Cursurious			Presumptuous
Cynical			Pretentious
			Problematic
			Prodigal
			Promiscuous
			Psittacine
			Psychopathic

Now its up to you to investigate your elected officials and decide for yourself if they are the ones you want in office. You can accomplish this by looking into Project Vote Smart. The goal of this database is to turn the table on politicians. Anyone can find it on the world wide web, or can call in and speak to an associate regarding your question. In my case, I wanted to know how Senator Dole voted on the 1985 Balanced budget act as well as the 1974 Balanced Budget Act. Because this information was not in their computers, they had to find the books and xerox the pages. Otherwise I probably would have received the answers the same day.

Project Vote Smart
129 NW Fourth Street, #204
Corvallis, OR 97330
Tel: 503-754-2746
Tel: 1-800-622-SMART
Fax: 503-754-2747
URL: http://www.vote.smart.org

Now that you have these tools, its up to you to make the difference. Harassing our Congressmen/Congresswomen into looking for new ideas and solutions is our responsibility. Simplistic and politically popular ideas that are short sighted will only create more problems for us in the future. We have to make some tough choices, including voting in people who will serve us and not themselves.

APPENDIX A

TRUST FUND PROGRAMS AND THE FEDERAL DEFICIT

By David Koit, Specialist in Social Legislation

Gene Falk, Analyst in Social Legislation
Education and Public Welfare Division

Philip Winters, Analyst in Government Finance
Economics Division

Overview

Trust fund programs have received a great deal of attention in recent discussions about the Federal budget and the budget deficit. The Federal Government, like most Governments, accounts for a variety of its activities through "trust funds." Trust funds serve useful purposes in budgeting and in the allocation of Federal spending authority. However, the "budgeting" and "accounting" features of trust funds are often confused with their impact on fiscal policy.

Fiscal policy concerns the Federal Government's transactions with the public: how much the Government spends and raises in the economy through tax receipts and borrowing. The effect of trust fund programs on the Federal deficit is simply put: it is how these programs affect the Federal Government's total revenues, spending and borrowing. This can be analyzed as separate from how the Government keeps its books. This paper concerns itself with how trust funds affect fiscal policy.

In a 1988 report, the General Accounting Office (GAO) identified one hundred sixty-seven Federal trust fund programs. However, while many in number, the bulk of their spending and revenues is concentrated among a few. In FY 1989, the eight largest ones accounted for 97% of all revenues and 99% of all spending caused by trust fund programs. Most of the big funds (in terms of revenues and spending) are for retirement- or pension-type programs, with the two Social Security programs— Old Age and Survivors Insurance (OASI) and Disability Insurance (DI)— accounting for 69% of all revenues and 58% of all spending caused by trust fund programs. The next seven largest include two for Medicare— Hospital Insurance (HI) and Supplementary Medical Insurance (SMI)— Civil Service Retirement, Military Retirement, Unemployment Insurance, and the Highway fund.

In FY 1989, trust fund programs collectively accounted for 35% of all Federal spending and 39% of all Federal receipts (aside from borrowing). Official budget documents show that in the aggregate their income exceeded their outgo by $124 billion. Including this apparent surplus, the Government ran a deficit overall of $152 billion. Consequently, many observers state that trust fund surpluses mask the "true" size of the deficit, which they would put at $276 billion (the official unified deficit of $152 billion plus the trust fund "surpluses" of $124 billion).

CHART 1
The Largest Federal Trust Fund Programs
Fiscal Year 1989

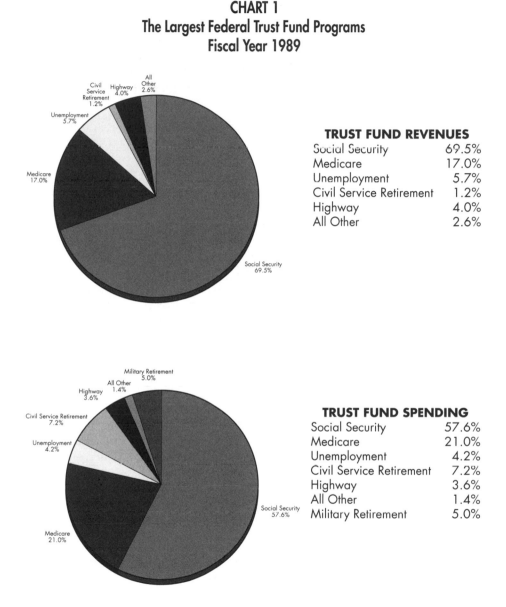

TRUST FUND REVENUES

Social Security	69.5%
Medicare	17.0%
Unemployment	5.7%
Civil Service Retirement	1.2%
Highway	4.0%
All Other	2.6%

TRUST FUND SPENDING

Social Security	57.6%
Medicare	21.0%
Unemployment	4.2%
Civil Service Retirement	7.2%
Highway	3.6%
All Other	1.4%
Military Retirement	5.0%

The perception that trust fund programs produce surplus cash for the Government is inaccurate, at least in the aggregate. In FY 1989 spending for them actually exceeded the receipts they generated from the public by $18 billion. The confusion arises in part from a misunderstanding of what trust fund income is. While specific taxes and premiums are often levied on segments of the population to help cover a trust fund program's expenditures, trust funds also "receive income" from the Government—i.e., "credit" from one Government account to another—or what in essence is *paper income*. No economic resources are moved, no actual money collected. In fact, in FY 1989, some 28%, or $147 billion of the aggregate "income" received by Federal trust funds, consisted of these Government "payments."

Also contributing to the confusion is the perception that Federal trust funds are independent financial entities, and that the taxes and premiums paid by the public to help finance their spending are deposited in them. The money actually goes into and out of the U.S. Treasury, not the trust funds. The trust funds are special accounts maintained by the Treasury Department. Their "income" and "outgo" are ledger entries. Usually "income" is recorded by posting Federal securities to them. "Outgo" is recorded by deleting securities from them. Typically, the securities are what are called *special issues*. They are non-marketable securities, meaning that they cannot be sold to the public.[66] Although less frequent, there also are times when the trust funds simply receive "credits" for cash taken in by the Treasury or for other reasons, i.e., no *special issue* or other security is actually recorded. The point is that the trust funds themselves do not hold money or other tangible assets.

What the trust fund securities, along with any other "credits" to the fund, do is represent "spending authority" for the programs involved. As long as there is a balance posted to a trust fund account, the Treasury Department has authority (that is either permanent in the law or periodically renewed by Congress) to continue to pay that program's bills.[67] But the money itself—the resources needed to make actual payments—comes from the receipts and public borrowing of the Government as a whole, through the U.S. Treasury.

In some instances, trust fund balances are based largely on how much revenues a program generates from the public (e.g., Social Security). As the revenues are received by the Treasury, the trust funds are credited with securities. Other times the balances are based only in small part on such revenues (e.g., Federal Civil Service Retirement). The revenues cause new securities to be posted to the trust fund account, but even larger postings are made to reflect Government "payments." Still other times,

---

[66] The Government could convert them into new marketable securities that it could then sell, but that is tantamount to the Government simply borrowing the money to pay the benefits, as it might borrow to cover any other form of spending it makes.

[67] In the case of entitlement programs such as Social Security and Medicare, the balances of their trust funds represent permanent spending authority. In the case of other programs, such as highway programs, the balances represent the amount available to be spent with *annual* or periodic approval by Congress.

the balances are based totally on Government "payments" (e.g., Military Retirement); the entire amount is *paper income*.

Thus, while the concept of trust funds and dedicated receipts connotes separate pots of money, the Federal Government really operates as a single financial entity. Revenues generated by trust fund programs are not handled separately, invested separately, or managed separately. Their operations are only separated from other accounts as bookkeeping entries. When money reaches the Treasury, it is commingled with other receipts, and the Treasury Department, after properly crediting the various accounts, uses whatever funds are available to pay its bills. Hence, the existence of a "trust fund" in the Treasury does not detach the program from the financial operations of the Government.

People sometimes argue that when a trust fund shows surplus income, this money is loaned to the Government, and the loan represents money the Government would otherwise have had to borrow from financial markets to cover other spending. In effect, the trust fund is presumed to have saved the Government from borrowing more from financial markets and from the interest expense such borrowing engenders.

In the case of some trust fund programs—in particular, Civil Service Retirement, Military Retirement and the SMI portion of Medicare—this is incorrect. Their receipts from the public are smaller than the expenditures they cause. But even when a trust fund program does run a cash surplus, as in the case with Social Security today, to conclude that these funds provide the Government with a substitute form of borrowing is speculative. There is no way of knowing whether over time a surplus leads to a reduction in Government borrowing from the public or whether it permits the Government to spend more or tax less.

A one time change that causes a trust fund program to have surplus receipts can be deemed to reduce Government borrowing from the public, in the absence of any offsetting fiscal policy. Fiscal policy, however, is not determined by any single program or change to it. It is the outcome of many actions taken by Congress. The resulting aggregate (unified) budget deficit today, and the borrowing from the public it causes, is a product of all the spending and taxation decisions made by Congresses and Administrations over many years. To say a surplus or a shortfall of Social Security taxes reduces or increases the deficit assumes that all other spending and taxation decisions have generally been made without any regard for Social Security's income and outgo, and vice versa.

Although the way Federal trust funds are labeled and portrayed leads many people to view them as separate money sources, the cash flow these programs create for the Government does not affect the financial markets and the economy independently of the rest of the Government.

What Are Federal Trust Funds & How Do They Work?

An account of the Treasury Department is designated as a "trust fund" by the Office of Management and Budget (OMB) in consultation with the Treasury Department, based on whether the law authorizes such a designation.[68] This differs from the private accounting concept of a "trust," which refers to the funds of one party held by a second party (the trustee) in a fiduciary (caretaker) capacity. For a Federal account, the term "trust fund" does not mean that the Federal Government is acting in a fiduciary capacity, it is merely a special account designation based in law.[69]

Federal trust funds typically have been established for programs that have very long-term purposes. Some were established with an understanding that in exchange for the public's paying certain new taxes or premiums, the Government would commit itself to finance some specific activity. Others do not require the payment of a specific tax, but still represent a long-term commitment of the Government to do something for a segment of the population. Yet a third group represents a blend, with partial funding coming from taxes or contributions paid by the affected population and the remaining funding coming from the Government. In some instances, trust funds were seen as a means of accumulating reserve spending authority for future Government spending. Others were intended to simply provide reserve spending authority to meet contingencies—no large buildup was intended.

Whatever their intended purposes, Federal trust funds are basically record keeping devices that account for the spending authority available for certain programs. Their "accounting" treatment by the Treasury is specified by law and it is important for internal bookkeeping purposes. Moreover, the existence of trust funds programs influences congressional

---

[68] U.S. General Accounting Office. *Budget Issues: Trust Funds and Their Relationships to the Federal Budget.* GAO/AFMD, Sept. 1988. In their report, GAO states that trust funds designations are sometimes inconsistently applied; that programs doing similar things in a similar manner are sometimes designated as trust funds and sometimes as accounts of the Treasury Department's general fund. They cite two similar programs: the Environmental Protection Agency's Hazardous Substance Superfund, which is designated a trust fund, and the Department of Energy's Nuclear Waste Fund, which is designated a "special fund."

[69] The distinction is made in U.S. Office of Management and Budget. *Historical Tables, Budget of the United States Government, Fiscal Year 1990.* Jan. 1989, pg. 14. There is one special account that the Government manages that may closely resemble a "trust" in the private accounting sense: the Federal Employees' Thrift Savings Plan (TSP). It is neither a trust fund nor an account in the general fund. The TSP is a special entity that establishes individual accounts owned by their contributors, with the owners capable of periodically shifting their funds among three investment options (Federal Government debt, common stock, and fixed income investments). Because of this feature, the TSP is not considered part of the Federal budget.

policy makers, Federal agencies, and the public in making economic decisions. However, whatever varied effects they have, trust funds are not "caretaker" entities of the Federal Government that hold and dispense funds. They are as much a part of Government as any other program and directly influence the overall financial condition of the Government.

Trust Fund Receipts & Spending

Federal trust fund programs can generate cash receipts from the public, such as from Social Security or gasoline taxes, or they may be simply credited with Government "payments" (i.e., income that does not reflect any receipts from the public) such as interest from the Government on their "holdings" of Government securities or Government "contributions" to the program involved. Most do generate at least some receipts from the public. Some, such as Social Security, Unemployment Insurance, Highway funding, and Medicare Health Insurance generate tax revenues that match or exceed their spending. However, two of the major ones generate receipts that only partially cover their expenditures, and another generates none. For instance, premiums paid by recipients cover only 27% of expenditures of the Medicare Supplemental Medical Insurance program. Civil service contributions similarly cover only 15% of the cost of the Civil Service Retirement system. Military Retirement requires no contributions at all from military personnel. These three programs are heavily or exclusively dependent on Government "payments".

Under current Government accounting rules, receipts from the public and Government "payments" are both counted and treated identically in Federal budget documents and individual reports of trust fund financial operations. They are combined to arrive at a figure for total income of a trust fund.

Table 1 on the following page shows a summary of income and outgo for the largest Federal trust funds under this traditional method of accounting, with income representing **both** receipts from the public and Government "payments." Table 2 shows only the receipts from the public and payments to the public for these programs.[70]

---

[70] There are forms of "paper outgo" as well, i.e., "payments" from one trust fund to another and "payments" from trust funds to the Treasury's general fund. They are reflected in table 1, but not in table 2. However, they account for a relatively small share of the aggregate difference in the figures reflected in the two tables—$5.4 billion in FY 1989.

TABLE 1
Total Income Credited to Trust Funds And
Total Outgo Recorded Against Trust Funds
FY 1989 ($ in billions)

Trust Fund	Total Income	Total Outgo	Difference
Social Security	286.1	233.6	52.5
Unemployment Insurance	25.5	18.7	6.8
Civil Service Retirement	48.8	29.2	19.6
Medicare	118.9	96.6	22.3
Military Retirement	34.0	20.2	13.8
Highway	16.9	14.5	2.4
All Other	30.2	24.0	6.2
Total	**$560.4**	**$436.8**	**$123.6**

TABLE 2
Receipts and Payments From and To The Public
For Trust Fund Programs
FY 1989 ($ in billions)

Trust Fund	Receipts from the Public	Payments to the Public	Difference
Social Security	267.4	232.5	34.9
Unemployment Insurance	22.0	16.8	5.2
Civil Service Retirement*	4.5	29.2	-24.7
Medicare	65.9	85.0	-18.6
Military Retirement	0	20.2	-20.2
Highway	15.6	14.5	1.1
All Other	10.3	5.1	5.2
Total	**$385.7**	**$403.3**	**-$17.6**

*Includes both the old Civil Service Retirement and disability system and the new Federal Employees Retirement System (FERS).

Note: In table 2 receipts from the public represent social insurance and other taxes. However, in conformity with budget accounting practices, payments to the public for trust fund programs are reduced here to take account of proprietary receipts (such as Medicare premiums) and "payments" from certain trust funds to the Treasury's general fund. See technical notes for details.

Source: Both tables were derived from data contained in the *Budget of the United States Government, Fiscal Year 1991*. January 1990.

Government "payments" to the trust funds account for most of the difference between the figures shown under the traditional accounting display (Table 1 above) and those in the display showing only the receipts and payments from and to the public (Table 2 above). In total, trust funds "received" about 28% of their FY 1989 total income, or $147 billion, in this form. While Congress has legislated these allocations for a variety of reasons to recognize and support the explicit goals and purposes of the programs, these "payments" do not represent receipts from the public and involve no exchange of money. They are bookkeeping entries, representing budgetary resources (authority to spend), having no direct effect on total Federal spending, revenues, or the deficit. Table 3 shows the various forms of these "payments" posted to the major trust fund accounts in FY 1989.

TABLE 3
"Government Payments" To Major Trust Funds
FY 1989 ($ in billions)

Trust Fund	Amount
Social Security	
Interest on Federal securities	$11.4
Government share of tax as employer	4.9
Special payments	2.4
Total Social Security	18.6
Unemployment Insurance	
Interest on Federal securities	3.3
Advances from the general fund	0.2
Total Unemployment Insurance	3.5
Civil Service Retirement*	
Interest on Federal securities	17.4
Government contribution as employer, including payment for past liabilities	26.9
Total Civil Service Retirement	44.3
Medicare (parts A & B combined)	
Interest on Federal securities	7.6
Government share of tax as employer	2.0
Government contribution to SMI & other payments	31.8
Total Medicare	41.4
Military Retirement	
Interest on Federal securities	5.6
Government contribution as employer, including payments for past liabilities	28.3
Total Military Retirement	33.9
Highway	
Interest on Federal securities	1.2
Total Highway	1.2

*See note at the bottom of table 2.
Source: Derived from the *Budget of the United States Government, Fiscal Year 1991*. January 1990.

Trust Fund Transactions with the Public

What happens to the money that trust fund programs do raise from the public? As with all other money taken in by the Government, it goes into the Treasury.[71] Does it remain there until needed to pay the trust fund program's bills? No, it goes out almost immediately to pay whatever obligations the Government has incurred. The Treasury Department, acting as the Government's banker, credits the proper trust fund account with the receipts. It typically does this by posting a non-marketable Federal security (a bill, note, or bond) to the account—in essence, providing the program with an IOU.[72] In some instances, it simply posts a "credit" (not a security), but this is a far less common practice. As expenditures are made for trust fund programs, the Treasury Department issues checks and reduces the amount of IOUs posted to the account—it reduces the trust fund's balance.

In other words, as in the case of almost all other Government financial operations, the actual money to and from the public for trust fund programs flows through the Treasury. The transactions are reflected as bookkeeping entries to the various trust fund accounts.

Chart 2 depicts the separation between the Treasury Department's handling of money and its accounting for trust fund transactions.

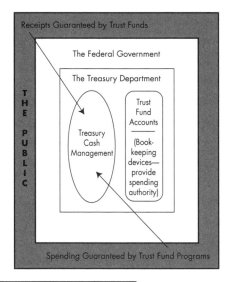

CHART 2
How the Treasury Manages Trust Fund Programs

---

[71] The Treasury is actually a generic term for cash management or depository accounts that the Government maintains with financial institutions across the country. Some 15,000 such institutions—mostly national banks—serve as conduits for money exchanged between the Government and the public. No money is exchanged between these institutions and Federal trust funds.

[72] The trust funds also may be credited with marketable Federal securities, however, this is done infrequently. As of the end of FY 1989, only about $15 billion of the holdings of Federal trust funds were in marketable form (out of total trust fund holdings of $660 billion).

The securities that the Federal trust funds hold represent a promise of future funding for the programs involved. Notably, they carry many of the same attributes as Federal securities sold to the public: a maturity date is set for each one, interest is accrued, and they count as part of the Federal debt. But they are not traded in the marketplace, and they do not fluctuate in value with rising and falling interest rates. Moreover, the interest they accrue, unlike securities held by the public, does not cause an exchange of economic resources. Although these interest "payments" are posted to the trust funds as income and as expenditures from the Treasury's general fund, they simply take the form of another non-marketable security (i.e., another IOU). And since no money is actually paid to anyone, this interest is excluded from the budget totals. However, if the trust funds were made independent of the Government, the interest they earn would be considered a budget expenditure. In this case, payments would flow from the Treasury, and money would have to be obtained to make them.[73]

Viewing the Federal Government as an extended family may be helpful. Assume that one bank account is used to collect all the family's income and to pay all its bills. The family keeps records of who has earned what and how much it will spend for each member. The gas company, the family doctor, and the grocer care about whether the family can pay its bills. The banker is concerned about whether the family can make its mortgage payments. Who earns the money or whether interest-bearing IOUs are exchanged between family members is really of no concern to them. To outsiders, it is the financial condition of the family as a whole that determines whether they will supply the family with goods and services and assist it financially.

In a similar vein, the gross Federal debt is comprised of two parts: 1) debt "held" internally by the Government (mostly by trust funds) and 2) debt held by the public.[74] When the Government sells new securities in the marketplace, it is asking individuals, businesses, and other Governments to lend it money. And by so doing, it is absorbing funds that would otherwise be available for investment in the financial markets. Internally issued debt to trust funds has no effect outside the Government. It is the portion of the Federal debt issued to and held by outsiders that influences the economy.

---

[73] It should be noted that if a trust fund program were taken out of the budget (i.e., placed "off budget") but not made independent of the Government, interest payments to the trust fund would show up as an expenditure in the budget totals, as would any other "Government payment" to a trust fund. In this situation, the budget would include expenditures that did not cause a flow of funds out of the Treasury.

[74] It should be noted that the Treasury Department can issue new debt only to the extent that the amount Federal debt outstanding at any given time stays within a limit established and periodically adjusted by Congress. This limit includes both debt held by the public and by Government accounts.

The Budget Impact Of Federal Trust Funds

The role of trust fund programs in the Federal budget and economy has expanded tremendously since World War II. Much of the increase is due to the growth of Social Security and other retirement programs (e.g., Civil Service and Military), and the creation in the mid-1960s of the Medicare program. Chart 3 on the following page shows these trends. Receipts from the public for trust fund programs increased steadily in the post war period as a percent of Gross National Product (GNP), while all other Federal receipts fell. By FY 1989, receipts for trust fund programs accounted for $4 out of every $10 collected by the Government (excluding borrowings from the public). Expenditures for trust fund programs also grew steadily as a percent of GNP, while all other Federal spending remained fairly constant. By FY 1989, trust fund programs accounted for $1 out of every $3 of Federal spending.

Share of Total Federal Receipts and Spending Caused by Trust Fund Programs, FY 1947-89 (Percent of GNP)

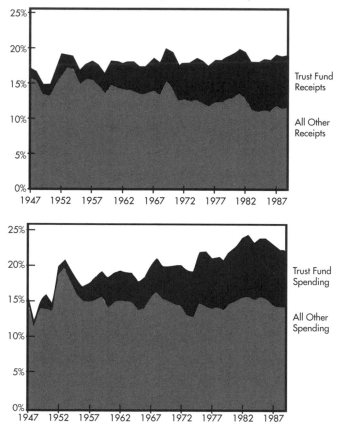

Source: Budget of the United States, FY 1991

Effect of Trust Fund Programs on the Federal Deficit

The unified budget deficit is the difference between total receipts and spending of the Government. It represents the amount of funds that must be raised by the Government through the sale of bonds, i.e., how much it must borrow. Said another way, only financial transactions with the public affect the amount of borrowing the Government must undertake in the financial markets. Internal transactions of the Government, such as the crediting of trust funds with interest, do not change governmental receipts and spending and therefore have no direct effect on how much the Government must borrow.[75]

Removing the internal transactions from the recorded trust fund income and outgo figures presents trust fund operations on the basis of what the Government receives and spends for them, i.e., a cash-flow basis. An excess of receipts from the public over spending would mean that they have run a cash "surplus"; an excess of spending over receipts indicates a cash "deficit."

Chart 4 shows the trends in the Government's cash flow for these programs from FY 1940 to 1989. Chart 5 shows the annual surpluses and deficits resulting from these trends. Together, they show a picture that is understandably very different from that usually described. Rather than running huge surpluses, these programs have been in chronic cash deficit since 1970. From 1940 to 1970, the surplus years outnumbered the deficit ones eighteen to twelve; however, the largest of these surpluses occurred during World War II, or immediately thereafter. Trust funds consistently ran surpluses from 1940 to 1948, and again during the early- to mid-1950s, but ran deficits from 1957 to 1966. Since 1969, the last year the Government ran a unified budget surplus, trust fund programs ran a surplus in only one year (1970). On a cash-flow basis, even Social Security experienced deficits in all but five of the years from 1957 through 1984. (See Tables A.1 and A.2 in the Appendix.)

It frequently is asserted that because trust funds generally are showing surpluses in their individual accounts, the Federal deficit is caused by everything else the Government does. On a cash-flow basis both parts of this assertion are misleading. First, as previously shown, for many years trust fund programs overall have not raised as much revenue from the

---

[75] The total Federal expenditure figure shown in budget documents (outlays) represents only payments to the public. All internal accounting transactions are "netted out" of that figure, since they do not cause the Treasury Department to write a check, pay cash, or make an electronic transfer of funds from the Government to the public. While internal transactions are displayed in individual accounts of the budget—most frequently in the form of Government "payments" to them—offsetting adjustments are made in arriving at the budget totals.

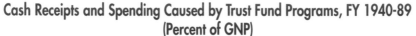

Cash Receipts and Spending Caused by Trust Fund Programs, FY 1940-89 (Percent of GNP)

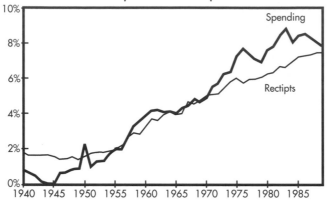

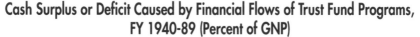

Cash Surplus or Deficit Caused by Financial Flows of Trust Fund Programs, FY 1940-89 (Percent of GNP)

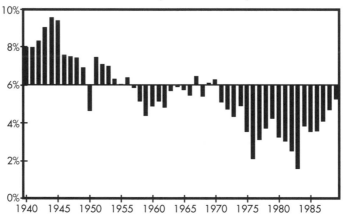

Source: Budget of the United States, FY 1991

public as they have spent—they ran deficits. This means that on a cash-flow basis, the rest of the Government—i.e., the non trust fund part—has not been exclusively responsible for Federal borrowing and the resulting build-up of debt held by the public. Second, the rest of the Government is currently running a surplus if interest on debt held by the public is excluded. Although this interest is often attributed to the non-trust fund part of the budget, trust fund programs—by running cash flow deficits—also can be considered responsible for the current level of publicly-held debt. Therefore, both trust fund and non-trust fund deficits have contributed to the current level of Government interest expenditures.

Table 4 represents the Federal deficits over the past decade in three parts: 1) trust fund transactions to and from the public, 2) other Government transactions to and from the public, and 3) interest payments to the public. The first column shows the total Federal deficits. The second column shows surpluses or deficits for trust fund programs on a cash-flow basis. The third column shows surpluses or deficits for the rest of the Government on a cash-flow basis (excluding interest). The fourth column shows interest expenditures on the publicly-held debt (what is often referred to as "net" interest).

| | | | Other | |
Fiscal Year	Total Deficit	Trust Funds Cash-flow Surplus/Deficit	Government Cash-flow Surplus/Deficit	Net Interest
1980	-73.8	-36.4	+15.1	-52.5
1981	-78.9	-43.6	+33.4	-68.7
1982	-127.9	-54.1	+11.1	-85.0
1983	-207.1	-72.4	-45.6	-89.9
1984	-185.3	-39.1	-35.1	-111.1
1985	-212.3	-47.9	-34.9	-129.4
1986	-221.2	-50.8	-34.4	-136.0
1987	-149.7	-41.4	+30.2	-138.6
1988	-155.1	-30.3	+27.0	-151.7
1989	-151.9	-17.6	+34.7	-169.1

TABLE 4
Federal Deficits, Fiscal Year 1989
($ in billions)

Effect of Trust Fund Programs on the Federal Debt

A rise in trust fund holdings, generated either from excess receipts from the public or Government "payments," increases the reported gross Federal debt. However, the portion of the debt held by trust funds does not represent a financial claim on the Government by anyone outside of the Government. A trust fund program may entitle people to certain benefits; but it is this entitlement to which people have claims, rather than the Government's accumulation of internal IOUs. Moreover, debt held by trust funds does not represent a resource that the Government can draw upon to fulfill any obligations incurred on behalf of trust fund programs. Therefore, building trust fund reserves and adding to debt held by Government accounts today does not *by itself* reduce future budget deficits. In fact, such action may increase future deficits (and hence raise the debt held by the public), since this internal debt is basically spending authority that may be available to trust fund programs without further congressional action.

Debt held by the public, on the other hand, represents financial claims by domestic households, businesses, and foreign entities on the Federal Government. For economic analysis, it is the debt held by the public, not the gross debt, that is relevant.

TABLE 5
Federal Debt Held By Trust Funds and the Public
November 30, 1989
($ in billions)

Trust Fund	Holdings
Social Security	$155.7
Medicare	98.5
Civil Service Retirement	216.3
Military Retirement	66.1
Unemployment Insurance	45.3
Highways	16.4
All other	66.4
Total trust fund holdings	659.7
Other Federal account holdings	25.7
Federal debt held by the public	2,260.7*
Gross Federal debt	2,946.1

*Includes $19.2 billion in net discounts on public debt securities.

Source: Derived from the *Monthly Treasury Statement*, November 30, 1989. For a more detailed summary, see table A.3 in the appendix.

CHART 6
Federal Debt Held By Trust Funds
As a Percent of Gross Federal Debt
November 30, 1989

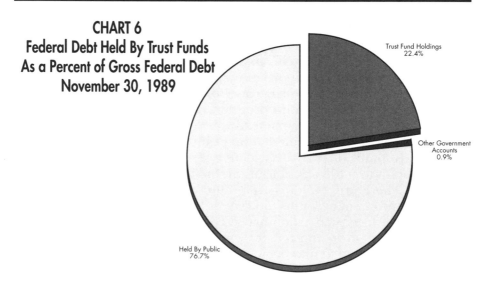

Trust Fund Holdings
22.4%

Other Government
Accounts
0.9%

Held By Public
76.7%

Conclusion

Federal trust funds generally are perceived as independent or quasi-independent financial entities. In reality, however, they are not. Their existence is based on Federal laws and policies; their programs are administered by agencies of the executive branch; their special taxes and premiums are collected by the Treasury Department and deposited in the U.S. Treasury, and their holdings are, for the most part, Federal non-marketable securities. More importantly, their financial operations are not separate transactions in the financing of the Government, and therefore, they are relevant in the formulation of overall budget and economic policies—their income and outgo to and from the Government matter. If they were considered irrelevant, the Government would be ignoring 39% of its revenues and 35% of its spendings.

A summary look at the Federal budget suggests that trust funds are more than carrying their load and that all other accounts are "overdrawn," but the formal presentation and accounting reflected in the budget is only one way of examining the data. Ignoring internal credits to trust funds—credits that are important for budget formulation and the Government's allocation of spending authority—reveals that trust funds have had cash-flow deficits with the public for many years. Even Social Security, which is currently running cash-flow surpluses, had cash-flow deficits for many years. If the overall Federal deficits are not completely caused by the non-trust fund part of Federal activities, then the resulting build-up of Federal debt held by the public and subsequent interest on that debt also are not exclusively attributable to the non-trust fund portion of Federal activities. And if interest expenditures are excluded from both trust fund and non-trust fund expenditures, the non-trust fund portion of Federal activities currently shows a surplus. The point is that, on a cash-flow basis, no one program or sector of the Government is responsible for deficits and the accumulation of Federal debt held by the public. It is the Government's operations in the aggregate that matter in determining the deficit.

The buildup of trust fund holdings adds to the gross Federal debt figure, but that buildup simply reflects the Government's holding of IOUs to itself. What really matters to the economy is the change in Federal debt held by the public. This is what has a market impact, affects interest rates, and causes expenditures from the Treasury for debt service. Debt service to a trust fund, although important for internal allocation purposes, is simply a ledger entry. Debt held by the public reflects the accumulation of unified budget deficits—or how much more overall the Government spent than it received in revenues—and interest payments on this portion of the debt require the Government to acquire and spend real resources.

Federal trust fund programs do not by themselves affect national savings, and their holdings do not necessarily represent national savings. They are claims *on* the Government, not *for* the Government. Their value depends on the Government's ability to draw money from the economy to honor them when program obligations are presented for payment. For their financial health, trust fund programs are just as dependent on the financial health of the Government as is any other Government program. The financial health of the Government comes from health of the economy and the Government's ability to draw resources from it. Many economists contend that greater national savings is important for the long-run health of the economy. Government borrowing from the public, however—for whatever reason—can run counter to that objective. Government borrowing takes funds from the financial markets, and the concern is that it limits the amount of potential private sector investment, causes interest rates to be higher than they otherwise would be, and makes the U.S. dependent upon foreign investment capital. Reducing this borrowing—i.e., the aggregate (or unified budget) deficits—is potentially one way that the Government can contribute to national savings.

Summary

The treatment of trust fund programs in the Federal budget is complicated and confusing. As a result, the impact of these programs on the financial condition of the Government is often misunderstood. Perhaps the biggest misconception today is that these programs are offsetting the Federal deficit by $124 billion and there by masking the true size of the deficit. Although attention has been drawn to the large Social Security trust fund surpluses, trust fund programs overall actually have been running cash deficits.

This aggregate cash deficit is not at first visible. Official budget documents show that overall income credited to Federal trust funds in FY 1989 exceeded the spending posted against them by $124 billion—an apparent surplus. However, what is commonly called trust fund income is not just the amount of receipts from the public generated by these programs. Trust funds also receive credits from the Treasury, what might be called *paper income*. It can be misleading to treat this *paper income* like cash when assessing the Federal deficit, which is the gap between total cash income and total expenditures in any given year. When only receipts from the public for trust fund programs—cash income—are compared to Federal spending for them, a deficit emerges; spending exceeded receipts by $18 billion.

Moreover, this is not an aberration. On the whole, trust fund programs ran deficits in their cash transactions with the public in nineteen of the last twenty-one years. Even Social Security went through a long period when its expenditures exceeded its revenues. And even Social Security receives paper credits that make its current surpluses appear larger.

Because the official or traditional approach to accounting for Federal trust funds shows them to be running surpluses, the blame for the Federal deficit frequently is placed on the rest of the Government. Thus, all the Government's borrowing is usually attributed to its non-trust fund activities, and the interest expense or debt service is generally considered part of this category. However, because trust funds have regularly run operating or cash-flow deficits, they too, can be considered responsible for the Government's need to borrow—i.e., for increasing the debt and the resulting interest expense. If interest expense were not included in the "rest of the Government" category of the budget, this category would show a *surplus*. The point is that no one program or sector of the Government is responsible for deficits and the resulting buildup of Federal debt. The Government borrows as it needs to, for whatever obligations it has to meet.

Trust fund programs are a major part of what the Government does. In FY 1989 they generated 39%—some $386 billion—of the Government's tax revenues and were responsible for 35%—$403 billion—of its spending. If deficit reduction efforts are based on the erroneous assumption that trust funds overall are *generating actual cash surpluses* for the Government, the result may be to distort the process by which Congress determines fiscal priorities—what Congress wants to spend money on and how it will raise the resources to do so.

Appendix

TABLE A.1
Receipts from the Public, Outlays, & Surplus/Deficit for All Federal Trust Funds Combined, FY 1940-1989
($ in millions)

Fiscal Year	Receipts From The Public	Payments To The Public	Surplus/ Deficit (-)
1940	1,678	721	953
1941	1,814	671	1,143
1942	2,297	620	1,677
1943	2,883	184	2,699
1944	3,279	*	3,279
1945	3,281	*	3,281
1946	2,935	1,234	1,701
1947	3,144	1,445	1,699

Fiscal Year	Receipts From The Public	Payments To The Public	Surplus/ Deficit (-)
1948	3,746	1,932	1,814
1949	3,572	2,333	1,240
1950	4,114	5,888	-1,774
1951	5,440	3,077	2,363
1952	6,188	4,257	1,931
1953	6,546	4,653	1,893
1954	6,952	6,313	640
1955	7,611	7,457	154
1956	9,025	8,119	906
1957	11,176	11,461	-285
1958	12,959	14,836	-1,877
1959	13,502	17,348	-3,846
1960	16,910	19,729	-2,819
1961	19,276	21,463	-2,187
1962	20,049	23,283	-3,234
1963	23,099	23,921	-822
1964	25,504	25,790	-286
1965	25,957	26,706	-749
1966	29,492	31,501	-2,009
1967	37,089	35,148	1,941
1968	38,346	40,798	-2,452
1969	43,667	42,996	671
1970	49,733	48,099	1,634
1971	53,449	58,075	-4,626
1972	58,568	65,694	-7,126
1973	69,563	79,988	-10,425
1974	82,207	89,775	-7,568
1975	91,725	110,220	-18,495
1976	97,153	130,098	-32,945
1977	114,427	142,000	-27,573
1978	129,329	153,771	-24,442
1979	147,919	168,933	-21,014
1980	166,623	203,065	-36,442
1981	189,566	233,177	-43,611
1982	209,269	263,346	-54,077
1983	220,347	292,772	-72,425
1984	256,889	295,988	-39,099
1985	285,685	333,550	-47,865
1986	304,578	355,356	-50,778
1987	324,692	366,052	-41,566
1988	357,425	387,754	-30,642
1989	385,740	403,296	-17,556

*Denotes negative outlays.

Source: Derived from Budget of the United States, Fiscal Year 1991. Jan. 1990.

TABLE A.2
Social Security Receipts from the Public, Outlays, and Surplus/Deficit, FY 1940-1989
($ in millions)

Fiscal Year	Receipts From The Public	Payments To The Public	Surplus/ Deficit (-)
1940	550	29	522
1941	688	91	597
1942	896	137	759
1943	1,130	176	964
1944	1,292	217	1,075
1945	1,310	267	1,043
1946	1,238	358	880
1947	1,459	467	992
1948	1,616	559	1,057
1949	1,690	661	1,030
1950	2,106	784	1,322
1951	3,120	1,568	1,552
1952	3,594	2,067	1,527
1953	4,097	2,717	1,380
1954	4,589	3,364	1,2226
1955	5,081	4,437	544
1956	6,425	5,485	940
1957	6,789	6,666	123
1958	8,049	8,221	-172
1959	8,296	9,737	-1,441
1960	10,641	11,609	-968
1961	12,109	12,475	-366
1962	12,271	14,367	-2,096
1963	14,175	15,790	-1,615
1964	16,366	16,622	-256
1965	16,723	17,463	-740
1966	19,085	20,701	-1,616
1967	24,401	21,726	2,675
1968	24,917	23,864	1,063
1969	28,953	27,298	1,655
1970	33,459	30,270	3,189
1971	35,845	35,873	-28
1972	39,907	40,158	-251
1973	46,084	49,090	-3,006
1974	53,925	55,867	-1,942
1975	62,458	64,658	-2,200
1976	66,389	73,899	-7,510
1977	76,817	85,060	-8,243
1978	85,391	93,851	-8,470
1979	97,994	104,073	-6,079
1980	113,209	118,559	-5,350

Fiscal Year	Receipts From The Public	Payments To The Public	Surplus/ Deficit (-)
1981	130,176	139,584	-9,408
1982	143,467	155,964	-12,497
1983	147,320	170,305	-22,985
1984	168,350	177,677	-9,327
1985	189,540	188,258	1,282
1986	203,786	198,598	5,188
1987	216,709	207,352	9,357
1988	244,882	219,340	25,542
1989	267,439	232,543	34,897

Source: Derived from *Budget of the United States, Fiscal Year 1991*. Jan. 1990.

TABLE A.3
Federal Debt Held by Federal Trust Funds
November 30, 1989
($ in billions)

Trust Fund	Amount
Old Age and Survivors Insurance	147.9
Disability Insurance	7.8
Hospital Insurance	82.6
Supplementary Medical insurance	10.9
Civil Service Retirement	216.3
Military Retirement	66.1
Unemployment Insurance	45.3
Highways	16.4
Airport & Airways	13.1
Railroad Retirement	8.6
All Other	44.7
TOTAL TRUST FUND HOLDINGS	**659.7**

Source: Table prepared by CRS based on data from the *Monthly Treasury Statement,* November 30, 1989.

TABLE A.4
Total Interest, Interest Paid to the Public, and Interest Credited to Government Accounts FY — 1962-1988
($ in billions)

Fiscal Year	Total	Public	Government Accounts	
			Trust Funds	Other
1962	9.5	7.9	1.4	0.2
1963	10.3	8.7	1.5	0.1
1964	11.0	9.2	1.6	0.2
1965	11.8	9.8	1.8	0.2
1966	12.6	10.4	1.9	0.2
1967	14.2	11.6	2.3	0.3
1968	15.6	12.6	2.7	0.3
1969	17.6	14.1	3.1	0.4
1970	20.0	15.6	3.8	0.6
1971	21.6	16.3	4.8	0.5
1972	22.5	16.6	5.1	0.7
1973	24.8	18.5	5.4	0.9
1974	30.0	22.4	6.6	1.1
1975	33.5	24.7	7.7	1.1
1976	37.7	28.7	7.8	1.2
1977	42.6	33.0	8.0	1.6
1978	49.3	39.2	8.5	1.7
1979	60.3	48.3	9.9	2.2
1980	75.2	60.4	12.0	2.8
1981	96.0	78.9	13.8	3.3
1982	117.5	97.7	16.1	3.8
1983	128.9	107.7	17.1	4.2
1984	154.1	129.0	20.4	4.8
1985	179.4	148.2	26.2	5.0
1986	191.5	155.4	27.9	8.3
1987	197.1	157.5	35.0	4.6
1988	216.5	169.8	41.8	4.9

Source: Derived from the *Budget of the U.S. Government, Fiscal Year 1990, Historical Tables.* Jan. 1989. U.S. Treasury. *Treasury Bulletin,* summer issue, Sept. 1989; *Final Monthly Treasury Statement of Receipts and Outlays for FY 1989.* September 1989.

TECHNICAL NOTES

The information on trust fund receipts and spending in this paper is from various documents released with the President's FY 1990 and 1991 budgets in January 1989 and 1990. Most important to this analysis is differentiating between total trust fund income and outgo, as reported in these budget documents, and receipts from the public and outlays made to the public. This was done using only the published information; therefore, some of the idiosyncrasies of Federal accounting may affect the accuracy of trust fund programs' transactions with the public reflected in this paper.

Trust fund "income" and "outgo" in this paper represent the figures shown in traditional analyses of trust fund transactions. Income is the amount credited to the trust fund over a year; outgo is the amount debited from the trust fund. These figures, however, do not represent the Government's transactions with the public that are generated by trust fund programs (that is, the cash flow to and from the Government). The transactions with the public are not reported as such in official budget documents but must be derived from the detailed information on trust fund activities shown therein.

Definitions of Receipts and Outlays

The Federal deficit is the difference between the Government's revenues received from the public and payments made to the public. A surplus or deficit for trust fund programs can similarly be defined as the difference between receipts from the public and payments to the public.

In the Federal budget, receipts from the public are accounted for in two ways: (1) as tax receipts and (2) as proprietary receipts. Tax receipts represent payments to the Government resulting from the exercise of the Federal Government's sovereign power to tax; that is, they represent compulsory payments from the public. Proprietary receipts are payments from the public for various "business activities" of the Government. For example, proceeds from sales of Government property and user fees are proprietary receipts. Medicare premiums for SMI similarly are considered proprietary and not tax receipts, since the program's recipients voluntarily enroll with the Government for SMI coverage.

The Federal budget accounts for tax receipts as "governmental receipts," and most analyses shown in the budget for total Federal receipts include only tax receipts. Likewise, the tables that show "trust fund receipts from the public" in this paper represent only the revenue raised through taxation. Proprietary receipts are accounted for in the Federal budget as an offset to outlays. (That is, rather than being added to total income to the Government, proprietary receipts are subtracted from total outgo from the Government.) In this case, trust fund outlays represent net payments to the public (spending minus proprietary receipts). While such an accounting may complicate an analysis that attempts to highlight income from and outgo to the public, the lack of a published historical series on trust fund proprietary receipts requires this report to conform with standard Federal accounting by having proprietary receipts reduce outlays. It should be noted that the accounting of proprietary receipts as either additions to the receipts-side of the budget or a subtraction from the spending-side of the budget does not affect the resulting deficit figure.

Trust Fund Receipts and Outlays

Trust fund tax receipts from the public were identified by using information from the historical tables section of the *Budget of the United States, Fiscal Year 1991* and from the budget *Appendices* for various years. Trust fund tax receipts represent:

1. Social insurance taxes and contributions and excise taxes identified as going to trust funds in Table 2.4 (p. A-288 to A-289).
2. Trust fund amounts included in "Other Receipts" in Table 2.5 (p. A-291).
3. Corporate income taxes for trust funds identified in the footnote of Table 2.1 (p. A-285).
4. Income taxes to the Medicare SMI trust fund for catastrophic health insurance (FY 1989 only), shown on Table 13.1 (p. A-329).

In addition, the trust fund tax receipt information shown in this report includes receipts from the income taxation of Social Security and railroad retirement benefits. In official budget documents, these taxes are receipts to the general fund and are then "transferred" (credited) to Social Security.

Trust fund net outlays (payments to the public minus proprietary receipts) are somewhat more complicated to derive because of the off-budget status of Social Security and the lack of a historical series on intragovernmental accounting transactions from trust funds to the Government's general fund. However, interfund payments from trust funds to the general fund are generally small; thus any errors in identifying these transactions would not substantially affect the data shown in this report.

In the historical data series, intragovernmental receipts to Social Security (for interest, for the Federal employer share of the tax, etc.) are deducted from the total off-budget outlay amount. Thus, the off-budget total outlay figures are smaller that total Social Security payments to the public. Social Security payments to the public are gross Social Security outlays without deduction for intragovernmental receipts.

Interfund transactions from non-Social Security and Medicare trust funds to the general fund were obtained from the *status of the funds* schedules in the FY 1991 budget and the *Special Analyses* accompanying earlier years' budgets. They were obtained from the early 1970s forward, when certain trust funds (for example, Unemployment Insurance), began borrowing "budget authority" credits from the general fund and repaying them. It is possible that some interfund transactions from non-Social Security and Medicare trust funds to the general fund were omitted from the calculations shown in this report.

References

U.S. GENERAL ACCOUNTING OFFICE. Budget issues: trust funds and their relationship to the Federal budget. GAO/AFMD, Sept. 1988.

U.S. CONGRESS. SENATE. Committee on the Budget. Social Security, Medicare, and the unified budget. CRS Report for Congress No. 99-83, 99th Congress, 1st Session. Prepared by the Congressional Research Service, Library of Congress. Washington, U.S. Government Printing Office, 1985. p. 112.

U.S. LIBRARY OF CONGRESS. Congressional Research Service. The Social Security surplus: a discussion of some of the issues. CRS Report for Congress No. 88-709 EPW, by David Koitz. Washington, 1988. p. 48.

U.S. PRESIDENT'S COMMISSION ON BUDGET CONCEPTS. Staff papers and other materials reviewed by the President's commission. Washington, U.S. Government Printing Office, 1967. p. 512.

PENNER, RUDOLPH G. Social Security off-budget: expensive idea. Wall Street Journal, March 29, 1989.

PUT NOT YOUR TRUST IN CONGRESS. The Economist, Nov. 11, 1989.

APPENDIX B

LEGISLATION & AGENCIES

State Agency

California State Prison Industry Authority

The California State Prison Industry Authority (PIA) is a "quasi state" (non tax-supported) agency that was established by State Statutes and operates enterprises using state inmates. A very unique and profitable recycling program has resulted from an arrangement with Folsom City and the PIA. The City of Folsom pays the PIA a per-ton processing fee to handle all of its municipal solid waste. In accordance with a service agreement, revenues generated from the sale of the sorted materials belong to the City of Folsom. The city collects all of the waste from its customers as it normally does and trucks it to an inmate-built material recovery facility next to the prison where the garbage is sorted by the prisoners. There are approximately one hundred prisoners working eight-hour shifts to sort the one hundred tons of garbage per day. These prisoners are minimum custody offenders who have violated their parole and earn an average 50¢ per hour wage with a day off their prison term for every day they work. Prisoners sort out all of the recyclables and the organic residue is currently being composted. Plans are in the works to build an anaerobic digestor that will produce methane gas that can be used to power a fuel cell and the electricity will be sold to the Sacramento Municipal Utility District.

In addition to the electricity, there are other benefits, which include:

➤ Work skills, responsibility, and the work ethic is taught to the prisoners.

➤ Revenues from the sale of the recyclable material can help offset the cost of incarceration.

➤ Meets and exceeds the State's mandate to reduce the garbage being buried in landfills.

➤ Stabilizes landfill costs by extending lives of existing facilities.

➤ Prisoners are beginning to pay back their debt to society.

For more information:
> Karen Hall
> Prison Industries Manager
> State of California Prison Industry Authority
> 560 E. Natoma Street
> Folsom, CA 95630
> (916) 358-2656

Trade Legislation

1934 Foreign Trade Zone Act

The Foreign Trade Zone Act of 1934 was designed to help offset the negative effects of imports by allowing corporations who employ American workers to add value to these imported goods without tariffs. These value added goods could enter these foreign trade zones without tariff. If no value were added to goods that entered the United States through the free trade zone, these goods would be subject to a tariff as if they did not enter the foreign trade zone at all. On the other hand, if goods entered into these foreign trade zones were stored, displayed, broken up, repackaged, distributed, sorted, graded, cleaned, assembled, mixed with foreign or domestic goods, or manipulated in any form, and then entered the United States, the tariff imposed on these manipulated goods would be less than it would be if it was directly imported into the United States. If these manipulated products were re-exported from the foreign trade zone, they would not be subject to any tariffs at all.[76]

---

[76] *United States Code*, 1988, Volume 7, p. 868.

GATT

GATT was started in 1947 and is an acronym for General Agreement On Tariffs and Trade. The latest version is commonly known as the Uruguay Round and it has twenty-two thousand pages of agreements and related tariff schedules. This latest version was signed in December of 1994. The World Trade Organization (WTO) administers the rules set forth by GATT and can authorize sanctions against violators of GATT. The goal of this document is to cut tariffs and bring trading nations down to a level playing field. One example of bringing everyone down to a level playing field regards patents. Prior to June of 1995, patent rights would expire seventeen years from the issue date of a patent in the United States. As a result of GATT, patent rights expire twenty years from the application date of the patent. Depending on how long (on average it can take three years) it takes to get a patent, this new ruling may or may not be in the favor of the patent designer. Regardless of its benefits to the patent applicant, GATT is attempting to bring everyone down to a level playing field. Patents is one method, tariffs is another.

Some tariffs will be completely eliminated and some import tariffs for the one hundred twenty-four participating nations will be lowered by an average of 38%.[77] There are new rules and laws pertaining to foreign investment in manufacturing, trade, and investment in services, protections for intellectual property (patents, copyrights, and trade marks), and the reduction of "technical" barriers to trade, i.e., consumer, environmental, and workplace safety regulations. Closely related to the "technical" barriers to trade is the food safety section of GATT. An international organization called Codex Alimentarius Commission (commonly referred to as Codex) exists to promulgate a long list of standards regarding food safety.[78]

NAFTA

NAFTA was created in 1994 and is an acronym for North America Free Trade Agreement. It is an approximately two thousand page document designed to eliminate tariffs and other trade obstacles over a fifteen year period between Canada, Mexico, and the United States. By lowering tariffs and trade barriers, NAFTA's goal is to encourage free trade and investment among these nations to bring about a higher standard of living for everyone involved. It is supposed to create jobs in Mexico and in the United States. By doing so, it was hoped to become an aid to limiting or stopping illegal immigration.

---

[77] Facts and figures form Hendricks, David. "Will GATT affect NAFTA? The Answer is: Yes, GATT will Make NAFTA Work Better," *Free Trade News*, Volume 01, Issue 09, 1995, p. 20.
[78] Weissman, Robert. "Trading The Future Away," *Environmental Action*, Winter 1995, pp. 31-35.

Internal Revenue Codes §§921-927 and §§991-996: FSC and DISC

FSC is an acronym for Foreign Sales Corporation and DISC is an acronym for Domestic International Sales Corporation. The Foreign Sales Corporation is described in Internal Revenue Codes §921, §922, §923, §924, §925, §926, and §927 and the Domestic International Sales Corporation is described in Internal Revenue Codes §991, §992, §993, §994, §995, and §996. Both the Foreign Sales Corporation and the Domestic International Sales Corporation receive substantial income tax breaks for exporting U.S.-made equipment and U.S.-grown crops. This tax benefit also extends to companies involved in construction projects outside the United States that render engineering and architectural services.[79]

Title 49 Code Of Federal Regulations Chapter V, Part 583: Automobile Parts Content Labeling

This code was designed to help consumers make more informed choices in their automobile purchases by providing them with information about the value of the U.S./Canadian and foreign parts content of each vehicle. This label is supposed to be attached to every new vehicle manufactured on or after October 1, 1994. This label is to have six basic components to it. These components include:

1. U.S./Canadian parts content
2. Major sources of foreign parts content
3. Final assembly point
4. Country origin of engine
5. Country origin of the transmission
6. Explanatory note[80]

Energy Legislation

1988 Alternative Motor Fuels Act

The Alternative Motor Fuels Act of 1988 was designed to help develop the alternative fuel market in the United States. This law was designed to encourage the widespread use of methanol, ethanol, and natu-

---

[79] Sanderson, Gregory. "Commercialization of Biomass Energy Projects: Outline for Maximizing Use of Valuable Tax Credits and Incentives," *BioEnergy '94, Technical Papers*, Volume 2, pp. 417-418.

[80] *Title 49 Code Of Federal Regulations* Chapter V, Part 583, pp. 725-727.

ral gas as fuels for vehicles. There are three sections of this law that are important in the development and demonstration of alternative-fueled vehicles. Those sections are Section 400AA, 400BB, and 400CC. Section 400AA encourages the use of alternative fuels in light-duty Federal vehicles by allocating money for that purpose. Section 400BB does the same thing, but applies to heavy-duty truck applications. Section 400CC provides a budget for alternative-fueled urban buses.[81]

1992 Energy Policy Act

The 1992 Energy Policy Act was designed to help save energy without sacrificing economic growth or the safety of the environment. This act redirects the Department Of Energy's emphasis into fossil fuels, renewable energy, nuclear energy, and energy conservation. This act has many provisions but the ones important to this book include the following:

➤ Mandates Federal Government to spearhead the use of alternative fuel vehicles and energy efficiency.

➤ Provisions to support electric and electric-hybrid vehicles.

➤ Mandates Federal agencies to improve energy efficiency in the buildings they own or lease.

➤ Assistance to U.S. manufacturers who wish to export advanced energy technologies.

➤ Tax provisions for fuels and electrical generation from renewable energy sources.[82]

Alcohol Fuels Incentives

INTERNAL REVENUE CODE §4041, §4081, & §4091: EXCISE TAX EXEMPTION FOR ALCOHOL FUELS

These internal revenue codes were put into place during the Carter Administration to induce substitution of ethanol and methanol for gasoline. Since then, the 1992 Energy Policy Act amended these codes. The current code gives a 5.45¢ per gallon excise tax exemption for any gasoline blend with at least a 10% mixture of alcohol (that is not produced from petroleum, natural gas, or coal). This 5.45¢ per gallon is being financed from the Highway trust fund and the Leaking Underground Storage trust fund. The amounts that are not deposited to those two trust funds are 5.4¢ per gallon and 5¢ per gallon respectively.[83]

[81] *United States Code Congressional And Administrative News*, Volume 5, 1988, pp. 3029-3031.
[82] Williams, Dan R. and Good, Larry. *Guide To The Energy Policy Act Of 1992*, Fairmont Press, 1994, pp. 20-22.
[83] Sanderson, Gregory. "Commercialization of Biomass Energy Projects: Outline for Maximizing Use of Valuable Tax Credits and Incentives," *BioEnergy '94, Technical Papers*, Volume 2, p. 415.

INTERNAL REVENUE CODE §40, ALCOHOL FUELS CREDITS

Internal Revenue Code §40 is a result of the 1980 Windfall Profit Tax Act and the Omnibus Budget Reconciliation Act of 1990. There are three types of credits available to producers of alcohol for fuel under Internal Revenue Code §40. Those three credits are:

1. Alcohol Mixture Credit
2. Alcohol Production Credit
3. Small Ethanol Producer Credit

The alcohol mixture credit and the alcohol production credit is a result of the 1980 Windfall Profit Tax Act while the small ethanol producer credit is a result of the Omnibus Reconciliation Act of 1990.

The alcohol mixture credit was amended by the 1992 Energy Policy Act and applies to methanol and ethanol that is not produced from petroleum, natural gas, or coal. Methanol receives a 60¢ per gallon credit if the methanol is at least 190 proof and 45¢ per gallon if the proof is between 150 to 190. In the case of ethanol with at least 190 proof, the alcohol mixture credit is 54¢ per gallon and the lower 150 to 190 proof ethanol will receive only 40¢ per gallon credit.

The alcohol production credit has been amended by the 1992 Energy Policy Act and applies to methanol and ethanol that is not produced from petroleum, natural gas, or coal. Methanol and ethanol will receive 60¢ per gallon if the alcohol has at least 190 proof. When the proof is between 150 and 190, the credit available is only 45¢ per gallon for both ethanol and methanol.

The small ethanol producer credit has not been amended by the 1992 Energy Policy Act. The credit is for small ethanol producers who produce less than 30 million gallons per year. In order to qualify for this credit, the ethanol cannot be produced from petroleum, natural gas, or coal. The credit is 10¢ per gallon for the first fifteen million gallons produced.[84]

---

[84] Sanderson, Gregory. "Commercialization of Biomass Energy Projects: Outline for Maximizing Use of Valuable Tax Credits and Incentives," *BioEnergy '94, Technical Papers*, Volume 2, p. 415.

INTERNAL REVENUE CODE §179A, SPECIAL DEDUCTION FOR ALCOHOL & CLEAN FUELS PROPERTY

Internal Revenue Code §179A resulted from the implementation of the 1992 Energy Policy Act which gives a special tax deduction for equipment to store and dispense clean fuels in addition to the purchase of new vehicles or retrofit of used vehicles that burns either ethanol or methanol or some other clean burning fuel. A "qualified clean-fuel" vehicle is one that uses any fuel that is at least 85% ethanol, methanol, or compressed natural gas, liquefied petroleum gas and hydrogen. The maximum deduction is $2,000 for cars, $5,000 for light trucks, and $50,000 for heavy trucks or buses. A maximum deduction of $100,000 can be obtained for qualifying refueling equipment. Qualifying refueling equipment includes natural gas compressing equipment that is located on site and dispenses the fuel into the vehicle.[85]

Electrical Generation Incentives

INTERNAL REVENUE CODE §45 RENEWABLE BIOMASS ELECTRICITY CREDIT

Internal Revenue Code §45 is a result of the 1992 Energy Policy Act. This tax code gives the producer of electricity from wind or "closed-loop biomass" an income tax credit of 1.5¢ per kilowatt hour of electricity (adjusted for inflation). Closed-loop biomass is defined by the Internal Revenue Service as any organic material derived from a plant that was for the sole purpose of producing electricity. In order to qualify for this income tax credit, a "qualified facility" must be put into service before July 1, 1999. A "qualified facility" is defined as a facility that uses closed-loop biomass or wind to generate electricity. To qualify for the income tax credit, an existing power plant can be converted to operate on either wind or closed-loop biomass.[86]

D.O.E. RENEWABLE ENERGY PRODUCTION INCENTIVE

Title 42 United States Code 13317 is titled The Renewable Energy Production Incentive. It gives a *payment* of 1.5¢ per kilowatt hour (ad-

---

[85] Sanderson, Gregory. "Commercialization of Biomass Energy Projects: Outline for Maximizing Use of Valuable Tax Credits and Incentives," *BioEnergy '94, Technical Papers*, Volume 2, p. 415.
[86] Sanderson, Gregory. "Commercialization of Biomass Energy Projects: Outline for Maximizing Use of Valuable Tax Credits and Incentives," *BioEnergy '94, Technical Papers*, Volume 2, pp. 413-414.

justed for inflation starting in 1993) to states, political subdivisions, and nonprofit electrical cooperatives that produce electricity from solar, wind, geothermal, or biomass sources. There are two exceptions that do not qualify: burning of municipal solid waste and certain dry steam geothermal reservoirs. A qualifying facility must be in use between October 1, 1993 and September 30, 2013. The facility cannot receive more than ten years of payments beginning with the first qualifying year.[87]

Executive Order 12759

On April 17, 1991, President George Bush signed Executive Order 12759 titled Federal Energy Management. Section 1 deals with energy efficiency on Federal buildings. By the year 2000, these buildings are supposed to reduce their energy consumption down to 20% of 1985's usage level. Section 2 deals with energy efficiency for other facilities. These facilities are supposed to increase their energy efficiency 20% by the year 2000. Section 3 mandates facilities to seek alternative energy sources other than petroleum products. In Section 4, the implementation strategy is defined for Sections 1, 2, and 3. Section 5 deals with the purchase of energy efficient goods and products. Section 6 deals with removing any barriers from the Government in participating in any rebate or incentive programs that the local utility companies may offer. Section 7 lays the groundwork for rules and regulations pertaining to energy management for Federal buildings. Section 8 sets guidelines for energy efficiency for newly constructed Federal buildings. Section 9 implements an outreach program for Federal employees to encourage ride sharing and the reduction of fuel usage for commuting. Section 10 is designed for Government agencies that operate more than three vehicles. These agencies are supposed to reduce their fuel consumption by 10% in 1995 compared to fiscal year 1991. Section 11 reiterates the 1988 Alternative Motor Fuel Act. The purchase of alternative fuel vehicles will be subject to the budget. Section 12 defines how the money will be spent on energy saving technologies. Section 13 mandates participating agencies to produce reports for the President. Finally, in Section 14, terms are defined.

---

[87] Sanderson, Gregory. "Commercialization of Biomass Energy Projects: Outline for Maximizing Use of Valuable Tax Credits and Incentives," *BioEnergy '94, Technical Papers*, Volume 2, pp. 414-415.

Environmental Legislation

1976 Resource Conservation & Recovery Act

This law currently mandates responsibilities for hazardous waste managers, e.g., generators, transporters, treaters, storers, and disposers. The responsibility of what is classified as a hazardous waste is up to the generator of the waste.[88] This is an unfunded mandate that places a financial burden on each individual state.

The individual states are responsible for implementing the 1976 Resource Conservation & Recovery Act. Each state has the option of developing their own hazardous waste programs, but their programs must meet or exceed Federal guidelines. In addition to guidelines that are generic (written without any reference to any specific industry and apply to all industries that generate hazardous waste), there are amendments to the Resource Conservation & Recovery Act that were put into place in 1984. These amendments have eighty-nine specific deadlines in seven categories.

The seven categories include the following:
1. Administrative Amendments
2. Financial Amendments
3. Enforcement Amendments
4. Solid Waste Amendments
5. Report Amendments
6. Miscellaneous Amendments
7. Hazardous Waste Amendments

1990 Clean Air Act

The 1990 Clean Air Act is a Federal law which was put into place to help clean up our air. This law is an unfunded mandate. That means the Federal Government sets the guidelines and the states are mandated to fulfill them. In order for the states to follow through with the law, they must develop *state implementation programs* (SIPs).

The 1990 clean air act will reduce air pollution:
1. By setting deadlines for EPA, states, local Governments, and businesses.
2. Enforcement Powers. The law enables the EPA to fine violators with increasing penalties.

---

[88] Freeman, Harry M. *Standard Handbook of Hazardous Waste Treatment & Disposal*, McGraw Hill, 1989, pp. 1-10.

3. Public Participation: the public is given opportunities to take part in determining how the law will be carried out.

4. Market Approach: provides economic incentives for cleaning up pollution. Each polluter is assigned credits for polluting. If the polluter is not using all of their credits, they could sell them for a price to a polluter who has used more credits than were given to them.

5. Chemical Safety Board: It investigates and reports upon accidental releases of hazardous air pollutants from industrial plants.

6. Mandates all oil companies clean up their motor fuels.

7. Auto makers must build some cars that use clean fuels such as alcohol.

8. Auto makers must build electric vehicles by 1999; 500,000 must be manufactured and sold in California.

9. In 1994 big diesel trucks must reduce particulate matter by 90%.

10. Air Pollution must be reduced by locomotives.

11. Phase I of The Acid Rain Reduction Program went into effect in 1995; 110 big coal burning boilers must reduce sulfur dioxide.

12. Phase II of The Acid Rain Reduction program goes into effect in 2000; reducing sulfur dioxide levels and will institute mandates against smaller polluter.

13. An allowance system of credits will be issued to power plants that permit sulfur dioxide emissions and encourages power plants to reduce their emissions. These allowances can be bought and sold on the stock exchange, thereby attributing a higher cost to those facilities that wish to pollute more, since profiteers will drive up the cost of these emission allowances.

14. Bonus allowances given to power plants for installing clean coal technology that reduces sulfur dioxide.

15. Sets a schedule for the elimination of chemicals that destroy the ozone.

16. Chemical allowances will be issued to chemical manufacturers who manufacture chemicals that destroy the ozone.

17. Chemical allowances can be sold on the open market by manufacturers who do not use up all of their allowances.

CATEGORIES OF SOURCES
1. Coal Burning Power Plants
2. Oil Refineries
3. Garbage incinerators
4. Steel manufacturers
5. Coal mining

6. Mobile Sources: cars, trucks and buses

➤ Motor Vehicles produce up to one-half of VOCs and Nitrogen Oxides (NO_x) and hazardous air pollutants.

➤ Motor vehicles produce more than one-half of the hazardous air pollutants.

➤ Motor Vehicles produce up to 90% of the carbon monoxide.

1993 Federal Acquisition, Recycling, And Waste Prevention

On October 20, 1993, President Clinton signed the Executive order #12873, titled Federal Acquisition, Recycling, and Waste Prevention. Section 506 of that order pertains to Procurement of Re-Refined Lubricating Oil and Retreaded Tires. This order mandates the use of retreaded tires on all Government vehicles. Section 506 specifically deals with this issue and is in its entirety below:

Sec. 506. *Procurement of Re-refined Lubricating Oil and Retread Tires.* Within one hundred eighty days after effective date of this order, agencies shall implement the EPA procurement guidelines for re-refined lubricating oil and retread tires.

a. Commodity managers shall finalize revisions to specifications for re-refined oil and retread tires, and develop and issue specifications for tire retreading services, as commodity managers shall take affirmative steps to procure these items in accordance with RCRA (1976 Resource Conservation & Recovery Act) section 6002.

b. Once these items become available, fleet managers shall take affirmative steps to procure these items in accordance with RCRA section 6002.[89]

Florida Advanced Disposal Fee

In 1993 the state of Florida adopted the Advance Disposal Fee on packaging. This piece of legislation was designed to help develop the market for recycled products. The one-cent fee per container is collected at the wholesale level for all containers from five ounces to one gallon.

---

[89] *Code of Federal Regulations*, 1993 Compilation and Parts 100-102, January 1994, p. 666.

Technology Legislation

1986 Federal Technology Transfer Act

This law removed many of the barriers that prevented private and public partnerships in the development and commercialization of innovative environmental technologies. This act made it possible for private industry to create partnerships with Federal laboratories and academic institutions. Each Federal agency is given the authority to enter into Cooperative Research And Development Agreements (CRADA). These agreements define responsibilities, financial terms, the free flow of ideas, technical expertise, materials, and royalties.[90]

Senate Bill 920

In the state of California, Senate Bill 920 was designed to promote seismic safety and prescribe certain earthquake protection standards for building and reconstruction. To accomplish these goals, this bill required the State Architect to do the following:

1. Develop a state policy to be submitted to the Legislature on acceptable levels of earthquake risk for new and existing state-owned buildings.
2. Adopt regulations for the application of earthquake hazard mitigation technologies to buildings.
3. Recommend to the Legislature a long term plan to study the retrofitting of existing state buildings and new earthquake hazard mitigation technologies where appropriate.
4. Assist in the development of information to increase public and professional understanding of earthquake hazard mitigation technologies and to perform other related duties.
5. Select suitable buildings for the use of earthquake hazard mitigation technologies on three state buildings as demonstration projects.

Welfare Legislation

1990 Farm Bill Act: Nutrition Programs

The 1990 Farm Bill Act re-authorized the food stamp program for five years. The bill excluded educational loans, grants and scholarships,

---

[90] *United States Code Congressional And Administrative News,* West Publishing Company, 1986, Volume 2, pp. 1785-1797.

and clothing allowances provided by state assistance programs, assistance payments, and general state welfare payments from the calculations in determining food stamp eligibility. This bill also authorized an online electronic benefit transfer system that uses plastic debit cards instead of food stamps in at least 15% of locations that accept food stamps. This expense was to be paid by the Department of Agriculture. Additional provisions included larger fines and longer prison terms for those caught laundering money in food stamp schemes as well as those involved in computer fraud regarding the electronic debit card.[91]

---

[91] *Congressional Quarterly Almanac*, Congressional Quarterly, 1990, Volume XLVI, p. 346

APPENDIX C
TECHNOLOGIES

I n this appendix, existing and emerging technologies will be discussed. Some of these technologies have been around for thousands of years, while some others are only now entering the marketplace. The purpose of this appendix is to inform you of the different options that are available to us today.

There are three main categories of technologies that are discussed within this appendix: energy, automotive, and construction. In the energy section, non-renewable, renewable, solar, and alternative energies will be discussed. The automotive section will cover basic technologies such as tire retreading, extended-life oil filters, fuel cells, hybrid and electric vehicles. In the construction section of this appendix, technologies that are progressive by nature, but will help reduce costs in the long run, will be discussed and include the following: shock absorbers for your building, manufactured wood products and polystyrene building panels.

Energy

Fuels

Our non-renewable energy sources will soon be used up. It took nature millions of years to create pockets of coal, natural gas, and crude oil, but in less than a century, we have managed to burn up most of the supply that we know to exist. The purpose of this section is to inform you of the cleaner possibilities of using our non-renewable energy supplies.

A-21 FUEL: NAPHTHA & WATER MIXTURE

The A-21 fuel is made from water, naphtha and a small amount of surfactant which binds the water and naphtha together. The surfactant has anti-corrosion properties and enables the fuel to be stored indefinitely without separating or causing corrosion. A small amount of ethanol or methanol is used as an antifreeze to prevent the fuel from freezing. The fuel will remain viscous even at -40° Fahrenheit.

The fuel has one favorable characteristic in that it can be used in many different types of engines. It can be used in lawnmowers, snow blowers, boats, cars, trucks, diesels and even turbine engines. Slight modifications can be done at modest costs that will enable these engines to burn this fuel and perform equal or better than their, gasoline, diesel or kerosene powered counterparts.

The fuel has been tested extensively by the inventor, Caterpillar tractors, Sierra Pacific Power Company, and even by the Citifare bus in Reno, Nevada. Initial tests demonstrated that the fuel provided equal or better power and fuel mileage. As an added bonus, nitrous oxide and carbon monoxide emissions were reduced by 80%, while hydrocarbons were reduced by 60%. These results were achieved without catalytic converters. In diesel engines, particulate matter was down by a factor of ten and nitrous oxide emissions were reduced by 80%.

These reductions can be achieved quite affordably since conversion costs are modest. It may cost $300 to convert a gasoline engine while a diesel is slightly more at $1,000. The payback period could be relatively short depending upon how much fuel one uses. The fuel will cost less than gasoline or diesel since it is mostly made from water and naphtha. Naphtha is a product of oil distillation that is normally used as feedstock for fertilizers, pesticides, and other chemicals.

ETHANOL

Ethanol has many different names. Some of these names are: ethyl alcohol, ethyl hydroxide, grain alcohol, booze, moonshine, or fuel alcohol. It can be used as a motor fuel that emits less hydrocarbons, benzene, and carbon monoxide than gasoline.[92] Ethanol can be produced through fermentation or fractional distillation of crude oil. Ethanol made from crude oil is used for the production of solvents used in paints, cosmetics, perfumes, soaps, and dyes.[93] Most of the ethanol produced for fuel purposes uses conventional feedstocks while it is also possible to produce ethanol from waste and biomass feedstocks.

Conventional Feedstocks

Most of the ethanol that is being produced today for fuel purposes comes from conventional feedstocks. These feedstocks include the sugar and starchy crops. Through the fermentation of these two feedstocks, byproducts are created that can be used and sold. These byproducts include carbon dioxide, woody residue materials, and concentrated protein. Carbon dioxide can be captured and sold to soft drink bottlers. The residual woody material can be dried and burned as fuel for heat to be used in the fermentation process. The concentrated protein results from the fermentation process that removes most of the carbohydrate from the plant material which is usually sold as animal feed. These byproducts add value to the fermentation process which would otherwise make the energy crops too expensive. For this reason, sugar and starch crops are used today as feedstocks for the production of ethanol.

Sugar crops are products such as sugarcane, molasses, sugar beets, sweet sorghum, Jerusalem artichoke, fodder beets, fruit crops, and cheese whey.[94] Unlike starch crops, the advantage of using sugar crops for the fermentation process of ethanol is that the six carbon sugar units are in the form that the yeast can use without any additional processing.

Starchy crops include items such as corn, sorghum, wheat, barley, cassava, potatoes, and sweet potatoes. Starch crops need additional processing in order for the yeast to act upon the six carbon sugars. This extra step is a relatively easy and inexpensive process involving heat and enzymes, or a mild acid solution. The main advantage of using a starch crop such as corn is the relative ease of storage.

Unconventional Feedstocks

Waste and biomass feedstocks include paper, wood waste (prunings, wood chips, sawdust, etc.), green waste (leaves, grass clippings, vegetable and fruit waste, etc.), agricultural residue (straws, corn stalks and cobs, cotton gin trash, etc.), municipal solid waste (only the cellulosic portion of the municipal solid waste), crops grown specifically for their biomass content (grasses, sweet sorghum, sugar cane, fast growing trees, etc.),

---

[92] Berger, Bill. *Modern Petroleum*, Penwell Publishing Company, 1992, p. 452.
[93] *The Dorling Kindersley Science Encyclopedia*, Dorling Kindersley, 1993, p. 99.
[94] Department of Energy. *Fuel From Farms*, Solar Research Institute Publication, 1980, p. 40.

and sewage sludge. If waste feedstocks are used for the production of ethanol, costs can be kept low because producers of waste feedstocks need to dispose of their materials. This will cost the producer of ethanol little or no money. When using waste or biomass feedstocks for the production of ethanol, a well known process called concentrated acid hydrolysis is used. The first step takes the feedstock and converts it into cellulose and hemicellulose. The second step of the process breaks down the hemicellulose and cellulose into sugars. After sugar is produced, it can be fermented with conventional or engineered microbes that will produce ethanol. Heat is necessary for this process and can be derived by burning the residual material (lignin) that is not transformed into sugars during the process. This process also creates byproducts such as carbon dioxide, agricultural gypsum, and a few minor fermentation products. This description of concentrated acid hydrolysis is a generic description of how to take waste and biomass feedstocks and transform them into usable sugars.

For further information contact:

Mark Carver
Vice President, Business Development
Arkenol
23046 Avenida De La Carlota
Suite 400
Laguna Hills, CA 92653
Tel: 714-454-4126
Fax 714-588-3973

Concentrated acid hydrolysis works well on most forms of biomass except for sewage sludge, but there is one technology that can transform sewage sludge into usable biomass. A system consisting of bacteria and hydroponics (water parks) has been tested at Cornell University. Anaerobic bacteria clean waste water as it passes through a special filter. Organic matter is then transformed into methane and carbon dioxide by the bacteria, collected and then diverted to either generate electricity (methane) or feed hydroponic plants (carbon dioxide). The hydroponic plants capture any remaining waste from constantly flowing water.[95] Once a sufficient amount of plant matter is generated, it could be harvested and processed with concentrated acid hydrolysis to create sugars that can be fermented into alcohol.

---

[95] May, Mike. "Sewage Solution," *Popular Science*, February 1994, p. 21.

BIODIESEL

Biodiesel is a petrodiesel substitute that can be made from beef tallow, vegetable oils such as canola, soybeans, safflower, and sunflower oils. Biodiesel has a higher flashpoint than diesel and is lower in toxicity, making it safer to handle and more benign to our environment. Biodiesel can be mixed with petrodiesel or it can run straight in a diesel engine without any modifications to the engine. Biodiesel can be handled by our normal fuel distribution system without any modifications. Biodiesel emits far less regulated pollutants than regular diesel. Furthermore, fuel economy and power are about the same as it is with petrodiesel.

Biodiesel has been tested by several transit authorities, two of which are Sioux Falls, South Dakota, and Southwest Ohio Transit Authority in Cincinnati, Ohio. Both of these authorities did not find any drawbacks to the fuel or the operation of its vehicles. In addition to these noteworthy results, the University of Missouri conducted emission tests and found dramatic reductions.[96]

To summarize the benefits of Biodiesel

➤ Reduces foreign imported oil and our trade deficit.

➤ Stimulates rural economies.

➤ Reduces emissions of particulate matter, hydrocarbons, CO_2 and SO_2.

➤ Its biodegradable and non-toxic.

➤ It's a renewable energy source that can be made from vegetable oils and animal fats.

➤ Provides more lubrication and better ignition qualities.

➤ Has a high flash point of over 300° F while diesel is about 175° F, making it safe to transport.

Electrical Generation Technologies

DIRECT FUEL CELL

The Direct Fuel Cell is an electrochemical device with no moving parts that takes fuel (gaseous or liquid) and converts it into electrical energy without combustion.

For further information contact:

Energy Research Corporation
3 Great Pasture Road
Danbury, CT 06813
203-792-1460

---

[96] "Transit Experts Discuss Advantages of Biodiesel," *Biologue*, 4th Quarter 94, pp. 23-24

Biomass Technologies

WHOLE-TREE-ENERGY TECHNOLOGY

Whole-Tree-Energy technology is a method of burning whole trees to generate electricity. Trees are harvested whole and delivered to the power plant for drying and eventual combustion. The trees are stacked up to one hundred feet high in a dome. Waste heat from the power plant is piped into the dome to dry the trees. After thirty days, the moisture content of these trees is approximately 20%. Once the trees reach this moisture content, they are ready to be burned. The trees are transported from the dome on a conveyor belt and then cut into twenty-eight-foot lengths and end up in the combustion chamber. Complete combustion of the trees is accomplished by injecting air into the combustion chamber both below and above the stack of trees. Heat from this combustion process boils water, which produces steam that drives a steam turbine and generator. The waste heat is captured by a heat exchanger and is piped back to the drying dome which completes the cycle.

Whole-Tree-Energy technology can be cost competitive with coal-fired power plants and much cheaper than conventional chipped-wood power plants. Since trees contain little nitrogen and sulfur, nitrogen and sulfur oxides are barely measurable when the trees are burned. There is less particulate matter and there is no release of toxic emissions. Therefore, this system requires no expensive emissions control equipment. It has been estimated by more than a half dozen state utility commissions that the environmental costs of coal add an additional 1¢ to 3¢ per kwh to install pollution control technologies.[97] Fuel handling savings up to 35% can be achieved when trees are harvested whole and do not have to be chipped prior to burning.[98] For this reason, this technology can be cost competitive with conventional coal-fired and wood-fired power plants.

SUPERTREE

Tree Technology Inc. has the rights to an "engineered" deciduous hardwood tree that grows 20 feet tall in one year. The tree matures in only seven years and is disease resistant and infertile. It won't grow unchecked in the wild. The tree is a clone of the Chinese paulownia tree and was developed by a group of scientists from the U.S., China, and Australia.[99]

---

[97] Morris, David and Ahmed, Irshad. "Rural Development, Biorefineries and the Carbohydrate Economy," *Institute For Local Self Reliance*, 1993, p. 2.

[98] Lamarre, Leslie. "Electricity From Whole Trees," *EPRI Journal*, Jan/Feb. 1994, pp. 16-24.

[99] Zmirak, John Patrick; Paul, Ken; and McCune Jenny C. "Eureka: It's a Breakthrough Idea," *Success*, October 1992, pp. 24-25.

WASTE GASIFICATION TECHNOLOGY

Thermogenics, Inc.

Thermogenics, Inc. produces small scale gasification equipment. This equipment is suitable for municipal solid waste, automobile shredder residue, shredded tires, wood and agricultural wastes, assuming these feedstocks are less than two inches in size and moisture content is below 30%. They have three models that can handle from 500 pounds per hour up to 6,000 pounds per hour. These machines do not require any staff once they are started, assuming they have a continuous flow of feedstocks. These gasifiers can run continuously or for short periods of time. The units are mounted on skids and are portable. They can be delivered by truck, and virtually no assembly is required.

The Thermogenics Gasifier is a continuously-fed, bottom feed, cross-draft gasifier. The technology is proprietary and a patent is pending. For this reason, no additional information on the technology is available at this time. The units produce gas at low pressures and moderate temperatures. The gas can be used as fuel to drive generators to produce electricity. The gasifier does not produce any emissions which means siting and permitting will be simple.

For further information contact:
Thermogenics, Inc.
3620 Wyoming Blvd., NE, Suite 210
Albuquerque, New Mexico 87111
Tel: 505-298-4381
Fax: 505-293-5150

GRINDERS & CHIPPERS

In order to process trees and/or refuse for gasification, liquification, or for paper pulp processing, the feedstocks need to be chipped into a size that is suitable for the various technologies. Morbark has a wide selection of equipment that can handle all types of feedstocks.

For further information contact:
Morbark Sales Corporation
8507 South Winn Road
P.O. Box 1000
Winn, MI 48896
Tel: 517-866-2381

BIOGAS

Waste Water Sludge

In Los Angeles, the Hyperion sewage treatment plant, serves nearly four million people, produces 250 dry tonnes per day of digested, dewatered sewage sludge; 220 tonnes per day of biogas (equivalent to 7.0 million cubic feet of gas per day); and generates about 16 MW of electricity.

This particular sewage plant accomplishes this feat by not using methane gas to heat the anaerobic digestors, but instead uses the gas as fuel to run four Allison 570K gas turbines which can generate 15 MW of electricity. The exhaust from these turbines is passed through a heat recovery steam generator which produces superheated steam. This steam is used for three purposes. First, it is used to power steam turbines that generate more electricity. Second, the steam is used to heat the anaerobic digestors. Finally, it is used to dry the wet sewage sludge.

Before the steam is used to dry the wet sewage sludge, the sludge is passed through a high-speed centrifuge where the mixture is reduced to 72% water content and 28% solids. Once the sludge is in this "wet cake" form, it passes through indirect rotary steam dryers.

Once the sludge is suitably dry, it can be burned in a furnace and the hot gasses can be used to generate additional steam that will pass through a 15 MW condensing steam turbine/generator.

Overall, this sewage plant produces about 25 MW of electricity. 15 MW is produced with the gas turbines and the remaining 10 MW is generated from the sewage sludge. The plant and its processes require 9.1 MW, which yields a net of 15.9 MW of electricity.[100]

Landfills

Biogas from landfill could fuel about 1% of the electrical needs of our country. An additional benefit of capturing the biogas for fuel would be the reduction of a greenhouse gas that is currently emitted every day. Biogas is a mixture of methane and CO_2 which is much more harmful to our environment than CO_2 alone. By capturing and using the biogas to produce only 1% of our electrical needs, we could eliminate the equivalent of 10% of the CO_2 that would normally be produced through conventional power plant combustion.

---

[100]Haug, Roger T.; Moore, Gary L.; and Harrison, David S. "Energy Recovery From Biosolids: The City of Los Angeles Experience," *Second Biomass Conference of the Americas: Energy, Environment, Agriculture, and Industry*, NREL, 1995, pp. 734-739.

Solar Technologies

SOLAR LIGHTING

Solar lighting can take the place of expensive electrical lights that add heat to the building and consumes electricity. There are two types of products of which I am aware. One type of product uses a clear plastic dome covering a reflective tube. This type of product is better suited for pitched roofs. The other type of product is an active daylighting system similar to a skylight and best suited for relatively flat roofs.

The first product is simply a reflective tube with a clear acrylic dome housing that uses a reflective tube with a reflective rating of around 87%. Some manufacturers may be higher and some may be lower. These products works well on sloped roofs and are unobtrusive. Most only stick up about twelve inches above the roof. This type of product is easy to install and can be retrofitted to existing structures.

These devices allow sunlight to enter the clear dome and reflect down to a translucent lens mounted on the ceiling. On a sunny or partly sunny day you may get 1500 watts of light. Depending on the manufacturer, more or less light may be produced. This factor depends upon the fixtures reflective capability. These units will outperform any skylight because a skylight will not bring in as much light as these solar units. For another, a skylight is very energy inefficient because it allows heat to escape in the winter and increases cooling costs during the summer. Simply stated, these devices bring in more light with less heat transfer than a skylight. Use of these devices will reduce heating, cooling and lighting costs.

For further information on these products you can contact:
Sun Tunnel Skylights
786 Mc Glincey Lane
Campbell, CA 95008
1-800-369-3664

The Sunpipe Company
P.O. Box 2223
Northbrook, IL 60065
1-800-844-4786
1-708-272-6977

Sola Tube
586 Wendell Drive, Suite 2
Sunnyvale, CA 94089
1-408-541-8930

The other type of device is like a skylight, but has different characteristics. It has an active daylight tracking system that causes a set of reflectors to follow the sun's path. This system directs the reflected light down the skylights shaft to an interior lens that diffuses the outdoor light. Unlike a skylight, a more uniform and consistent light is captured throughout the day. These units also have reflective shafts that bring in more available light. Unlike a normal skylight, these units have an interior lens that diffuses the light and acts as an additional thermal barrier. With the interior lens in place, an air space is created that helps insulate the building from solar gain or loss.

For further information on these products you can contact:
So-Luminaire Daylighting Systems Corp.
4444 Quay Avenue #6
Los Angeles, CA 90744
Tel: 310-952-8990

Recycling Technologies

Tire Recycling: TRTM-60

The TRTM-60 is a tire recycling plant that takes chipped tires and reduces them to steel (from steel-belted tires), carbon black, and fuel grade oil at a cost of a few cents per tire without creating any pollution. This plant is capable of handling one hundred tons of chipped tires (approximately 10,000 car size tires) per day. The chipped tires are first preheated to about 250°F to remove any moisture. Afterwards, they are moved by augers through a hotter stainless steel chamber where the chipped tires react with a catalyst and heat to create hydrocarbon vapors, carbon black, steel fibers, and ash. The hydrocarbon vapors are condensed to form the fuel grade oil. The remaining gases are sent back through the system to be used as fuel in the heating process.

The plant costs approximately $5 million excluding land, buildings, and other optional equipment, and should generate approximately $4.4 million in revenue per year. On a daily basis, the plant is capable of producing 250 barrels of fuel grade oil, 30,000 pounds of steel, 50,000 pounds of carbon black, and enough light gases to power itself with only a five-person shift.

For further information contact:
Tire Recycling Technologies Corp.
3206 Candelaria Road North
Albuquerque, NM 87107
Tel: 505-884-0272

Waste Recycler: Proler SynGas Process

THE PROCESS

Proler SynGas Process is a versatile recycling method that can take a wide variety of waste feedstocks and convert them to syngas and residual material. The process is economical and benign without negative air or water emissions. The syngas can be used for electrical energy production, thermal energy, and as feedstocks in making plastics. The process can handle municipal solid wastes and sludge, automobile shredder residue, recycled cardboard residue, and paper mill sludges, tires, agriculture and food industry wastes, wood chips, industrial solid wastes and sludges, special and hazardous wastes such as medical wastes, hydrocarbon-contaminated sludges and soils, petroleum refining waste sludges, and chemical waste solutions and solvents.

The volume of residue from feedstocks such as municipal solid waste can be reduced over 90%, assuming moisture content does not exceed 40%. Individual units are sized at 250 tons per day and multiple units can be assembled together to handle a higher volume. A single unit can handle up to 500 tons per day and down to 200 to 250 tons per day efficiently. In order to efficiently use the syngas for plastic production, the facility needs to be close enough to pipe the gas to a petrochemical refinery. If not, the syngas can be used to generate electricity.

THE TECHNOLOGY

The feedstock is introduced into a rotary gasification reactor where high-temperature gaseous carbon dioxide and water vapor are injected into the mix. Instantly, a high-temperature gaseous product is produced which dynamically reacts with the feedstock by melting, decomposing, vaporizing, and dissociating it. Once the feedstocks is reduced to a gas, it is scrubbed to produce a high-quality syngas.

ACQUIRING THE TECHNOLOGY

Currently, Proler International prefers to own and operate the equipment. Under this arrangement, Proler International will build a facility within an industrial complex where wastes generated on site are recycled into syngas and utilized on or near the premises. Costs to recycle most wastes are cheaper than other alternatives. Revenues are generated by creating electricity, steam, plastics, or methanol. The end product will depend upon many factors such as their proximity to a refinery or the demand for electricity. This will save landfill space and money for the industry, city or county that has the responsibility of dealing with the waste.

For further information:
> Mr. Harold Burnham or Pamela Merritt
> Proler International Corp.
> 4265 San Felipe Street, Suite 900
> Houston, TX 77027
> Tel: 713-627-3737

Automotive Technologies

Tire Retreading

The retread industry suffers from a poor image resulting from misinformation that is wholly undeserved. Tire retreading is safe, and it saves oil and money.

Tire retreading encompasses various names with subtle differences between names and the products. A tire that has its old tread removed and a new tread applied is called a retreaded tire. An antiquated name for this same procedure is called the recap tire. A retreaded tire with a new rubber veneer applied to the sidewall is often called a remolded or a remanufactured tire. Another name for this same procedure is bead-to-bead retreading.

RETREADS GET A BAD RAP

Tire failure and rubber on the road is a common sight on the highway. Much of this strewn rubber is mistaken for the remnants of retreaded tires. This is a fallacy. With closer inspection of the casings on the road, one would find that the rubber has steel strands protruding from the casings. This indicates that the tire casing failed and that the failure was not a result of retreading. Failure of any tire, whether it be new or a retread, will come about from driver error. Such errors may be caused by any of the following:

➤ Inadequate attention to air pressure and maintenance
➤ Overloading beyond a tire's rated capacity
➤ Using tires which are unsuited for particular applications
➤ Lack of vehicle maintenance, especially wheel alignment and front tire balancing
➤ Cracking caused by weather

RETREADS ARE SAFE

Retreaded tires are as safe as new tires. This has been proven by millions of users over many years. In 1994, truckers purchased sixteen million retreaded tires, while they purchased only eleven million new ones. In fact, retreaded tires are so safe, all forms of industry use them on their vehicles and crafts. Here is just a brief list of applications that use retreaded tires:

➤ Commercial Jets
➤ Military Jets
➤ Fire Engines
➤ Ambulances
➤ Race Cars
➤ Trucking Companies
➤ Taxi Fleets

There are many companies that use retreaded tires. A few national names that you might recognize include: United Parcel Service, Federal Express, Georgia Pacific, Weyerhaeuser, and McDonell Douglas. There are thousands of additional companies that use retreaded tires and if you are interested in knowing who else is on this list, you can contact the Tire Retread Information Bureau, 900 Weldon Grove, Pacific Grove, CA 93950. Not only do companies use retreaded tires for trucks and automobiles, they are used on some school buses and on heavy equipment. In the case of the CAT model 994 loader, new tires cost approximately $28,000, while a retreaded tire may cost as little as $18,000.

When buying a retreaded tire, it is important that the tire retreader has been certified through the Tire Retreading Institute. For the best quality retreads, insist on doing business with an "A" rated retread plant. An "A" rated retread plant has had an in-depth inspection of the retread facilities by the Tire Retreading Institute. This inspection has found the plant to offer the best in plant efficiency, technology, and product quality. In their evaluation of the plant, the Tire Retreading Institute examines the plant's initial casing inspection, repair, buffing and measuring, tire building, curing, and final inspection. The Tire Retreading Institute also examines the plant's equipment, its retreading material, employee performance and safety procedures, as well as how well the plant complies with OSHA (Occupational Safety and Health Administration) regulations.

There are two ways to retread a tire. The first method is the Mold Cure and the second is the Pre Cure. Both methods produce a high quality tire. The only difference between the two processes lies in the third step of a five-step process. Otherwise, each prior and subsequent step in the retreading process is identical. Those steps are:

1. INSPECTION: Each tire is subjected to a very rigorous visual inspection to eliminate substandard tires.
2. BUFFING: The old tread is removed, the tire is trued, and the exact diameter of the tire is accomplished with high speed buffers.
3. NEW RUBBER: New tread is applied by the Mold Cure or Pre Cure Method.
4. FINAL INSPECTION: All tires are inspected for quality and workmanship.
5. TRIMMING & PAINTING: Any excess rubber is removed and the tire is painted.

MOLD CURE METHOD: An unvulcanized rubber tread is applied to the buffed tire and then placed into a rigid mold that has the tread design. The mold is then heated, resulting in the tread design, and this vulcanization process (which is similar to new tire construction) adheres the tire tread to the casing.

PRE CURE METHOD: A vulcanized rubber tread with tread pattern is applied to the buffed tire that has been treated with a thin layer of cushion gum. The tire tread is adhered to the tire casing by placing the tire in a curing chamber where the vulcanizing process (which is similar to new tire construction) takes place.

RETREADS SAVE MONEY

Retreads save money. A retreaded tire consists of up to 85% of recycled materials (the worn casing itself) and can cost 30% to 50% less than a new tire. The reason a retreaded tire cost so much less is that the casing of any tire accounts for approximately 70% of the tire's total cost. The only raw material used in retreading a tire is the rubber that is used for the new tread. Because retreaded tires can be retreaded two or three times, the life cycle cost is lower, and savings can be substantial. High quality retreaded tires can often accumulate more mileage than new tires. Depending on how many miles a person drives, the savings can be substantial. These savings come in the form of direct savings and indirect savings. The direct savings would be the amount of money you would directly save by using a retreaded tire. The indirect savings is a far more important number. That number will vary depending upon our trade deficit situation with the oil producing countries. When we manufacture a new truck tire, it takes 22 gallons of oil to make that tire. By comparison, it only takes 7 gallons of oil to retread that same truck tire, which results in a 15 gallons per tire savings. A passenger car tire takes 7 gallons of oil to produce, and the retreading of that same tire only takes 2-1/2 gallons of oil. As you can see, the 15 gallons of oil savings in a truck retreaded tire can save millions of gallons of oil. In 1994, the production of retreaded tires saved America over 400 million gallons of oil.

TF Purifiner™ On-board Oil Purification System

Here is an automotive technology that has been certified by the California EPA's Department of Toxic Substance Control and endorsed by American Oceans Campaign. California has given it a seal of approval as a "Pollution Prevention Technology." It is an "electric on board oil purification system that continually cleans the engine oil while the vehicle is running. If the unit is installed on a brand new engine, it will help break in the new engine. It protects hydraulic systems by reducing pitting and scoring of pumps, control valves, and cylinders. The unit works in all climates with up to 50 weight lubricating oil including synthetics. It cannot harm any engine or equipment, therefore it will not affect the manufacturers warranty. The unit itself has a limited ten year warranty and the heating element has a five year warranty.

The unit has been field tested for over ten years. It has been discovered that engines and equipment outfitted with the TF Purifiner™ have had their lives greatly extended. The research has shown that the sub micron particles that cannot be filtered out act as polishing agents in the motor oil. It accomplishes this task by reducing solid particles down to one micron in size. This process virtually eliminates the ridges and grooves normally left by standard filtration.

When oil enters the TF Purifiner™ On-board Oil Purification System, it must pass through a small metering jet under pressure supplied by the equipment's oil pump. The metering jet prevents any drop in oil pressure and slows the oil flow down so that it flows through the tightly compressed filter very slowly, 6 gallons per hour (23 liters). The cotton is compressed to a specific density to prevent channeling and to provide maximum particle retention. The special filter used in conjunction with the TF Purifiner™ equipment is designed to keep the oil suitable for ongoing use. The combination of the two types of filtration gives the equipment maximum protection.

After oil passes through the filter, it enters a dry heat evaporation chamber at atmospheric pressure. The chamber is electrically heated to approximately 200°F (95° C). This process is accomplished through the use of an electric heater that is totally isolated from the oil and gases for safety. The oil passes over the electrically heated diffuser plate in a thin film. Because the plate is heated and the oil is in a thin film at atmospheric pressure, the heated liquids rise to the top of the oil, vaporized and are vented out through their own pressure before they can recondense. The gaseous blow-by is also vented at this time. The contaminants are vented back into the induction system and consumed in the combustion process. The oil is now free of solid and liquid contaminants and flows by gravity back to the oil sump. This continuous process keeps the oil consistently clean, suitable for continuous use almost indefinitely.

In addition to these benefits it will have a positive impact upon the environment and will save money and oil. A more detailed list of benefits is shown below.

Significantly Reduce Operating Expense

1. Reduce frequency of regular oil changes
2. Reduce new oil purchases up to 90%
3. Increase engine efficiency, thereby improving fuel economy
4. Reduce down time, thereby improving bottom line profits
5. Increase manpower productivity by reducing the necessity for maintenance

Significantly Reduce Maintenance Costs

1. Minimizes sludge build up and resulting engine wear
2. Minimizes acids that cause pitting and corrosion to engine parts
3. Minimizes fuel dilution that causes oil to become too thin
4. Minimizes water-oil emulsion which causes the oil to become too thick
5. Reduces waste oil handling and disposal costs
6. No maintenance of the unit, (The TF Purifiner™ has no moving parts)

Significantly Reduces Capital Expenses

1. Extends engine life and time between overhauls
2. TF Purifiner™ has a rapid payback period
3. Maximizes the resale value of the vehicle
4. The TF Purifiner™ is reusable. It will outlast several engines
5. Does not void manufacturers' warranty

Significantly Enhances the Environment

1. Reduce environmental pollution by decreasing toxic waste storage and disposal
2. Reduce possibility of oil spills
3. Filter elements can be incinerated (disposal problem eliminated)

For further information on the TF Purifiner™ On-board Oil Purification System, contact:

TF Purifiner, Inc.
3020 High Ridge Road, Suite 100
Boynton Beach, Florida 33426-8701
1-800-488-0577
1-561-547-9499
FAX: 1-561-547-4025

Fuel Cell Vehicles

Hydrogen-powered buses are already on the streets of some cities in the U.S. as part of government testing of fuel cells and other alternative fuels. These buses run cleaner than any other buses, including electric ones. By using a special fuel cell that runs on hydrogen and carbon dioxide converted from methanol, it generates electricity that powers electric motors. The fuel cell is so versatile, it can run on other gaseous and liquid fuels such as gasoline, diesel, and propane. The fuel cell is so efficient, emissions are almost 100% lower than diesel-powered buses.[101]

Hybrid Vehicles

A hybrid vehicle is typically a vehicle that has an electric drive motor supported by a series of batteries. The batteries are charged by some form of internal combustion engine. With this combination, hybrid vehicles can obtain up to an amazing 80 mpg!

A promising example of the hybrid vehicle belongs to Volvo. Consisting mostly of batteries, a diesel-powered turbine propels a generator that charges the batteries and yet manages a top speed of 110 mph. With an average speed of 55 mph, the car can go more than 400 miles on a full tank and average 45 mpg. A heat exchanger uses exhaust energy to preheat intake air thereby bypassing harmful emissions. Technologies such as this can antiquate internal combustion engines, resulting in cleaner air and lower fuel consumption.[102]

Another demonstration of a hybrid vehicle is being tested by the Marines. It is an amphibious assault vehicle built by United Defense L.P. of Santa Clara, California. It weighs 30 tons and is as efficient as other amphibious assault vehicles with traditional drive motors.[103]

In the fall of 1993, President Clinton announced that the Government's national defense and weapons laboratories and the domestic auto companies would collaborate on a massive effort to sharpen the competitiveness of the U.S. auto industry.

Companies can license technologies developed at labs, contract with labs to do research, or sign Cooperative Research and Development Agreements (CRADAs) where costs are shared, usually fifty-fifty. The Department of Energy has authorized more than 500 CRADAs during the last three years.

---

[101]Nadis, Steve. "The Fuel Cells Are Coming," *Popular Science*, June 1994, p. 34.
[102]Frank, Len. "Volvo's Environmental Turbine Car," *Popular Science*, January 1994, p. 48.
[103]"Big Green Electric-Drive Machine," *Popular Mechanics*, July 1994, p. 22.

In 1993, the Department of Energy signed a CRADA with the Big Three car manufacturers to cover a number of research efforts. In return, the CRADA provided $16 million for research and provided "one-stop shopping" for the car makers. This enables the car companies to turn to a designated lab representative who refers it to labs with expertise in the field.

The program constitutes researching advanced manufacturing technology and investigating automobile efficiency, safety, and emissions. It also includes building a prototype car capable of up to three times the gas mileage of today's conventional cars.

Argonne National Laboratory Argonne, IL	Flywheels, fuel cells, batteries, recycling, high temperature lubrication
Brookhaven National Engineering Laboratory, Upton, NY	Natural Gas Storage
Idaho National Engineering Laboratory Idaho Falls, ID	Gas turbines, laser beam welding techniques, finishing, assembly, and joining
Lawrence Berkeley Laboratory Berkeley, CA	Batteries, electrochromic switching devices, fuel cells
Lawrence Livermore National Laboratory Livermore, CA	Flywheels, aerogel, ultracapacitors, batteries, high performance computer modeling, superplastic steel, composites, machine tooling.
Los Alamos National Laboratory, Los Alamos, NM	Fuel cells, plasma-source ion implantation for surface hardening, ultracapacitors, high performance computer modeling, combustion dynamics
National Renewable Energy Laboratory, Golden, CO	Alternative fuels, hybrid vehicles, batteries
Oak Ridge National Laboratory Oak Ridge, TN	Motors, generators, flywheels, ceramics and coatings for high temperature engines, rapid prototyping, composites
Pacific Northwest Laboratories, Richland, WA	Superplastic forming of aluminum alloys, hydrocarbon traps for catalytic converters, advanced fuel-combustion systems, emissions sensors
Sandia National Laboratories Albuquerque, NM	High performance computer modeling, microelectronics, automated manufacturing, machine tooling, aluminum alloys, ultracapacitors, combustion dynamics

Supposedly this supercar would use technology already developed in advanced weapons research to make this car affordable to everyone. This technology will have great impact on future gasoline consumption not only in the U.S., but world-wide. The exploding technology of third-world countries, particularly Asia, is expected to increase by hundreds of millions the number of gas-guzzling cars on the roads of the world. If this prediction is true, we definitely need a fuel efficient car, otherwise our gas and oil resources will not support the need by early next century.

In order to achieve the proposed 80 mpg from an automobile requires a complete reassessment of the basic structures and components of the car. The exact approach is still being debated, but there is virtually a universal agreement that the car would use some hybrid drive, a combination of fuel-burning power plant generating electrcity, and a final electric drive.

There are three fundamental systems in a hybrid: a power source, a power storage unit, and control system. The power source can be engine-driven by a generator, turbine, or by a fuel cell.

Fuel cells show great potential. They can convert practically any gaseous fuel into hydrogen to produce electricity. They work best when producing low power at constant loads, which would be ideal for automobiles.

The conventional power storage unit is a battery, but most battery systems cannot handle the high current loads resulting from regenerative braking. A sudden stop at 60 mph would push loads up by several hundred amps and volts.

Europeans are already using flywheel systems in some of their buses. It is estimated that these diesel electric buses save approximatcly one-third the fuel cost and use less energy.

Another solution might be an ultracapacitor, a high-energy storage device. Already developed by defense labs, ultracapacitors power a projectile along a rail. It is also one of the oldest known ways of storing electricity. It allows a charge to build up between two conductive plates separated by an insulator and would allow storage like that of a large battery or flywheel.

TURBINE ENGINE

The turbine engine is a mature technology that has many benefits over conventional internal combustion engines. A turbine engine can burn a variety of fuels such as alcohol, gasoline, diesel, home heating oil, or practically any type of gaseous or liquid fuel. Since this engine can burn various liquid fuels, it is highly adaptable to the existing infrastructure of filling stations and repair shops. Turbines can attain thermal efficiencies in the mid 40's, while the best piston engines can only achieve efficiencies in the upper 20's.[104] In addition to being thermally efficient, turbine engines are clean burning without the addition of any sort of smog device and will pass the strictest standards set by the Environmental Protection Agency. The engine itself weighs less, lasts longer, and breaks down less often than a conventional internal combustion engine. Pound for pound, the turbine engine used as a generator can produce more electricity than batteries or fuel cells.

One promising turbine engine being developed by Allied Signal of Torrance, California is compact, lightweight and only has one moving part. That part is the turbine/generator/compressor unit which eliminates the need for a gearbox since the generator rotates at the same speed of the compressor and turbine. A normal turbine engine spinning at 60,000 rpm would usually require a gearbox to reduce the drive shaft speed so the alternator could generate a current that batteries and electrical equipment can accept.

For further information contact:
        Allied-Signal Inc.
        Aerospace Equipment systems
        2525 W. 190th Street
        Torrance, CA 90504-6099
        310-512-4127

ELECTRIC BATTERIES

There are numerous entries into the electric battery race. Everyone is familiar with the lead acid battery that we all have in our cars. Other battery technologies are now entering the marketplace that will provide both a long service life and a long driving range.

The testing of nickel-metal batteries is being tested in Germany for possible use as a replacement for the nickel-cadmium car battery. Nickel-metal batteries last nearly twice as long as conventional car batteries and can be recharged in an hour. The only drawback is that they are expensive and long-term testing hasn't been completed yet.[105]

FLYWHEEL BATTERIES

A 147 pound carbon fiber flywheel is being used as an energy storage device in Chrysler's Patriot race car using a turbine engine to supply electric power to an AC induction motor. Other companies are also de-

---

[104]These numbers refer to the amount of usable energy produced per unit of fuel. The rest is wasted in friction and heat.
[105]*Popular Science*, June 1994, p. 37.

veloping flywheel systems as primary power sources. So far, testing has proven greater acceleration, lower operating cost, and better mileage than conventional cars. If this hybrid technology is successful, fast-spinning flywheels may soon be the key to energy storage for hybrid vehicles.[106]

Construction Technologies

Quake Shock Absorbers

There are various companies that develop base isolators for buildings and bridges. These isolators work well on buildings between two and fourteen stories on firm and moderately-firm soil. Shorter buildings, unlike tall skyscrapers, are not as flexible and cannot "throw off" quake generated energy. Shorter buildings tend be extremely rigid and try to absorb an earthquake's energy instead of dissipating it, which usually results in heavy damage. Buildings designed in this fashion are prime candidates for retrofitting with base isolators.

Buildings designated for earthquake retrofitting are reviewed on a case-by-case basis to determine if base isolator installation is the correct technology to use in the retrofit. If base isolators are specified, the architects basically have two choices. One design is made of rubber, steel, and sometimes with a lead inner core. This design has layers of rubber and steel plates vulcanized together which is used to support the loads of steel support columns in a building. Depending on the placement within the building's foundation, a base isolator with a lead inner core is used.

The other basic design of base isolators uses a shallow metal dish in which a structural steel ball-bearing supports the load of the column. As the earth shakes, both styles of base isolators dissipate the earth's energy, saving the building and its contents from damage. If these technologies are used during new construction, it may add 1% to 5% to the total cost of construction.

For further information contact:
Ray Enos
Marketing Representative, Building Applications
Dynamic Isolation Systems, Inc.
3470 Mt. Diablo Blvd., Suite A200
Lafayette, CA 94549
Tel: 510-283-1166
Fax: 510-283-4307

---

[106]*Popular Science*, April 1994, p. 41.

Steel & Foam Building Panels

Here is an innovative product that is completely recyclable. The product is made of sheet metal and expanded polystyrene (styrofoam). The product has many advantages over conventional stick buildings. The first advantage over a wood house is that it is termite and mildew resistant. The wall panels are made of steel and foam and both components are resistant to most termites. Unlike wood, these panels will not warp, rot, or mildew. These building panels also offer superb insulation values.

A 2x4 wall with fiberglass insulation only offers an R-15 value of insulation while this building panel offers an R-19 for the same thickness. In a 2x6 wall, wood gives an R-19, while this panel gives you an R-23 rating. This building panel also has superior structural values. It is wind resistant up to 150 mph, can support 10,000 lbs, and requires no plywood sheeting for shear resistance. This panel has been tested and in use for over twenty-five years and is accepted and approved by: ICBO #PFC4216, SBCCI Report #84200, BOCA Research Report #81-47, HUD Structural Engineering Bulletin #1072, the United States Military, and FMHA. It is dimensionally stable, which means it will not warp or shrink. In addition to being a stable building product, it is also fire retardant. It has a Class A Flame Spread Rating, and when it was tested by Federal laboratories, the product was considered one of the least toxic materials in the event of a fire. It is also considered environmentally safe. The panel will not outgas toxic fumes and it is not made with any chlorofluorocarbons.

For further information contact:
Bob Dressler
General Sales Manager
Wallframe, Inc.
1436 East 6th Street
Corona, CA 91719
1-800-922-2221

TrimJoist

TrimJoist is an open-web floor joist that can be trimmed at both ends to adapt to those situations when inconsistencies or changes occur during construction. Each end of the joist has an oriented strand board web that can be trimmed up to 12 inches. Each joist is made up of 2x4s which means it has a 3-1/2 inch nailing and gluing surface which helps strengthen the floor. The joist is available in up to 30-foot lengths in 2-foot increments. Like the traditional open-web floor joist, installation of ductwork, plumbing, and wiring is much easier. The product is available from Rebel Building Components at 215-695-7128.

Plastic Building Materials

There are all forms of plastic building materials that require no up-keep and can be recycled when the building is no longer needed. The most common plastic building material is vinyl which is used for siding, windows, lattice, fencing, and decking. Another plastic called Noryl, which is manufactured by GE Plastics, is now showing up on some homes as roofing material. This plastic is made from recycled computer housings. The panels look like cedar shakes, but install faster and offers better flame retardance. The product is maintenance free and has a fifty-year warranty.

THE VINYL INSTITUTE

The Vinyl Institute is a national trade association representing the leading manufacturers of vinyl (polyvinyl chloride or PVC) plastics, as well as makers of vinyl feedstocks, additives, and film and sheet products. The Institute is a division of The Society of the Plastics Industry, Inc. and is headquartered in Morristown, New Jersey. The Institute was established in 1982, with a dual character to promote and protect the growth of the vinyl industry. It maintains an active program of technical research designed to help integrate vinyl products into all phases of the solid waste management process, and also operates an information center to answer questions about vinyl and the environment.

For further Information contact:
>Directory of Companies Manufacturing Products
>From Recycled Vinyl
>The Vinyl Environmental Resource Center
>One Cascade Plaza, 19th Floor
>Akron, OH 44308-1121
>Tel: 1-800-969-VINYL
>Fax: 216-276-9379

>The Vinyl Institute
>155 Route 46 West
>Wayne Interchange Plaza II
>Wayne, NJ 07470

LiftPlate International

LiftPlate International, a Miami based company, specializes in professional house lifting. They use a patented system which is faster and safer than conventional methods. They bolt a steel lifting grid to the walls and floor that enables them to raise the house on steel posts via synchronized hydraulic jacks which keeps the building level at all times. The building can be raised to any height. If the house needs to be on a berm of earth, they can lift the structure high enough to allow equipment and earth to be moved in under the house to provide a compacted surface. Once the desired height is achieved, the house is lowered onto the soil. If a new lower story is recommended, the house is lifted high enough to construct the supporting walls and then the jacks and lifting grids are removed.

For further information contact:
Peter Vanderklaauw
LiftPlate International
P.O. Box 430253
7020 SW 71st Avenue
Miami FL
Tel: 305-665-3541
Fax: 305-667-1256

APPENDIX D

BIOMASS RESOURCES

Alabama
Lynn Greer Russel
Moore Division of Science,
    Technology, & Energy
Alabama Dept. of Economic &
    Community Affairs
P.O. Box 5690
Montgomery, AL 36103-5690
Tel: (205) 242-5292
Fax: (205) 242-5515

Alaska
Peter Crimp
State of Alaska Department of
    Community & Regional
    Affairs
Division of Energy
333 W. 4th Avenue
Anchorage, AK 99501-2341
Tel: (907) 269-4631
Fax: (907) 269-4645

Arizona
Dr. James Kuester
Arizona State University
Dept. of Chemical & Biomaterials
Engineering Building B210
Tempe, AZ 85287
Tel: (602) 965-5071

Arkansas
Joe Gentry
Arkansas Science & Technology
    Authority
100 Main Street, Suite 450
Little Rock, AR 72201
Tel: (501) 324-9006
Fax: (501) 324-9012

California
Mike Smith
Manager Research &
    Development
Office California Energy
    Commission
1516 9th Street
Sacramento, CA 95814-5512
Tel: (916) 654-4604

Colorado
Mark Roper
Colorado Office of Energy
    Conservation
1675 Broadway, #1300
Denver, CO 80202-4613
Tel: (303) 620-4288

Connecticut
Allan Johanson
Assistant Director
Office of Policy & Management
80 Washington Street
Hartford, CT 06106
Tel: (203) 566-2800
Fax: (203) 566-6295

Delaware
Austin Short
Box 354 Route 4
Georgetown, DE 19947
Tel (302) 856-5084
Fax: (302) 856-5039

Florida
Larry Stokely
Department of Community Affairs
Florida Energy Office
2740 Centerview Drive
Tallahassee, FL 32399-2100
Tel: (904) 488-2475
Fax: (904) 488-7688

Georgia
Tommy Loggins
John Wells
Georgia Forestry Commission
P.O. Box 819
Macon, GA 31298-4599
Tel: (912) 751-3521
Fax: (912) 751-3465

Hawaii
Maurice H. Kaya
Energy Program Administrator
Room 110
335 Merchant Street
Honolulu, HI 96813
Tel: (808) 587-3812

Idaho
Gerald Fleischman
Idaho Department of Water
    Resources
P.O. Box 83720
Boise, ID 83720-0098
Tel: (208) 327-7959
Fax: (208) 327-7866

Illinois
Norm Marek
Illinois Department of Energy &
    Natural Resources
325 West Adams, 3rd Floor
Springfield, IL 62706
Tel: (217) 785-0184

Indiana
Niles Parker
Division of Energy Policy
Indiana Department of
    Commerce
1 North Capitol
Indianapolis, IN 46204
Tel: (317) 232-8970

Iowa
Sharon Tahtinen
Division of Energy & Geological
    Resources
Iowa Department of Natural
    Resources
Wallace Building
Corner of E. 9th & Grand
Des Moines, IA 50319
Tel: (515) 281-7066

Kansas
Dr. Richard Hayter
Director Kansas Extension Service
Engineering Extension Program
Kansas State University
Room 133 Ward Hall
Manhattan, KS 66506-2508
Tel: (913) 532-6026

Kentucky
John M. Stapleton
Geoff Young
Department of Natural Resources
Division of Energy
691 Teton Trail
Frankfort, KY 40601
Tel: (502) 564-7192
Fax: (502) 564-7484

Louisiana
Michael Buchart
Office of Marketing
Louisiana Department of
    Agriculture & Forestry
P.O. Box 3334
Baton Rouge, LA 70821
Tel: (504) 922-1280
Fax: (504) 922-1289

Maine
James Connors
Economic Division
State Planning Office
State House Station #38
Hallowell Annex
Augusta, ME 04333
Tel: (207) 624-6040
Fax: (207) 624-6023

Maryland
Dr. Donald Milsten
Maryland Energy Administration
45 Calvert Street
Annapolis, MD 21401
Tel (410) 974-3755
Fax: (410) 974-2250

Massachusetts
Irving Sacks
Division of Energy Resources
100 Cambridge Street
Room 1500
Boston MA 02202
Tel: (617) 727-4732
Fax: (617) 727-0030

Michigan
Ms. Jan Patrick
Michigan Public Service
    Commission
P.O. Box 30221
6545 Mercantile Way
Lansing, MI 48910
Tel: (517) 334-6262

Minnesota
Narv Somdahl
Energy Division
Minnesota Department of Public
    Service
121 7th Place East, Suite 200
St. Paul, MN 55101-2145
Tel: (612) 297-2117

Mississippi
Wes Miller
Energy & Transportation Division
510 George Street
Jackson, MS 39202
Tel: (601) 359-6600
Fax: (601) 359-6642

Missouri
Cher Stuewe-Portnoff
Orville Travis
Department of Natural Resources
P.O. Box 176
Jefferson City, MO 65102
Tel: (314) 751-4000
Fax: (314) 751-6860

Montana
Howard Haines
Energy Division
DNRC 3rd Floor
1520 East Sixth Avenue
Helena, MT 59620
Tel: (406) 444-6773

Nebraska
Larry Pearce
Assistant Director for Planning &
    Research
Nebraska Energy Office
State Capitol Building
14th & Lincoln Mall
Lincoln, NE 68509-5085
Tel: (402) 471-2867

Nevada
Dave McNeil
Energy Specialist
Nevada State Energy Office
1050 East William, Suite 435
Carson, NV 89710
Tel: (702) 687-4909
Fax: (702) 687-4914

New Hampshire
Norwood H. "Woody" Keeney III
Governor's Energy Office
57 Regional Drive
Concord, NH 03301-8519
Tel: (603) 271-2611
Fax: (603) 271-2615

New Jersey
Ed Lempicki
Supervising Forester
Department of Environmental
    Protection & Energy
Division of Parks & Forestry
501 East State Street
4th Floor Plaza 5
Trenton, NJ 08625
Tel: (609) 292-2531
Fax: (609) 984-0378

New Mexico
Dr. Walter Zachritz
Southwest Technology
    Development Institute
New Mexico State University
Box 30001/Dept. 3SOL
Las Cruces, NM 88003-0001
Tel: (505) 646-1846

New York
Jeffrey Peterson
New York State Energy Research
    & Development Authority
2 Rockefeller Plaza
Albany, NY 12223
Tel: (518) 465-6251 ext. 288
Fax: (518) 432-4630

North Carolina
Doug Culbreth
Tim Butler
Department of Commerce
Energy Division
430 N. Salisbury Street
Raleigh, NC 27611
Tel: (919) 733-2230
Fax: (919) 733-2953

North Dakota
Shirley Dykshoorn
Director
Office for Intergovernmental
    Assistance
14th Floor State Capitol
Bismarck, ND 58505-0170
Tel: (701) 224-2094

Ohio
Claude Eggleton
Carl Tucker
Ohio Public Utilities Commission
180 E. Broad Street
3rd Floor
Columbus, OH 43215-3793
Tel: (614) 466-7707
Tel: (614) 644-8301

Oklahoma
Fenton Rood
Department of Environmental
    Quality
1000 NE 10th Street
Oklahoma City, OK 73117-1212
Tel: (405) 271-3775

Oregon
Alex Sifford
Oregon Department of Energy
625 Main Street, NE
Salem, OR 97310
Tel: (503) 378-2788

Paul Bell
Oregon Department of Forestry
2600 State Street
Salem, OR 97310
Tel: (503) 378-6459

Pennsylvania
Mike Palko
Forestry Advisory Services
Department of Environmental
    Resources
P.O. Box 8552
Harrisburg, PA 17105-8552
Tel: (717) 787-2105
Fax: (717) 783-5109

Rhode Island
Julie A. Capobianco
Rhode Island of Housing
Energy & Intergovernmental
    Relations
275 Westminster Street
Providence, RI 02903-3415
Tel: (401) 277-3370
Fax: (401) 277-1260

South Carolina
Janet Lockhart
Jean-Paul Gouffray
South Carolina Governor's Office
Division of Energy, Agriculture, &
    Natural Resources
Edgar Brown Building
1205 Pendleton Street
3rd Floor
Columbia, SC 29201
Tel: (803) 734-0349
Fax: (803) 734-0356

South Dakota
Steve Wegman
South Dakota Public Utilities
    Commission
500 East Capitol
Pierre, SD 57501-5070
Tel: (605) 773-3201

Tennessee
Brian Hensley
Department of Economic &
    Community Development
Energy Division
320 6th Avenue North
Nashville, TN 37219-5308
Tel: (615) 741-2994
Fax: (615) 741-5070

Texas
Mike Wiley
General Services Commission
State Energy Conservation Office
201 East 11th Street
Austin, TX 78711-3047
Tel: (512) 463-1931

Utah
State of Utah
Division of Community
    Development
Office of Energy Services
324 S. State Street, Suite 230
Salt Lake City, UT 84104
Tel: (801) 538-8690

Vermont
Norm Hudson
Department of Public Services
Energy Efficiency Division
State Office Building
120 State Street
Montpelier, VT 05620
Tel: (802) 828-2393
Fax: (802) 828-2342

Virginia
Jennifer Byrd
Division of Energy
Office Building
9th Street
8th Floor
Richmond, VA 23219
Tel: (804) 692-3218
Fax: (804) 692-3238

Washington
Jim Kerstetter
Washington State Energy Office
925 Plum Street
P.O. Box 43165
Olympia, WA 98504-3165
Tel: (206) 956-2069

West Virginia
John F. Herholdt
Bill Willis
West Virginia Fuel & Energy
    Office
Capitol Complex
Room 553 Building 6
Charleston, WV 25305
Tel: (304) 558-4010
Fax: (304) 558-3248

Wisconsin
Dan Moran
Wisconsin Division of State Energy
P.O. Box 7868
Madison, WI 53707
Tel: (608) 266-1067

Wyoming
Dale Hoffman
Economic Development &
    Stabilization Board
Herschler Building
122 W. 25th Street
Cheyenne, WY 82002-3096
Tel: (307) 777-7284

Source: National Directory of Federal and State Biomass Tax Incentives and Subsidies by Gregory A. Sanderson in Association with the U.S. Department of Energy, Tennessee Valley Authority, Southeastern Regional Biomass Energy Program.

Legal Resources

Legal interpretation of the tax codes regarding renewable energy requires expertise in that area. For your convenience, two sources that can possibly assist you are listed below.

Keith Martin
Chadbourne & Parke
1101 Vermont Ave. NW
Washington, DC 20005
Tel: 202-289-3000
Fax: 202-289-3002

Gregory Sanderson, P.C.
Gomel & Davis
700 Marquis II Towers
285 Peachtree Center Ave. NE
Atlanta, GA 30303
Tel: 404-223-5900
Fax: 404-524-4755

APPENDIX E

ECOLOGICAL

Co-Op America

Co-Op America is a non profit organization interested in promoting a green sustaining economy. They accomplish this task through their National Green Pages. This book lists hundred of companies in over one hundred different categories of products and services that are ecologically responsible, companies that minimize waste, recycle, create green jobs, promote energy efficiency, make products that last, and support sustainable agriculture. Co-Op America believes that the customer who votes with their dollars can make a difference in the way America does business.

For more information, contact:

Co-Op America
1612 K Street NW, Suite 600
Washington, DC 20006
Tel: 202-872-5307

CALMAX

CALMAX is a free service designed to conserve energy, resources, and landfill space by helping businesses find markets for materials that have been traditionally discarded. CALMAX is a program indigenous to California and is provided by the California Waste Management Board. It can benefit businesses and communities in may ways. By finding new markets for materials that would normally end up in the waste stream, disposal costs are reduced, landfill life is extended, and businesses, schools, art groups and non profit organizations can benefit from free or inexpensive materials. CALMAX produces a catalog of items that are available for free or very little cost. The catalog is divided into three main sections. Items that are available, items that are wanted, and a regional listing that list the items in the first two sections by regions. Other material exchange programs are scattered throughout the United States and that list can be obtained from CALMAX.

For further information contact:
CALMAX
916-255-2369

APPENDIX F

INTERNET SITES

For those who are interested in bioenergy and alternative fuels, here are a few internet sites that can be helpful:

Center for Renewable Energy & Sustainable Technology (CREST):
http://solstice.crest.org/

Center of the Analysis and Dissemination of Demonstrated Energy Technologies (CADDET):
http://www.ornl.gov/CADDET/caddet.html

Energy Ideas Clearinghouse:
http://eicbbs.wseo.wa.gov

Great Lakes Regional Biomass Energy Program:
http://www.great-lakes.net/partners/cglg/biomass/

Oak Ridge National Laboratory:
http://beijing.eid.anl.gove/ee-cgi-bin/bio_bibwaisq.pl

National Renewable Energy Laboratory:
http://nrelinfo.nrel.gov:700/1/information/nrel/publications/biofuels

Alternative Fuels Data Center:
http://afdc.nrel.gov:70/

Efficiency and Renewable Energy Network (EREN):
http://www.eren.doe.gov

Biomass Energy Alliance's homepage:
http://www.biomass.org

Biomass Resource Information Clearinghouse:
http://asd.nrel.gov/projects/rrdec/data/biomass

United BioEnergy Commercialization Association:
http://www.paltech.com/ttc/ubeca/index.htm

Biofuels Information Network:
http://www.esd.ornl.gov/BFDP/BFDPMOSAIC/binmenu.html

APPENDIX G

POLITICAL RESOURCES

Americans for Tax Reform
1320 18th Street, N.W., Suite 200
Washington, DC 20036
202-785-0202

Citizens Against Government Waste
1301 Connecticut Avenue, N.W., Suite 400
Washington, D.C. 20036
202-467-5300
1-800-BE-ANGRY

Concord Coalition
1019 19th Street, N.W., Suite 810
Washington, DC 20036
202-467-6222

Congressional Accountability Project
P.O. Box 19446
Washington, DC 20036
202-296-2787

League of Conservation Voters
1707 L Street, N.W., Suite 750
Washington, DC 20036
202-785-8683

National Empowerment Television (NET)
717 Second Street, N.E.
Washington, DC 20002
202-546-3000

National Taxpayer Union
108 North Alfred Street
Alexandria, VA 22314
703-683-5700
1-800-TAX-HALT

Perot Reform Committee
7617 LBJ Freeway, Suite 727
Dallas, TX 75251
214-450-8800

Public Citizen
1600 20th Street, N.W.
Washington, DC 20036
202-588-1000

Tax Foundation
1258 H Street, N.W., Suite 750
Washington, DC 20005
202-783-2760

The National Center on Public Policy Research
300 I Street, N.E., Suite 3
Washington, DC 20002
202-543-1286

Vote Smart
1-800-622-SMART

FURTHER READING

Aguayo, Rafael. *Dr. Deming*. Fireside: New York, New York, 1990

Barlett, Donald L. and. Steele, James B. *America: What Went Wrong?* Andrews and McMeal: Kansas City, MO, 1992

Barlett, Donald L. and Steele James B. *America: Who Really Pays The Taxes*. Touchstone: New York, NY, 1994

Berle, Gustav. *The Green Entrepreneur*. Liberty Hall Press: 1991

Brown, Lester R. *Who Will Feed China? Wake Up Call For A Small Planet*. W.W. Norton & Company: New York, NY, 1995

Buckley, Adrian *The Essence of International Money*. Prentice Hall: 1990

Calleo, David P. *Bankrupting of America, How the Federal Budget is Impoverishing the Nation*. Avon Books: New York, NY, 1992

Carless, Jennifer. *Renewable Energy, A Concise Guide to Green Alternatives*. Walker Publishing: 1993

Caves, Richard E., Frankel, Jeffrey A., and Jones, Ronald W. *World Trade and Payments, An Introduction*. Harper Collins Publishers: 1990

Ferguson, Charles H. and Morris, Charles R. *Computer Wars, How the West Can Win in a Post-IBM World*. Times Books: New York, NY, 1993

Freeman, Harry M. *Standard Handbook of hazardous Waste Treatment and Disposal*. McGraw-Hill: 1989

Gillespie, Ed and Schellhas, Bob, editors. *Contract With America, The Bold Plan by Representative Newt Gingrich, Representative Dick Armey, and the House Republicans to Change the Nation*. Times Books: 1994

Greenberg, Jonathan and Kistler, William, editors. *Buying America Back*. Council Oak Books: Tulsa, OK, 1992

Gross, Martin L. *A Call For Revolution*. Ballantine Books: New York, NY, 1993

Gross, Martin L. *The Government Racket, Washington Waste From A to Z*. Bantam Book: New York, NY, 1992

Howes, Ruth and Fainberg, Anthony. *The Energy Sourcebook, A Guide to Technology, Resources and Policy*. American Institute of Physics: New York, NY, 1991

Krueger, Anne O. *Economic Policies At Cross-Purposes, The United States and Developing Countries*. The Brookings Institution: Washington, DC, 1993

Krugman Paul R. and Obstfeld, Maurice. *International Economics, Theory and Policy*. Harper Collins: New York, NY, 1992

League of Women Voters. *Plastic Waste Primer, A Handbook for Citizens*. Lyons & Burford: New York, NY, 1993

League of Women Voters. *The Garbage Primer, A Handbook for Citizens*. Lyons & Burford: New York, NY, 1993

Mankiw, Gregory N. *Macroeconomics*. Worth Publishers: New York, NY, 1992

Osborne, David and Gaebler, Ted. *Reinventing Government, How the Entrepreneurial Spirit is Transforming the Public Sector*. Plume: New York, NY, 1993

Samuelson, Paul A. and Nordhaus, William D. *Economics*. McGraw-Hill: 1992

Stein, Herbert and Foss, Murray. *An Illustrated Guide to the American Economy*. The AEI Press: Washington, DC, 1992

Williams, Dan R. and Good, Larry, CEM. *Guide to the Energy Policy Act of 1992*. The Fairmont Press: Lilburn, GA, 1994

GLOSSARY

Alcohols:

Organic compounds that are distinguished from hydrocarbons by the inclusion of a hydroxyl group. The two simplest alcohols are methanol and ethanol.

Appropriation Act:

A statute under the jurisdiction of the House and Senate Committees on Appropriations that provides budget authority. Enactment generally follows adoption of authorizing legislation unless the authorization itself provides the budget authority. Currently, thirteen regular appropriation acts are enacted each year. When necessary, the Congress may enact supplemental or continuing appropriations.

Aromatics:

Hydrocarbons based on the ringed six-carbon benzene series or related organic groups. Benzene, toluene, and xylene are the principal aromatics, commonly referred to as the BTX group. They represent one of the heaviest fractions in gasoline.

Biochemical Conversion:

The use of enzymes and catalysts to change biological substances chemically to produce energy products. For example, the digestion of organic wastes or sewage by microorganisms to produce methane is a biochemical process.

Biodiesel:

A biodegradable transportation fuel for use in diesel engines that is produced through transesterfication of organically derived oil or fats. Biodiesel is used as a component of diesel fuel. In the future it may be used as a replacement for diesel.

Biomass:

Renewable organic matter such as agricultural crops, crop-waste residues, wood, animal and municipal wastes, aquatic plants; fungal growth, etc., used for the production of energy.

Budget Authority:

Legal authority to incur financial obligations that will result in the spending of Federal Government funds. Budget authority may be provided in an authorization or an appropriation act. Offsetting collections, including offsetting receipts, constitute negative budget authority.

Budget Deficit:

Amount by which budget outlays exceed budget revenues during a given period.

Budget Enforcement Act of 1990 (BEA):

Title XIII of the Omnibus Budget Reconciliation Act of 1990. This act amended both Congressional Budget Act of 1974 and the Balanced Budget and Emergency Deficit Control Act of 1985. The BEA provides for new budget targets, sequestration procedures, pay-as-you-go procedures, credit reform, and various other changes. The discretionary spending caps and the pay-as-you-go process were extended through 1998 by the Omnibus Budget Reconciliation Act of 1993. See **discretionary spending caps** and **pay-as-you-go**.

Budget Function:

One of twenty areas into which Federal spending and credit activity are divided. National needs are grouped in seventeen broad budget functions, including national defense, international affairs, energy, agriculture, health, income security, and general Government. Three functions—net interest, allowances, and undistributed offsetting receipts—do not address national needs but are included to complete the budget.

Budget Resolution:

A resolution, passed by both House of Congress, that sets forth a Congressional budget plan for the next five years. The plan must be carried out through subsequent legislation, including appropriations and changes in tax and entitlement laws. The resolution sets guidelines for Congressional action, but it is not signed by the President and does not become law. The Congressional Budget Act of 1974 established a number of mechanisms that are designed to hold spending and revenues to the targets established in the budget resolution.

Budgetary Resources:

All sources of budget authority that are subject to sequestration. Budgetary resources include new budget authority, un-obligated balances, direct spending authority, and obligation limitations. See **sequestration.**

Business Cycle:

Fluctuations in overall business activity accompanied by swings in the unemployment rate, interest rates, and profits. Over a business cycle, real activity rises to a peak (its highest level during the cycle), then falls until it reaches its trough (its lowest level following the peak), whereupon it starts to rise again, defining a new cycle. Business cycles are irregular, varying in frequency, magnitude, and duration. (National Bureau of Economic Research)

Carbon Dioxide (CO_2):

A product of combustion has become an environmental concern in recent years. CO_2 does not directly impair human health but is a "greenhouse gas" that traps the earth's heat and contributes to the potential for global warming.

Carbon Monoxide (CO):

A colorless, odorless gas produced by the incomplete combustion of fuels with a limited oxygen supply, as in automobile engines. CO is poisonous if inhaled, entering the bloodstream through the lungs and forming carboxyhemoglobin, a compound that inhibits the blood's capacity to carry oxygen to organs and tissues. CO can impair exercise capacity, visual perception, manual dexterity, and learning functions.

Carcinogens:
Chemicals and other substances known to cause cancer.

Catalyst:
A substance whose presence changes the rate of chemical reaction without itself undergoing permanent change in its composition. Catalysts may be accelerators or retarders. Most inorganic catalysts are powdered metals and metal oxides, chiefly used in petroleum, vehicle, and heavy chemical industries.

Central Bank:
A Government-established agency responsible for conducting monetary policy and overseeing credit conditions. The Federal Reserve System fulfills those functions in the Untied States.

Civilian Unemployment Rate:
Unemployment as a percentage of the civilian labor force—that is, the labor force excluding armed forces personnel. (Bureau of Labor Statistics)

Clean Diesel:
An evolving definition of diesel fuel with lower-emission specifications, which strictly limit sulfur content to 0.05% by weight; in California, aromatics content is further limited to 10% by volume (for large refineries).

Compressed Natural Gas (CNG):
Natural gas that has been condensed under high pressures, typically between 2,000 and 3,600 psi, held in a container. The gas expands when released for use as a fuel.

Consumer Confidence:
A measure of consumer attitudes and buying plans indicated by an index of consumer sentiment. One such index is constructed by the University of Michigan Survey Research Center based on surveys of consumers' views of the state of the economy and their personal finances, both current and prospective.

Consumer Durable Goods:

Goods bought by households for their personal use that, on average, last more than three years—for example, automobiles, furniture, or appliances.

Cooperative Research and Development Agreement (CRADA):

Federal and private joint research and development program that is used to further technology commercialization.

Corporate Average Fuel Economy (CAFE):

(Public Law 94-163) Law passed in 1975 that set Federal fuel economy standards. The CAFE values are an average of city and highway fuel economy test results weighted by vehicle sales.

Cost of Capital:

The total expected rate of return that an investment must generate in order to provide investors with the prevailing market yield consistent with risk after accounting for corporate taxes (if applicable) and depreciation.

CPI-U:

An index of consumer prices based on the typical market basket of goods and services consumed by all urban consumers during a base period—currently 1982 through 1984. (Bureau of Labor Statistics)

Credit Crunch:

A significant, temporary decline in the normal supply of credit, usually caused by tight monetary policy or a regulatory restriction on lending institutions.

Credit Reform:

A revised system of budgeting for Federal credit activities that focuses on the cost of subsidies conveyed in Federal credit assistance. This process was authorized by the Federal Credit Reform Act of 1990, which was part of the Budget Enforcement Act of 1990.

Credit Subsidies:

The estimated long-term costs to the Federal Government of direct loans or loan guarantees calculated on the basis of net present value, excluding administrative costs and any incidental effects on Governmental receipts or outlays. For direct loans, the subsidy cost is the net present value of loan disbursements less repayments of interest and principal, adjusted for estimated defaults, prepayments, fees, penalties, and other recoveries. For loan guarantees, the subsidy cost is the net present value of the estimated payments by the Government to cover defaults and delinquencies, interest subsidies, or other payments, offset by any payments to the Government, including origination and other fees, penalties, and recoveries. See **present value**.

Current-Account Balance:

The net revenues that arise from a country's international sales and purchases of goods and services, net international transfers (public or private gifts or donations), and net factor income (primarily capital income from foreign-located property owned by residents less capital income from domestic property owned by nonresidents). The current account balance differs from net exports in that the former includes international transfers and net factor income. (Bureau of Economic Analysis)

Cyclical Deficit:

The part of the budget deficit that results from cyclical factors rather than from underlying fiscal policy. The cyclical deficit reflects the fact that, when GDP falls, revenues automatically fall and outlays automatically rise. By definition, the cyclical deficit is zero when the economy is operating at potential GDP. Compare with **standardized-employment deficit**. (Congressional Budget Office)

Debt Held By The Public:

Debt issued by the Federal Government and held by nonfederal investors (including the Federal Reserve System).

Denatured Alcohol:

Ethanol that contains a small amount of a toxic substance, such as methanol or gasoline, which cannot be removed easily by chemical or physical means. Alcohols intended for industrial use must be denatured to avoid Federal alcoholic beverage tax.

Depreciation:

Decline in the value of a currency, financial asset, or capital good. When applied to a capital good, depreciation usually refers to loss of value because of obsolescence or wear.

Direct Spending:

The Budget Enforcement Act of 1990 defines direct spending as (a) budget authority provided by an authorization, (b) entitlement authority (including mandatory spending contained in appropriation acts), and (c) the Food Stamp program. A synonym is **mandatory spending**. Compare with **discretionary spending**.

Discount Rate:

The interest rate the Federal Reserve System charges on a loan that it makes to a bank. Such loans, when allowed, enable a bank to meets its reserve requirements without reducing its loans.

Discouraged Workers:

Jobless people who are available for work but who are not actively seeking it because they think they have poor prospects of finding jobs. Because they are not actively seeking jobs, discouraged workers are not counted as part of the labor force or as being unemployed. (Bureau of Labor Statistics)

Discretionary Spending:

Spending for programs whose funding levels are determined through the appropriation process. The Congress has the discretion each year to determine how many dollars will be devoted to continuing current programs and funding new ones. The Budget Enforcement Act of 1990 divided discretionary spending among three categories: defense, international, and domestic. Compare with **direct spending**.

Discretionary Spending Caps:

Annual ceilings on budget authority and outlays for discretionary programs defined in the Balanced Budget Act of 1985, as amended by the Budget Enforcement Act of 1990 and the Omnibus Budget Reconciliation Act of 1993. For fiscal years 1991 through 1993, the caps were divided among the three categories of discretionary spending—defense, international, and domestic. For fiscal years 1994 through 1998, there is one cap for all discretionary spending. Discretionary spending caps are enforced through Congressional rules and sequestration procedures.

Domestic Demand:

Total purchases of goods and services, regardless of origin, by U.S. consumers, businesses, and Governments during a given period. Domestic demand equals gross domestic product minus net exports. (Bureau of Economic Analysis)

E10 (Gasohol):

Ethanol/gasoline mixture containing 10% denatured ethanol and 90% gasoline, by volume.

E85:

Ethanol/gasoline mixture containing 85% denatured ethanol and 15% gasoline, by volume.

E93:

Ethanol mixture containing 93% ethanol, 5% methanol, and 2% kerosene, by volume.

E95:

Ethanol/gasoline mixture containing 95% denatured ethanol and 5% gasoline, by volume.

Entitlements:

Programs that make payments to any person, business, or unit of Government that seeks the payments and meets the criteria set in law. The Congress controls these programs indirectly by defining eligibility and setting the benefit or payment rules. Although the level of spending for these programs is controlled by the authorizing legislation, funding may be provided in either an authorization or an appropriation act. The best-known entitlements are the major benefit programs, such as Social Security and Medicare; other entitlements include farm price supports and interest on the Federal debt. See **direct spending**.

Ester:

An organic compound formed by reacting an acid with an alcohol, always resulting in the elimination of water.

Ethanol (Also known as Ethyl Alcohol, Grain Alcohol, or CH_3CH_2OH):

Can be produced chemically from ethylene or biologically from the fermentation of various sugars from carbohydrates found in agricultural crops and cellulosic residues from crops or wood. Used in the United States as a gasoline octane enhancer and oxygenate, it increases octane 2.5 to 3.0 numbers at 10% concentration. Ethanol also can be used in higher concentration in vehicles optimized for its use.

Ether:

A class of organic compounds containing an oxygen atom linked to two organic groups.

Etherification:

Oxygenation of an olefin by methanol or ethanol. For example, MTBE is formed from the chemical reaction of isobutylene and methanol.

Ethyl Ester:

A fatty ester formed when organically derived oils are combined with ethanol in the presence of a catalyst. After water washing, vacuum drying and filtration, the resulting ethyl ester has characteristics similar to petroleum-based diesel motor fuels.

Ethyl Tertiary Butyl Ether (ETBE):

An aliphatic ether similar to MTBE. This fuel oxygenate is manu-factured by reacting isobutylene with ethanol. Having high oc-tane and low volatility characteristics, ETBE can be added to gaso-line up to a level of approximately 17% by volume.

Evaporative Hydrocarbon:

Hydrocarbon vapors that can escape from a gasoline storage tank, vehicle gasoline tank during refueling or vehicle fuel system.

Exchange Rate:

The number of units of a foreign currency that can be bought with one unit of the domestic currency. (Federal Reserve Board)

Excise Tax:

A tax levied on the purchase of a specific type of good or service, such as tobacco products or telephone services.

Federal Funds Rate:

Overnight interest rate at which financial institutions borrow and lend monetary reserves. A rise in the Federal funds rate (com-pared with other short-term rate) suggests a tightening of mon-etary policy, whereas a fall suggests an easing. (Federal Reserve Board)

Federal Open Market Committee (FOMC):

The group within the Federal Reserve System that determines the direction of monetary policy. The open market desk at the Federal Reserve Bank of New York implements the policy with open market operations—the purchase or sale of Government securities—which influence short-term interest rates and the growth of the money supply. The FOMC is composed of twelve members, including the seven members of the Board of Gover-nors of the Federal Reserve System and five of the twelve presi-dents of the regional Federal Reserve Banks.

Federal Reserve System:

As the central bank of the United States, the Federal Reserve is responsible for conducting the nation's monetary policy and over-seeing credit conditions.

Feedstock:

Any material converted to another form of fuel or energy product. For example, corn starch can be used as a feedstock for ethanol production.

Fermentation:

The enzymatic transformation by microorganisms of organic compounds such as sugars. It is usually accompanied by the evolution of gas, as in the fermentation of glucose into ethanol into CO_2.

Fiscal Policy:

The Government's choice of tax and spending programs, which influences the amount and maturity of Government debt as well as the level, composition, and distribution of national output and income. An "easy" fiscal policy stimulates the short-term growth of output and income, whereas a "tight" fiscal policy restrains their growth. Movements in the standardized-employment deficit constitute one overall indictor of the tightness or ease of Federal fiscal policy; an increase relative to potential gross domestic product suggests fiscal ease, whereas a decrease suggests fiscal restriction. The President and the Congress jointly determine Federal fiscal policy.

Fiscal Year:

A yearly accounting period. The Federal Government's fiscal year begins October 1 and ends September 30. Fiscal years are designated by the calendar years in which they end—for example, fiscal years 1995 began October 1, 1994 , and will end on September 30, 1995.

Fuel Cell:

An electrochemical engine (no moving parts) that converts the chemical energy of a fuel, such as hydrogen, and an oxidant, such as oxygen, directly to electricity. The principal components of a fuel cell are catalytically activated electrodes for the fuel (anode) and the oxidant (cathode) and an electrolyte to conduct ions between the two electrodes.

Gasification:

Any chemical or heat process used to convert a feedstock to a gaseous fuel.

Gasohol:

In the United States, gasohol refers to gasoline that contains 10% ethanol by volume. This term was used in the late 1970s and early 1980s but has been replaced by terms such as E10, Super Unleaded Plus Ethanol or Unleaded Plus.

Global Warming:

The theoretical escalation of global temperatures caused by the increase of greenhouse gas emissions in the lower atmosphere.

Government Purchases of Goods and Services:

Purchases from the private sector (including compensation of Government employees) made by Government during a given period. Government purchases constitute component of GDP, but they encompass only a portion of all Government expenditures because they exclude transfer payments (such as grants to state and local Governments and net interest paid). (Bureau of Economic Analysis)

Greenhouse Effect:

A warming of the earth and its atmosphere as a result of the thermal trapping of incoming solar radiation by CO_2, water vapor, methane, nitrous oxide, chlorofluorocarbons and other gases, both natural and man-made.

Gross Domestic Product (GDP):

The total market value of all goods and services produced domestically during a given period. The components of GDP are consumption, gross domestic investment, Government purchases of goods and services, and net exports. (Bureau of Economic Analysis)

Gross National Product (GNP):

The total market value of all goods and services produced in a given period by labor and property supplied by residents of a country, regardless of where the labor and property are located. GNP differs from GDP primarily by including the excess of capital income that residents earn from investments abroad less capital income that nonresidents earn from domestic investment.

Hybrid Electric Vehicle (HEV):

A vehicle that is powered by two or more energy sources, one of which is electricity. HEVs combine the engine and fuel tank of a conventional vehicle with the battery and electric motor of an electric vehicle in a single drive train.

Inflation:

Growth in a measure of the general price level, usually expressed as an annual rate of change.

Investment:

Physical investment is the current product set aside during a given period to be used for future production; in other words, an addition to the stock of capital goods. As measured by the national income and product accounts, private domestic investment consists of investment in residential and nonresidential structures, producers' durable equipment, and the change in business inventories. *Financial investment* is the purchase of a financial security. *Investment in human capital* is spending on education, training, health services, and other activities that increase the productivity of the workforce. Investment in human capital is not treated as investment in the national income and product accounts.

Labor Force:

The number of people who have jobs or who are available for work and are actively seeking jobs. *Labor force participation rate* is the labor force as a percentage of the non-institutional population age sixteen years or older. (Bureau of Labor Statistics)

Liquefied Natural Gas (LNG):

Natural gas that has been condensed to a liquid typically by cryogenically cooling the gas.

Liquefied Petroleum Gas (LPG):

A hydrocarbon and colorless gas found in natural gas and produced from crude oil, used principally as a home heating fuel or motor vehicle fuel. Also known as propane.

M85:

85% methanol and 15% unleaded gasoline by volume, used as a motor fuel in flexible fueled vehicles.

M100:

100% (neat) methanol.

Means of Financing:

Sources of financing Federal deficits or uses of Federal surpluses. The largest means of financing is normally Federal borrowing from the public, but other means of financing include any transaction that causes a difference between the Federal (including off-budget) surplus or deficit and the change in debt held by the public. The means of financing include changes in checks outstanding and Treasury cash balances seigniorage (that is, Government revenue from the manufacture of money), and the transactions of the financing accounts established under credit reform.

Means-tested Programs:

Programs that provide cash or services to people who meet a test of need based on income and assets. Most means-tested programs are entitlements—for example, Medicaid, the Food Stamp program, Supplemental Security Income, family support, and veterans' pensions—but a few, such as subsidized housing and various social services, are funded through discretionary appropriations.

Methane (CH_4):

The simplest of the hydrocarbons and the principal constituent of natural gas. Pure methane has a heating value of 1,012 Btu per standard cubic foot.

Methanol (Also known as Methyl Alcohol, Wood Alcohol, or CH_3OH):

A liquid fuel formed by catalytically combining CO with hydrogen at a 1:2 ratio under high pressure and temperature. Commercially, it is typically manufactured by steam reforming natural gas. Also formed in the destructive distillation of wood.

Methyl Ester:

A fatty ester formed when organically derived oils are combined with methanol in the presence of a catalyst. Methyl ester has characteristics similar to petroleum-based diesel motor fuels.

Methyl Tertiary Butyl Ether (MTBE):

An ether manufactured by reacting methanol and isobutylene. The resulting ether has high octane and low volatility. MTBE is a fuel oxygenate and is permitted in unleaded gasoline up to a level of 15% by volume.

Monetary Policy:

The strategy of influencing movements of the money supply and interest rates to affect output and inflation. An "easy" monetary policy suggests faster money growth and initially lower short-term interest rates in an attempt to increase aggregate demand, but it may lead to a higher rate of inflation. A "tight" monetary policy suggests slower money growth and higher interest rates in the near term in an attempt to reduce inflationary pressure by reducing aggregate demand. The Federal Reserve System conducts monetary policy in the United States.

National Income and Product Accounts (NIPAs):

Official U.S. accounts that detail the composition of GDP and how the costs of production are distributed as income. (Bureau of Economic Analysis)

National Saving:

Total savings by all sectors of the economy: personal savings, business saving (corporate after-tax profits not paid as dividends), and Government saving (budget surplus or deficit-indicating dissaving-of all Government entities). National saving represents all income not consumed, publicly or privately, during a given period. (Bureau of Economic Analysis)

Natural Gas:

A mixture of gaseous hydrocarbons, primarily methane, occurring naturally in the earth and used principally as a fuel.

Near Neat Fuel:

Fuel that is virtually free from admixture or dilution.

Neat Fuel:

Fuel that is free from admixture or dilution with other fuels.

Neat Alcohol Fuel:

Straight or 100% alcohol (not blended with gasoline), in the form of either ethanol or methanol.

Net Exports:

Exports of goods and services produced in a country less its imports of goods and services produced elsewhere.

Net Interest:

In the Federal budget, net interest includes Federal interest payments to the public as recorded in budget function 900. Net interest also includes, as an offset, interest income received by the Government on loans and cash balances. *In national income and products accounts* (NIPAs), net interest is the income component of GDP paid as interest—primarily interest that domestic businesses pay, less interest they receive. The NIPAs treat Government interest payments as transfers, so they are not part of the GDP.

Net National Saving:

National saving less depreciation and physical capital.

Nominal:

Measured in the dollar value (as in nominal output, income, or wage rate) or market terms (as in nominal exchange or interest rate) of the period under consideration. Compare with **real**.

Octane Enhancer:

Any substance such as MTBE, ETBE, toluene and xylene that is added to gasoline to increase octane and reduce engine knock.

Octane Rating (Octane Number):

A measure of a fuel's resistance to self ignition, hence a measure as well of the antiknock properties of the fuel.

Off Budget:

Spending or revenues excluded from the budget totals by law. The revenues and outlays of the two Social Security trust funds and the transactions of the Postal Service are off-budget and (except for discretionary Social Security administrative costs) are not included in any Budget Enforcement Act calculations.

Offsetting Receipts:

Funds collected by the Federal Government that are recorded as negative budget authority and outlays and credited to separate receipt accounts. More than half of offsetting receipts are intragovernmental receipts that reflect agencies' payments to retirement and other funds on behalf of their employees; these receipts simply balance payments elsewhere in the budget. An additional category of receipts (proprietary receipts) come from the public and generally represent voluntary, business-type transactions. The largest items are the flat premiums for Supplementary Medical Insurance (Part B of Medicare), timber and oil lease receipts, and proceeds from the sale of electric power.

Organization of Petroleum Exporting Countries (OPEC):

The group of oil-rich countries that tries to determine the price of crude oil (given demand) by agreeing to production quotas among its members.

Outlays:

The liquidation of Federal obligation, generally by issuing a check or disbursing cash. Sometimes obligations are liquidated (and outlays occur) by issuing agency promissory notes, such as those of the former Federal Savings and Loan Insurance Corporation. Unlike outlays for the other categories of spending, outlays for interest on the public debt are counted when the interest is earned, not when it is paid. Outlays may be for payment of obligations incurred in previous fiscal years or in the same year. Outlays, therefore, flow in part from unexpended balances of prior year budget authority and in part from budget authority provided for the current year.

Oxides of Nitrogen (NO_x):

Regulated air pollutants, primarily NO and NO_2 but including other substances in minute concentrations. Under the high pressure and temperature conditions in an engine, nitrogen and oxygen atoms in the air react to form various NO_x. Like hydrocarbons, NO_x are precursors to the formation of smog. They also contribute to the formation of acid rain.

Oxygenate:

A term used in the petroleum industry to denote fuel additives containing hydrogen, carbon and oxygen in their molecular structure. Includes ethers such as MTBE and ETBE and alcohols such as ethanol and methanol.

Oxygenated Gasoline:

Gasoline containing an oxygenate such as ethanol or MTBE. The increased oxygen content promotes more complete combustion, thereby reducing tailpipe emissions of CO.

Ozone:

Tropospheric ozone (smog) is formed when volatile organic compounds (VOCs), oxygen, and NO_x react in the presence of sunlight (not to be confused with stratospheric ozone, which is found in the upper atmosphere and protects the earth from the sun's ultraviolet rays). Though beneficial in the upper atmosphere, at ground level, ozone is a respiratory irritant and considered a pollutant.

Particulate Matter (PM):

Unburned fuel particles that form smoke or soot and stick to lung tissue when inhaled.

Pay-As-You-Go (PAYGO):

A procedure required in the Budget Enforcement Act of 1990 to ensure that, for fiscal years 1991 through 1995, legislation affecting direct spending and receipts does not increase the deficit. Pay-as-you-go is enforced through Congressional rules and sequestration procedures. The pay-as-you-go process was extended through fiscal year 1998 by the Omnibus Budget Reconciliation Act of 1993.

Personal Saving:

Saving by households. Personal saving equals disposable personal income minus spending for consumption and interest payments. *Personal saving rate* is personal saving as a percentage of disposable income. (Bureau of Economic Analysis)

Potential Real GDP:

The highest level of real GDP that could persist for a substantial period without raising the rate of inflation. CBO's calculation relates potential GDP to the nonaccelerating inflation rate of unemployment, which is the unemployment rate consistent with a constant inflation rate. (Congressional Budget Office)

Present Value:

A single number that expresses a flow of current and future income (or payments) in terms of an equivalent lump sum received (or paid) today. The calculation of present value depends on the rate of interest. For example, given an interest rate of 5%, today's 95¢ will grow to $1 next year. Hence, the present value of $1 payable a year from today is only 95¢.

Private Saving:

Saving by households and businesses. Private saving is equal to personal saving plus after-tax corporate profits minus dividends paid. (Bureau of Economic Analysis)

Productivity:

Average real output per unit of input. *Labor productivity* is average real output per hour of labor. The growth of labor productivity is defined as the growth of real output that is not explained by the growth of labor input alone. *Total factor productivity* is average real output per unit of combined labor and capital inputs. The growth of total factor productivity is defined as the growth of real output that is not explained by the growth of labor and capital. Labor productivity and total factor productivity differ in that increases in capital per worker would raise labor productivity but not total factor productivity. (Bureau of Labor Statistics)

Real:

Adjusted to remove the effect of inflation. *Real (constant dollar) output* represents volume, rather than dollar value, of goods and services. *Real income* represents power to purchase real output. *Real data* are usually constructed by dividing the corresponding nominal data, such as output or a wage rate, by a price index or deflator. *Real interest rate* is a nominal interest rate minus the expected inflation rate. Compare with **nominal**.

Receipt Account:

Any budget or off-budget account that is established exclusively to record the collection of income, including negative subsidies. In general, receipt accounts that collect money arising from the exercise of the Government's sovereign powers are included as revenues, whereas the proceeds of intragovernmental transactions or collections from the public arising from business-type transactions (such as interest income, proceeds from the sale of property or products, or profits from Federal credit activities) are included as offsetting receipts—that is, credited as offsets to outlays rather than included in receipts.

Recession:

A phase of the business cycle extending from a peak to the next trough—usually lasting six months to a year—characterized by widespread declines in output, income, employment, and trade in many sectors of the economy. Real GDP usually falls throughout a recession. See **business cycle**. (National bureau of Economic Research)

Recovery:

A phase of the business cycle that lasts from a trough until overall economic activity returns to the level it had reached at the previous peak. See **business cycle**. (National Bureau of Economic Research)

Reformulated Gasoline (RFG):

Gasolines that have had their compositions and/or characteristics altered to reduce vehicular emissions of pollutants, particularly pursuant to EPA regulations under the Clean Air Act.

Residential Investment:

Investment in housing primarily for construction of new single-family and multifamily housing and alterations plus additions to existing housing. (Bureau of Economic Analysis)

Retained Earnings:

Corporate profits after tax that are used for investment rather than paid out as dividends to stockholders. (Bureau of Economic Analysis)

Revenues:

Funds collected from the public arising from the sovereign power of the Government. Revenues consist of receipts from income taxes (individual and corporate), excise taxes, and estate and gift taxes, social insurance contributions, custom duties, miscellaneous receipts such as Federal Reserve earnings, gifts, and contributions; and fees and fines. Revenues are also known as Federal Government receipts but do not include offsetting receipts, which are recorded as negative budget authority and outlays.

Sequestration:

The cancellation of budgetary resources to enforce the discretionary spending caps and pay-as-you-go process established under the Budget Enforcement Act of 1990 and the Omnibus Budget Reconciliation Act of 1993. Sequestration is triggered if the Office of Management and Budget determines that discretionary appropriations exceed the discretionary spending caps or that legislation affecting direct spending and receipts increases the deficit. Changes in direct spending and receipt legislation that increase the deficit would result in reductions in funding for entitlements not otherwise exempted by law. Discretionary spending in excess of the caps would cause the cancellation of budgetary resources within the discretionary spending category.

Short-term Interest Rate:

Interest rate earned by a debt instrument that will mature within one year.

Smog:

A petrochemical haze caused primarily by the reaction of hydrocarbons and NO_x with sunlight.

Standardized-Employment Deficit:

The level of the Federal budget deficit that would occur under current law if the economy was operating at potential GDP. It provides a measure of underlying fiscal policy by removing the influence of cyclical factors from the budget deficit. Compare with **cyclical deficit**. (Congressional Budget Office)

Supply Shock:

A large and unexpected change in the production of a good or service. Examples include bumper crops, crop failures, or sudden restrictions on the supply of oil as occurred in 1973-1974 and 1979-1980. A supply shock that restricts output will raise the price of the good in short supply; a surfeit will lower the price of the good.

Ten-Year Treasury Note:

Interest-bearing note issued by the U.S. Treasury that is redeemed in ten years.

Tetraethyl Lead:

An organometallic octane enhancer. One gram of lead increases the octane of one gallon of gasoline about six numbers. The EPA has phased down the use of lead in gasoline as it has been determined to be a health hazard. Lead will not be permitted in gasoline beginning in 1996.

Three-Month Treasury Bill:

Security issued by the U.S. Treasury that is redeemed in ninety-one days.

Toluene:

Basic aromatic compound derived from petroleum and used to increase octane. The most common hydrocarbon purchased for use in increasing octane.

Transesterification:

A process in which organically-derived oils or fats are combined with alcohol (ethanol or methanol) in the presence of a catalyst to form esters (ethyl or methyl ester).

Transfer Payments:

Payments in return for which no good or service is currently received—for example, Welfare or Social Security payments or money sent to relatives abroad. (Bureau of Economic Analysis)

Trust Fund:

A fund, designated as a trust fund by statute, that is credited with income from earmarked collections and charged with certain outlays. Collections may come from the public (for example, taxes or user charges) or from intrabudgetary transfers. More than one hundred fifty Federal Government trust funds exist, of which the largest and best known finance several major benefit programs (including Social Security and Medicare) and certain infrastructure spending (the Highway and the Airport and Airway trust funds). The term "Federal funds" refers to all programs that are not trust funds.

Underlying Rate of Inflation:

Rate of inflation of a modified CPI-U that excludes from the market basket the components most volatile in price—food, energy, and used cars.

Unemployment:

Joblessness. The measure of unemployment is the number of jobless people who are available for work and are actively seeking jobs. The *unemployment rate* is unemployment as a percentage of the labor force. (Bureau of Labor Statistics)

Volatile Organic Compound (VOC):

Hydrocarbon gases released during combustion or evaporation of fuel and regulated by EPA. VOCs combine with NO_x in the presence of sunlight and form ozone.

Xylene:

An aromatic hydrocarbon derived from petroleum and used to increase octane. Highly valued as a petrochemical feedstock. Xylene is highly photochemically reactive and, as a constituent of tailpipe emissions, is a contributor to smog formation.

Yield:

The average annual rate of return on a security, including interest payments and repayment of principal, if held to maturity.

N

National Association of Home Builders
    12
national debt 7, 8, 20, 21, 22, 23, 24,
    32, 42, 44, 50, 51, 52, 53, 62, 69,
    70, 71, 73, 76, 115, 121, 141,
    188, 189, 195, 196, 199, 200
National Flood Insurance Program 82
national ID card 86
national security 72
National Technical Information Service
    116
natural disasters v, 7, 40, 82, 83
net operating loss 8
New Madrid fault zone 80
Northridge earthquake 79, 80, 82

O

oil ii, 2, 11, 26, 30, 35, 36, 37, 57,
    58, 66, 67, 68, 77, 78, 92, 93, 94,
    96, 99, 112, 125, 128, 130, 137,
    139, 140, 141, 142, 143, 148, 157,
    158, 160, 161, 162, 163, 164, 165,
    166, 167, 168, 169, 170, 171, 172,
    175, 177, 184, 185, 188, 199,
    241, 245, 246, 247, 249, 254, 256,
    258, 259, 263, 286, 297, 301, 306
oil crisis of 1973 160, 166, 167
oil companies 2, 30, 36, 37, 57, 77,
    112, 128, 130, 140, 148, 157, 162,
    164, 165, 166, 167, 168, 169, 170,
    171, 172, 175
oil industry 36, 140, 142, 161, 165,
    168, 170, 172, 175, 188
oil plants 93, 94, 96
oligopolies 54
online service 29, 115
OPEC 26, 29, 109, 137, 160, 161,
    164, 168, 169, 172, 173, 301
open market 25, 42, 89, 91, 94, 96,
    182, 240, 294
opportunity cost 56, 57, 177
OSHA 38, 257

P

PAC money 96, 201
Pacific Rim nations 24
paper pulp 31, 90, 93, 94, 95, 251
pass through rebate 148
Patriot race car 264

Pebble Beach 11, 61
pensions, government 3, 48, 199
plastic 36, 101, 165, 166, 170, 171,
    175, 177, 243, 253, 255, 267
policies, trade 5, 38
pollution ii, 11, 33, 54, 105, 106, 109,
    125, 127, 128, 136, 162, 163, 167,
    177, 239, 240, 250, 254
pollution, no point 167
power plants 28, 32, 58, 95, 125, 127,
    136, 141, 156, 157, 240, 250
President i, 1, 8, 14, 21, 45, 47, 49,
    68, 72, 79, 83, 96, 106, 120, 159,
    165, 180, 188, 193, 199, 228, 230,
    238, 241, 248, 261, 287, 295
President Clinton 47, 83, 84, 85, 96,
    120, 159, 165, 188, 193, 241, 261
President Bush 68, 238
Prison Industry Authority 4, 37, 39,
    104, 109, 176, 231, 232
prisoners 14, 39, 91, 93, 97, 104, 110,
    143, 176, 182, 187, 188, 231, 232
programs, entitlement
    20, 50, 71, 192, 195, 208
programs, retirement 69, 75, 216
programs, trust fund 3, 8, 41, 42, 43,
    45, 46, 47, 48, 49, 50, 51, 69, 71,
    73, 189, 192, 193, 195, 206, 207,
    209, 211, 212, 214, 216, 217, 219,
    222, 228
Progress Entrepreneurs Actualizing
    Creative Enterprises (PEACE) 151
Project Vote Smart 203
Proler International 105, 106, 109,
    170, 176, 255, 256
propane 164, 261, 297
property taxes 120, 180, 187
Proposition 13 187
protectionistic trade policies 5, 38
publicly owned debt 21, 71
Puerto Rico 9

R

Rabushka, Alvin 123
racial tensions 182
real estate ii, 10, 11, 40, 58, 59, 61,
    124, 141, 144, 171, 172, 198
recession ii, 141, 145, 304

Ordering Information

YES! I want to read OPERATION PROSPERITY and find out what can be done to keep America strong while there's still time.

Paperback books available for only $14.95 (price subject to change) each plus $3.25 shipping and handling for the first book, add $1.00 for each additional book.

CA residents add $1.23 (8.25%) sales tax.

Please send me:

_____ Paperback books @ $14.95 each	$ _____
CA residents add 8.25% sales tax	$ _____
Subtotal	$ _____
Postage	$ _____
GRAND TOTAL	$ _____

Please allow six to eight weeks for delivery.

Name _____

Address _____

City _____

State _____ Zip _____

Phone _____

Form of payment:

❑ Check or money order enclosed

❑ MasterCard   ❑ VISA   ❑ AMEX   ❑ Discover

Name on credit card _____

Account number_____

Expiration _____

Mail to:
    Candor Press, P.O. Box 27037, Concord, CA 94527-0037

Credit card orders call TOLL FREE:
1-888-226-3671